Asian American S Higher Education

Asian American Students in Higher Education offers the first comprehensive analysis and synthesis of existing theory and research related to Asian American students' experiences in postsecondary education. Providing practical and insightful recommendations, this sourcebook covers a range of topics including critical historical and demographic contexts, the complexity of Asian American student identities, and factors that facilitate and hinder Asian American students' success in college. The time has come for institutions of higher education to develop more holistic and authentic understandings of this significant and rapidly growing population, and this volume will help educators acquire deeper and more intricate knowledge of Asian American college students' experiences. This resource is vital for college educators interested in better serving Asian American students in their institutions.

Samuel D. Museus is an Associate Professor of Higher Education at the University of Denver, USA.

KEY ISSUES ON DIVERSE COLLEGE STUDENTS

Series Editors: Marybeth Gasman and Nelson Bowman III

Asian American Students in Higher Education
Samuel D. Museus

Asian American Students in Higher Education

Samuel D. Museus

Routledge
Taylor & Francis Group

NEW YORK AND LONDON

First published 2014
by Routledge
711 Third Avenue, New York, NY 10017

and by Routledge
2 Park Square, Milton Park, Abingdon, Oxon OX14 4RN

Routledge is an imprint of the Taylor & Francis Group, an informa business

Library of Congress Control Number:
2013951563

ISBN: 978-0-415-84430-7 (hbk)
ISBN: 978-0-415-84431-4 (pbk)
ISBN: 978-0-203-75300-2 (ebk)

Typeset in Perpetua and Bell Gothic
by Florence Production Ltd, Stoodleigh, Devon, UK

Printed and bound in the United States of America by Publishers Graphics,
LLC on sustainably sourced paper.

To the scholars who have fought to give voice to Asian American students, this book is a product of your work. To the educators who have dedicated their careers to empowering Asian Americans through education, this book was inspired by your vision. To today and tomorrow's Asian American students in pursuit of their dreams, this book is a consequence of your existence. To all of those with an interest in the welfare of Asian American students in higher education, this book is yours.

Contents

Series Editor Introduction

We are very pleased to include Sam Museus's book *Asian American Students in Higher Education* in our "Key Issues on Diverse College Students" series with Routledge Press. Museus's work exemplifies the quality of research that we aim to foster within the series.

Although there is growing research on Asian Americans in higher education, myths and stereotypes continue to exist. Museus's deeply personal book, which builds upon the salient literature in the field, allows the reader to connect with the experiences of Asian American students. He draws upon literature from across disciplines and makes connections between K-12 and higher education literature to paint a picture of the struggles, successes, and experiences of Asian American students.

Not only does Museus provide the reader with a rich historical overview and corresponding demographic information, but he also explains Asian American racial identity and also race relations with other underrepresented racial and ethnic groups. He situates the issues of Asian Americans within the larger racialized America, even questioning the very use of the words Asian and Asian American.

Scholars and students alike will benefit from reading Museus's book as will the field of higher education. It is well-researched, beautifully written, and important in our quest to understand the methods, strategies, and reasons behind and for college student success.

Marybeth Gasman & Nelson Bowman III,
Series Editors

Preface

I am Asian American. For many, the label "Asian American" can invoke simplistic and racist images of Geishas, kamikazes, tiger moms, marital artists, or socially awkward math nerds. Of course, the term "Asian American" embodies much more complexity than the term or these stereotypes that society attaches to it could ever reflect. For me, being Asian American is an intricate fusion of identities, experiences, and cultural knowledge that I have internalized from my existence within and navigation through many different ethnic communities.

My mother spent her childhood living in various regions of the islands of Okinawa, and my father was born and raised in Saint Paul, Minnesota. When they were in their late teens, my father joined the United States Navy and was stationed in Okinawa, where he met my mother. After they married and my mother gave birth to my oldest brother in Okinawa, they moved to Minnesota and my mother gave birth to her second son and me. So, I am a second-generation Okinawan American and a product of Okinawan cultural values and beliefs that were transmitted to me through generations.

Long before my mother was born, Okinawa was colonized by Japan, so my mother also identifies as Japanese, and she passed values and beliefs from Japanese culture and communities on to my brothers and me as well. My father is racially White and is descendent from several generations of European Americans from a wide range of ethnic origins, including English, German, Irish, Norwegian, and others. Therefore, I am a multiracial Japanese American and undoubtedly am shaped by these identities as well.

I spent my early years in an almost all-White neighborhood and school, never quite fitting in socially because of my obvious racial and cultural differences. One of the few vivid memories from these early years is my two closest friends in elementary school repeatedly and jokingly calling me "the Jap" and, in doing so, unconsciously drawing a clear invisible racial line between us. When I entered middle school, it became apparent that the Saint Paul population was undergoing a process of rapid racial and ethnic diversification. During this time, my friendship groups became increasingly racially and ethnically diverse and, by the time that I had entered high school, I had friends from many different racial and ethnic backgrounds and communities.

One of the demographic changes taking place in Saint Paul and its neighboring twin city of Minneapolis, as I was navigating middle and high school, was the settlement and growth of many Southeast Asian refugee communities that had migrated to the United States after the end of the Vietnam War. During high school, I made more connections and became much more immersed in these Southeast Asian American communities—especially Cambodian and Vietnamese American communities—in Saint Paul and Minneapolis. And, although I am not genetically Southeast Asian, I am no doubt as much a product of these communities as any other.

During my undergraduate years at the University of Minnesota's Twin Cities campus, I had strong connections with groups of Cambodian, Chinese, Hmong, Filipino, Laotian, Korean, and Vietnamese American peers. My deep connections to and sense of belonging in each of these communities have shaped my identity as an Asian American.

I eventually graduated with bachelor's degrees in History and Sociology from the University of Minnesota. It is important to note that, contrary to common racial constructions of Asian American parents as "tiger parents," my decision to pursue college and eventual completion of the bachelor's degree cannot be attributed to any excessive parental pressure to achieve educational and professional perfection. In fact, although my parents certainly taught my siblings and me moral values and good work ethic, they never received college degrees themselves and were candid about the fact that they would not disapprove if I chose not to pursue a college education. In contrast to common racial constructions of Asian Americans as model minorities, I also doubt that my educational success was a result of a genetic predisposition to achieve academically or cultural values that fuel overachievement in college. After all, my first three years at the University of Minnesota were spent without purpose and moving in a direction that would more likely lead me to prison than a professorship.

Although many people and experiences influenced my educational trajectory, one important factor that likely contributed to my pursuit of a college degree was an Affirmative Action initiative, called the Minority Encouragement Program (MEP), which was focused on encouraging students of color to pursue college and giving them opportunities to explore their postsecondary options. Although my immediate and extended family did not have the cultural or social capital to teach me extensively about higher education options, the MEP program provided information and offered college and university tour opportunities that made the idea of pursuing postsecondary education a real consideration. Given this experience, I could be called an Affirmative Action baby, and I am proud of that reality.

There were surely other factors that led to my completing college and pursuing graduate school. For example, there were a few professors in my undergraduate years that inspired me with their intellectual curiosity and passion for social justice. In addition, I experienced an identity crisis during college, when a complex interplay of events and experiences led to a transformation of my worldview and development of a sense of purpose. Yet another influential factor that contributed to my decision to finish college and interest in pursuing a doctoral degree and career in academia was the reality that many of my friends had dropped out of college due to various cultural, economic, and social challenges, leaving me with a sense of responsibility to remove some of those hurdles for those from our communities who went to college after us.

When I transitioned to Penn State University in State College, Pennsylvania, to pursue my doctoral degree, I encountered fantastic faculty and students in its Higher Education Doctoral Program. However, I also discovered a larger campus environment that was hostile toward people of color. Right before I went to Penn State, the President of the Campus Republicans had a race-themed party and dressed up as a Ku Klux Klan member and his friends wore black face paint. Within months of living at Penn State, I observed a White male college student making *ching-chong, ching-chong* noises to Asian American students who were passing by on the street at the perimeter of the campus, death threats made to Black student leaders, xenophobic comments printed in the campus newspaper, and many more incidents that contributed to a diminished sense of safety and belonging among many students of color at the institution.

Although there were no Asian Americans interested in studying these issues of race, ethnicity, and culture in my doctoral program, I connected with my eventual dissertation Chair and some of his advisees, who were all Black and became my closest intellectual community at the time. Through these experiences, my connections to other communities of color with whom I found mutual interests deepened. As a result, both my identity and scholarly agenda shifted, and my research began to focus on race, ethnicity, and culture in the college student experience.

After completing my doctorate at Penn State, I assumed my first faculty position in Higher Education Administration and Asian American Studies at the University of Massachusetts, Boston. For the first time, I connected with an actual community of Asian American and multiracial scholars and students, who were ethnically diverse and interested in examining issues relevant to and advocating for these populations. This community made me increasingly aware of the deprivation I had been experiencing—the deprivation of space and voice in higher education arenas as a multiracial Asian American. As a result of this new context, my connections to Asian American and multiracial communities became deeper and more complex than they had previously been. Moreover, my identity as a multiracial Asian American evolved, along with my scholarly agenda, to include a greater commitment to solving problems within and advocating for Asian American and multiracial communities.

I share the preceding story to underscore the complexity of concepts, such as "Asian American," "Asian American identity," and "Asian American success." The story shows how my identification as an Asian American signifies my association with and commitment to many different ethnic communities. It also shows that my life has been shaped by a variety of distinct international, national, and local contexts—with international relations between the U.S. and Asia creating the conditions for my existence and shaping the communities in which I grew up, national policies such as Affirmative Action facilitating my trajectory, and a complex combination of cultures making me who I am today. And, the story paints a much more complex picture of what being Asian American means, one that far transcends racial and ethnic stereotypes that are often imposed upon us by dominant narratives in society.

Of course, the true complexity of Asian American identity and experiences cannot be captured in one story, or even in one book for that matter. But, in this volume, I hope to paint a more coherent and complex picture of the Asian American college student experience than currently exists so that postsecondary scholars and educators can construct a deeper and more intricate understanding of and be more equipped to serve this population. As I discuss in the following introduction, the time has come for institutions of higher education across the nation to develop more holistic and intricate understandings of this significant and rapidly growing Asian American population, to acknowledge and honor their voices, and to address their needs.

The current volume was written with multiple purposes in mind. First, the current text is aimed at stimulating thought and discourse around literature on Asian American students in postsecondary education and how college educators can improve the lives of these individuals. Second, the current volume is aimed at providing the most comprehensive synthesis of Asian American college students' experiences to date. In doing so, the book complicates oversimplified stereotypes of Asian American college students and offers a more intricate understanding of this student population through an analysis of their experiences in higher education. Third, in producing this text, I take stock of the literature on Asian American college students to inform future scholarly research on this population. The hope is that this text can provide a modest building block for the next wave of cutting-edge scholarship on Asian American college students and the development of new theory and research to shed light on the complex realities of the Asian American student experience in higher education.

Given the contexts discussed above, the current synthesis is a timely one. Although many recent contributions to the knowledgebase on Asian American students in higher education are valuable, a comprehensive and coherent picture of Asian American experiences in college remains elusive. It can certainly be argued that an adequately holistic and cohesive picture of Asian Americans in college is impossible to construct given the complexity and diversity of their experiences. Yet, the complementary bodies of scholarship that exist on Asian American experiences outside the field of higher education and on Asian American undergraduate experiences within the field can be synthesized to generate a more comprehensive and cogent understanding of this population than that which previously exists. Accordingly, in the following sections, I draw from the fields of K-12 and higher education, Critical Race Theory, ethnic studies, sociology, and psychology, and integrate the bodies of knowledge that are relevant to Asian American experience in these different disciplines to offer such a synthesis.

In the Introduction, I discuss the context for this volume, underscoring recent signs of progress and stagnation in the emergence of Asian American voice in higher education research, policy, and practice. The next three chapters of this volume are focused on understanding critical contexts that are necessary for developing a comprehensive understanding of Asian American college students' lives. Chapter 1 focuses on the racial context of Asian American college students' experiences. Specifically, I synthesize literature in the areas of Critical Race Theory (CRT), ethnic studies, psychology, sociology, and education to discuss the ways in which race and racism shape the experiences of Asian Americans in general and Asian American students in higher education in particular. Chapter 1 also includes an overview of a new Asian Critical Theory (AsianCrit) perspective that can be used to critically analyze and understand the experiences of Asian American people and communities through a critical race lens. This perspective can also provide one useful framework through which to interpret and understand subsequent chapters.

In Chapter 2, I utilize existing literature primarily from the field of Asian American Studies to offer a synthesis of the historical context of Asian American college students' lives. In this chapter, I discuss the immigration histories of various Asian American populations, which provide important context for understanding the current conditions of their communities and experiences in higher education. I also provide an overview of critical historical cases in Asian American higher education history. These incidents, together, can provide a foundation for the future development of a collective history relevant to this population in higher education.

In Chapter 3, I analyze national data to illuminate critical demographic contexts that highlight key characteristics of current Asian American popula-tions. This discussion includes an analysis of trends in the growth of the Asian American racial group, the diversity that exists within this population, and the inequalities that permeate this community. This context provides a snapshot of the communities from which Asian American students come and underscores the importance of paying attention to this population and responding to their needs.

Chapters 4 through 6 synthesize literature from Asian American Studies, psychology, sociology, and education to synthesize theories, models, and research on Asian American students' identity, race relations, and success in higher education. Each of the first six chapters concludes with a discussion of how the ideas within it can inform institutional policy and practice in higher education. Finally, Chapter 7 discusses future directions for research on Asian American students, highlighting gaps in research and knowledge about this population that can inform postsecondary education policy and practice. The hope is that this final chapter can help stimulate critical scholarly discourse on Asian American students in higher education and spark a new wave of cutting-edge scholarship on this population.

Introduction

The story of Asian Americans in postsecondary education has historically been a paradoxical one of both inclusion and exclusion. Of course, Asian Americans have not been completely excluded from our system of higher education. After all, as is the case with other racial and ethnic populations, many Asian American students pursue college degrees and enroll in American colleges and universities. In this sense, Asian Americans are a visible population in higher education nationally, and a highly visible group at specific colleges and universities.

At the same time, however, Asian Americans have often been excluded in higher education research, policy, and practice. My colleagues and I have written in depth about this exclusion (Ching & Agbayani, 2012; Museus, 2009a, 2009c; Museus & Kiang, 2009; Osajima, 1995; Suzuki, 2002). In the higher education scholarly arena, Asian American graduate students in the field of higher education can pick up some of the most highly visible and widely used texts in the field and find the voices of their communities absent from them, or those students can go through graduate school without ever seeing themselves or their communities reflected in the graduate curriculum altogether (Museus, 2009c). As a result, Asian Americans are arguably the most misunderstood population in higher education (M. J. Chang, 2008). In higher education policy, many federal agencies exclude Asian Americans from opportunities, resources, and discussions that are focused on underserved populations of color. Moreover, Asian American students find themselves excluded from scholarship opportunities reserved for people of color (Ching & Agbayani, 2012; Museus, 2009a). In higher education practice, Asian American students are often made to feel like they do not belong in support service arenas because they are assumed to be genetically superior and should not need help, and they are ignored by postsecondary educators who assume that they do not need support (e.g., Museus & Park, 2012; Suzuki, 2002).

The combination of the significant increasing presence of Asian American students in postsecondary institutions and their historical exclusion from higher education research, policy, and practice is highly problematic (Museus, 2009a).

To go a step further, given the rapid growth of the Asian American population and reality that this community does face challenges, the continued exclusion of Asian Americans from postsecondary education research, policy, and practice is unacceptable (Museus, 2009a, 2013). More than ever before, it is important that higher education scholars, policymakers, and practitioners acquire evidence-based understandings of this growing population and respond to their interests and needs.

In the remainder of this introduction, I set the stage for the review of research on Asian American college students. In the following section, I discuss the contemporary context for the current volume by highlighting the signs of both progress and stagnation in the inclusion of Asian American students in higher education research, policy, and practice. These signs constitute the conditions within which this volume is written. Then, I offer an existing conceptual framework as a backdrop for the following analysis and synthesis of research on Asian American college students. Finally, before transitioning into the comprehensive analysis and synthesis of literature, I offer an important caveat regarding the racial classification of Asian Americans and use of the term Asian American in the current volume.

CONTEMPORARY CONTEXTS OF THE VOLUME

As mentioned, the last decade has included both signs of progress and signs of stagnation with regard to the inclusion or the authentic voices and realities of Asian Americans in postsecondary education research, policy, and practice (Ching & Agbayani, 2012; Museus, 2013; Museus, antonio, & Kiang, 2012; Museus, Maramba, & Teranishi, 2013). In the sphere of higher education research, with few exceptions (e.g., Nakanishi, 1995), Asian Americans were almost completely invisible and voiceless before the transition into the 21st century. However, since that transition, several scholars have been making efforts to give voice to Asian Americans in postsecondary education and generate more authentic understandings of their lives.

It could be argued that the most notable advances in this scholarly arena are the collective volumes that Asian American scholars and their allies within the Asian American community have mobilized to produce. In 2002, for example, McEwen, Kodama, Alvarez, Lee, and Liang made history when they published the first collective volume on *Working with Asian American College Students*. In 2009, Museus and colleagues produced the first volume focused on issues related to *Conducting Research on Asian Americans in Higher Education* (2009b). In 2012, Ching and Agbayani published *Asian Americans and Pacific Islanders in Higher Education: Research and Perspectives on Identity, Leadership, and Success*, which represented the most comprehensive collection of work on Asian Americans in postsecondary education yet. Finally, in 2013, Museus, Maramba, and Teranishi published

The Misrepresented Minority: New Insights on Asian Americans and Pacific Islanders, and the Implications for Higher Education. Many other articles, books, and book chapters have emerged over the past decade, and they are discussed throughout the following chapters. However, I underscore these collective volumes herein because they represent a shared rising consciousness of the need to advance current levels of knowledge about Asian Americans in postsecondary education, as well as the collective mobilization of scholars to increase understandings of this population.

Another promising development regarding the inclusion of Asian Americans in the scholarly arena is the increase in the number of Asian American scholars and the emergence of research and policy organizations dedicated to serving Asian Americans in the postsecondary education arena. Regarding the former point, although still few and far between, there are an increasing number of Asian American scholars who study Asian Americans in higher education than ever before, and many of these researchers have contributed to the collective volumes discussed above. In addition, several Asian American—or Asian American and Pacific Islander (AAPI)—organizations that are involved in the production of scholarly activity on these populations have emerged in education. Important organizations, such as the National Commission on Asian American and Pacific Islander Research in Education (CARE) Project, Research on the Education of Asian and Pacific Americans (REAPA), and the Southeast Asia Resource Action Center (SEARAC) have all been involved in fostering scholarship on and advocating for Asian Americans in policy arenas. And, in 2012, a national group of AAPI scholars formed the Asian American and Pacific Islander Research Coalition (ARC), which is aimed at providing a collective voice for AAPI scholars in education, generating mentoring networks and opportunities for the development of a new generation of AAPI scholars, promoting collaborations among AAPI scholars and community members to collectively advance knowledge about these populations, cultivating a scholarship–policy–practice nexus to facilitate the involvement of AAPI researchers in policymaking efforts, and increasing avenues for the mass dissemination of research to education policymaker and practitioner audiences.

Several signs of progress have emerged in higher education policy and practice arenas over the past decade as well. For example, several highly visible national policy reports and briefs have shed important public light on Asian American issues, from their experiences in community colleges to the impact of Affirmative Action on Asian American experiences and outcomes (CARE, 2008, 2010, 2011; GAO, 2007; Park, 2012a; Poon, 2012). In addition, the federal government has established the Asian American Native American and Pacific Islander Serving Institutions (AANAPISI) designation and AANAPISIs are now eligible to secure federal funding to provide programs aimed at serving AAPI college student populations. Moreover, President Barack Obama has re-established the previously

3

dormant Advisory Commission and White House Initiative on Asian Americans and Pacific Islanders (WHIAAPI), which is aimed at bringing attention to the unmet needs of AAPI communities, expanding opportunities for this population, and improving the quality of life with the AAPIs across the nation.

Despite the many advances discussed above, signs of stagnation regarding the exclusion of authentic Asian American perspectives continue to manifest in these arenas as well (Museus, antonio, & Kiang, 2012). For example, although scholarship on Asian Americans is emerging faster than ever before, they remain underrepresented in the knowledge base. Less than 1 percent of articles published in the most widely visible peer-reviewed journals in the field of higher education include any focus on this population (Museus, 2009a). Similarly, while the aforementioned policy reports have shed light on the authentic realities of Asian American communities, other highly visible national policy reports, as well as international and national discourse, continue to exclude the voices of Asian Americans in higher education and reinforce simplistic and stereotypical views of this population as monolithic model minorities and perpetual foreigners in America (e.g., Findlay & Kohler, 2010; Pew Research Center, 2012). Therefore, while the aforementioned achievements in postsecondary education arenas are noteworthy, they should be tempered with the reality that the field of higher education has a long way to go in efforts to authentically include Asian Americans in discourse in research, policy, and practice spheres.

A CONCEPTUAL BACKDROP FOR THE VOLUME

The sparse research on Asian American college students is couched within a larger body of literature on AAPIs in society in general and education in particular. And, although the current volume represents the first extensive analysis and synthesis of theory and research related to the experiences of Asian American college students, scholars have conducted reviews of extant research on AAPIs in education in general. At the 2012 inaugural summit of the ARC, for example, Museus, antonio, & Kiang (2012) presented the findings of an analysis and synthesis of more than 300 pieces of literature on AAPIs in both K-12 and postsecondary education in a paper titled *The State of Scholarship on Asian Americans and Pacific Islanders in Education*. In the current section, I provide a summary of the major findings of this review, which can constitute an important conceptual foundation upon which the current volume builds. These major findings include (1) a synthesis of four main ways in which AAPIs have been viewed in educational research and (2) four core themes in the literature on this population.

Regarding the ways in which AAPIs have been perceived and conceived in education research, Museus, antonio, & Kiang (2012) concluded that AAPIs have been viewed as a monolith, subjected to fragmentation, imbued with integrity, and recognized as a community engaged in self-determination. The *monolithic view* of AAPIs aggregates this diverse population into a singular racial category, with the group's meanings derived from its classification and comparison with other racial groups. A substantial amount of research, for example, has constructed AAPIs as a successful monolith relative to other racial groups. The *fragmentation view* is characterized by the disaggregation of data by ethnicity, nationality, socioeconomic status, and other social groupings to highlight problems inherent in the monolithic view, generate better understandings of differences between and among AAPI subpopulations, and give greater visibility and voice to underserved AAPI populations. The *integrity view* moves beyond aggregation and fragmentation to examine AAPIs as complex social actors within racial, cultural, and structural contexts in society and education. Finally, the *self-determination view* illuminates the potential power and influence of AAPI populations in education through their engagement in leadership, politics, social activism, and resistance to oppression.

With regard to core themes in the scholarship on AAPIs in education, Museus, antonio, & Kiang (2012) identified four areas of greatest density within this body of knowledge and these areas were characterized by anti-essentialism, inequality, context, and relevance. Congruent with the fragmentation view discussed above, the *anti-essentialism* theme refers to the significant and growing body of research that focuses on deconstructing oversimplified monolithic views of AAPIs and complicating understandings of this population by disaggregating data and examining the ethnic, socioeconomic, and other forms of heterogeneity that exist within this population and analyzing how intersecting identities interact to shape the experiences of AAPIs in complex ways. Closely connected to the anti-essentialism theme is the *inequality* theme, which encompasses the large body of literature that problematizes the status of AAPIs in education by illuminating the inequalities and inequities that this population faces in various education sectors. The *context* theme refers to the body of literature that underscores the critical role of historical, racial, cultural, and structural contexts within which education institutions exist and that exhibit salient influences on AAPI experiences in education. Finally, the *relevance* theme describes the ways in which scholars discussed the importance of educators constructing and delivering education that is relevant to the AAPI cultures and communities. Specifically, this body of knowledge highlights the ways in which AAPIs are excluded from the mainstream cultures of educational institutions and illuminates the ways in which culturally relevant spaces, curricula, and pedagogies can empower AAPIs within education systems.

These four views of AAPIs and four dominant core themes within existing literature on this population constitute a valuable backdrop for the following analysis and synthesis of research on Asian American students in higher education. For example, the current text illuminates the problems inherent in the aforementioned monolithic perspective. This volume also demonstrates how viewing

Asian American college students through fragmentation, integrity, and self-determination lenses can help generate more accurate understandings of this population and intricate visions of education that can empower and facilitate the development and success of these students. Moreover, anti-essentialism to deconstruct overgeneralizations of Asian American college students, the illumination of inequalities faced by this community, and the critical role of context and relevance in understanding the experience of this population are themes that permeate the current volume in ways that also contribute to more complex and authentic understandings of Asian American students in postsecondary education.

With this backdrop in mind, I move forward to discuss the literature on Asian American students in higher education. However, before doing so, an important caveat regarding the use of the racial classification and the Asian American label is warranted.

A WORD ON THE RACIAL CLASSIFICATION OF ASIAN AMERICANS IN THE VOLUME

Before proceeding to the following chapters, it is important to distinguish between the concepts of race and ethnicity, which are utilized throughout the chapters within this volume. Whereas *race* has to do with how society socially categorizes people based on hereditary skin color and physical traits, *ethnicity* refers to a social identity that is based on historical nationality or tribal group identity (Helms, 1994). Thus, each racial group is comprised of many different ethnicities, and Asian Americans include more than two dozen ethnic communities.

Before moving forward, it is also important to discuss the nature and use of race-related terms like "Asian" and "Asian American." Today, many people in America take racial categories and racial labels (e.g., Asian or Asian American) for granted, as if they are a natural occurrence. In reality, however, racial classifications are socially constructed or, in other words, a human invention (Delgado & Stefancic, 2001; Omi & Winant, 1996). In the mid-1800s, when the first large wave of Asian immigrants began entering the United States, they did not identify themselves with an "Asian" or "Asian American" racial group and had little in common with individuals who belonged to Asian ethnic groups other than their own (Takaki, 1998). Even today, some people of Asian descent and living in the United States would not prefer to be labeled "Asian" or "Asian American," but prefer identifying with their own ethnic group.

However, when Asian immigrants began entering the United States in large numbers, dominant society and the racism that existed within it led the White majority to utilize the term "Asian" to refer to those who originated from the continent of Asia and were phenotypically and culturally different from themselves (Takaki, 1998). The racialization of Asians in America as different or the "other" provided a foundation for the dominant majority to separate themselves from and discriminate against Asians in America in the years and decades that followed. This racial construction of an "Asian" group has also permeated society and persisted through generations, eventually normalizing the use of the term "Asian."

The term "Asian American" did not emerge until the Asian American Movement that occurred the 1960s (Espiritu, 1993; Shilpa, Pawan, Sunaina, & Partha, 2000). During this era, Asian American ethnic groups witnessed an increased racial consciousness and understanding regarding how racism shaped their lives. As a result, Asian American activists coalesced to construct a collective pan-ethnic "Asian American" identity for purposes of solidarity and political power to combat systemically racist social structures and advocate for the well-being of their communities. I discuss these events in more detail in Chapter 2, but it is important to note here that racial terms utilized to categorize Asian Americans emerged from societal racism and from the emergent pan-ethnic consciousness and identity in the 1960s Movement.

It is also important to note that the terms "Asian" and "Asian American" can present significant challenges for researchers, policymakers, and practitioners seeking to understand the condition of this population in higher education. As I discuss in Chapter 3 of this volume, the Asian American population includes peoples from a wide range of distinct histories, generational statuses, ethnicities, communities, languages, socioeconomic statuses, etc. The lumping of this entire population into one Asian or Asian American racial category conflates recent immigrants from Pakistan and Chinese Americans who were born and raised within the United States. This aggregation also conflates fourth-generation Japanese Americans in Hawaii with first-generation Vietnamese refugees in Minnesota. In sum, the racial categorization of Asians or Asian Americans conflates many drastically different peoples and communities. In the context of research on Asians and Asian Americans, this aggregation can often lead to smaller subgroups within the Asian and Asian American community being silenced as their voices and experiences become lost in the aggregated data and analyses.

The simplistic aggregation of Asians and Asian Americans into a singular racial population disadvantages subgroups within Asian America in other ways as well. For example, scholars have noted that, with Asian American Studies circles, East Asian Americans (e.g., Chinese, Japanese, and Korean Americans) have dominated discourse. They have convincingly asserted that Southeast Asian Americans (e.g., Cambodian, Hmong, Laotian, Mien, and Vietnamese Americans) and South Asian Americans (e.g., Bangladeshi, Indian, Pakistani, and Sri Lankan Americans) have been marginalized within the field and their voices and needs have been ignored, or at least not adequately addressed (Kiang, 2004, 2008; Shilpa et al., 2000).

At the same time, it is important to clarify that, in the context of contemporary society's racial realities, not *all* aggregation is inevitably negative or harmful (Ching & Agbayani, 2012; Museus, antonio, & Kiang, 2012). Indeed, as I discuss in the following chapters, since the 1960s, Asian Americans have recognized that aggregation and pan-ethnic identification can be important political tools for advocating for the rights, voices, visibility, and well-being of the Asian American community. And, the potential value of aggregation and pan-ethnic coalitions as a political tool remains relevant today. Thus, both disaggregation and aggregation are imperative for researchers, policymakers, practitioners, and community members to generate authentic knowledge of Asian American populations and advocate for Asian Americans in higher education. However, analysts and activists who utilize either one of these methodological tools must do so thoughtfully and critically, so that they are constructing images and narratives that help and do not hurt Asian American populations and other communities of color in the process.

Throughout the current volume, I use the term "Asian American" to refer to residents of the United States who are of Asian descent. Despite the reality that this racial classification can contribute to social problems and pose many challenges, I choose to use the term "Asian American" because it is congruent with Asian American activists' past and continued calls for collective Asian American consciousness, acknowledges that the racialization of Asian Americans as a racial group is an unavoidable aspect of contemporary American society, and underscores the common racialized experiences of Asian American peoples. Yet, readers should consume this text, as well as other writing on Asian Americans, with caution and a critical eye so that they are aware of which voices within the Asian American community are represented in the discussion and which ones are not. As higher education scholars, policymakers, and practitioners, we must develop an understanding of both the bigger picture and the complexities that underlie it.

Chapter 1

Critical Racial Contexts

In 2000, two White men and one White woman abducted two Japanese female college students who were on their way to class, raped the students, and videotaped the crime. The assailants threatened that, if the incident was reported, they would release the video footage of the rape to the victims' families. The victims helped police locate the perpetrators, and the offenders were charged with kid-knapping, rape, and intimidation.

When the offenders were questioned, they admitted to targeting Asian women because they believed that Asians are submissive, averse to shaming their families, and therefore less likely to report these incidents to authorities.

In 2011, a White undergraduate student at the University of California, Los Angeles (UCLA) posted a YouTube rant called "Asians in the Library." Throughout the video, she described her discontent with the "hordes of Asian people" getting into UCLA, shared an array of racist views about Asians and Asian Americans at UCLA, and mocked Asian and Asian American people with "ching, chong, ling long, ting tong" noises. The video ignited a backlash from Asian Americans at UCLA and throughout the nation, and the White student eventually discontinued her enrollment at the university.

In 2010, the highly visible and widely read Canadian magazine, Maclean's published an article that was titled "Too Asian?" and expressed fears that Asian students are taking over top colleges and universities in Canada. The article shared stories that suggested this trend is driving away White students from some of the most prestigious Canadian colleges because they do not want to compete with Asian students who always study and do not know how to have fun. After the article sparked outrage in both Asian Canadian and Asian American communities, Maclean's refused to offer an apology or remove the piece from the Internet. Instead, they decided to change the title of the article.

In 2012, the well-respected Pew Research Center released a report, titled "The Rise of Asian Americans." The report asserted that Asian Americans have taken over as the largest percentage of immigrants to the United States, lead others in education and income, and have a superior work ethic. The Asian American community responded with discontent with the Pew Center's simplistic message about a diverse and complex population, as well as their reinforcement of long-standing and harmful stereotypes of Asian Americans as perpetual foreigners, yellow perils, model minorities.

It is difficult to deny that race and racism play a significant role in shaping the lives of Asian American students in higher education. Although the disconcerting stories presented above range from individual hate crimes to national policy discussions, and vary from a seemingly harmless policy report that reinforces harmful racial stereotypes to a rape, they all constitute real life examples of the ways in which race and racism influence the experiences of Asian American students. For postsecondary education scholars, policymakers, and practitioners to understand the Asian American undergraduates with whom they work, they must understand the racial context of those students' lives.

In this chapter, I discuss the significance of race and racism in the lives of Asian Americans. First, I introduce the nature of racial dynamics and processes in American society and delineate and define the different types of racism that affect the experience of people within society. Second, I offer a brief critique of the Black–White nature of racial discourse in American society and discuss some of the most salient ways that society racializes Asian Americans. In doing so, I illuminate the most salient racist constructions of Asian Americans that, at least in part, define Asian American experiences in society. Finally, I present an AsianCrit framework that offers a useful conceptual lens for understanding Asian American experiences specifically in higher education and beyond.

RACIAL PROCESSES IN AMERICAN SOCIETY

Although many people think of race as a natural, commonsense, or biological reality, it is a socially constructed concept. Indeed, the emergence of race as a significant element of society can be traced back to the initial contact between European and non-European populations occurring hundreds of years ago (Omi & Winant, 1994). European explorers, who encountered people inhabiting distant lands and exhibiting physical characteristics different from their own, socially constructed a racial worldview that allowed them to make sense of these differences and racially categorize their own communities as not only different than, but also superior to, other people and communities. As a means of harnessing power, race and racial categories were also used to justify the oppression of people of color through the denial of their rights, imposition of coercive labor, creation and perpetuation of slavery, and even extermination. Moreover, because race and racial categorization are not natural but are constructed realities, racial categories and meanings that are attached to them vary across societies and over time. The term *racial formation* refers to this process by which economic, political, and social forces shape racial categories, their meanings, and their importance (Omi & Winant, 1994).

Despite the fact that race is not natural and is socially constructed, it is a powerful and pervasive aspect of society (Delgado & Stefancic, 2001; Omi & Winant, 1994). On an individual level, one of the first things we notice about people when we meet them is their race, and this recognition of race influences our understanding of these people and how to interact with them (Omi & Winant, 1994). On a systemic level, despite the implementation of laws prohibiting racial discrimination, most social indicators suggest that racial inequalities and inequities continue to permeate almost every aspect of society (Bonilla-Silva, 2006). Moreover, the persistence and pervasiveness of race and racism has led some to argue that race is a permanent aspect of American society (Bell, 1992; Omi & Winant, 1994).

Within societal systems of racism, racial minority groups are racialized. The term *racialization* refers to the process of creating a racial category, associating that category with a previously unclassified population, and attaching racial meanings to that category and community (Omi & Winant, 1994). History illuminates how society racialized Asian Americans. As mentioned in the preceding introduction, the first wave of people who emigrated from Asia to the United States in the mid-1800s did not identify with a racial group (Takaki, 1998). However, historical accounts illuminate how the dominant majority in America racialized these immigrants throughout history (see Chapter 2 for more thorough discussion). Speaking to the permanence and pervasiveness of race and racism is the fact that racialized constructions of Asians in the 1800s reflect persisting stereotypes that still permeate discourse about Asian Americans today, which I discuss in greater detail in the following sections.

RACISM IN AMERICAN SOCIETY

Although racism is often viewed in simplistic ways, it is a complex concept. The nature of racism and its meanings are certainly not obvious or commonsense, and they can vary across individuals, communities, and time. Therefore, before discussing the role of racism in Asian American students' experiences in postsecondary education, it is important to offer some definitions of racism and clarifications regarding the meaning of racism as it is used herein.

The general term *racism* can be defined as a social system that benefits a dominant racial group and allows that population to maintain disproportionate power and privilege over minority racial groups, their experiences, and their access to resources (Harrell, 2000). In addition to this general term, several scholars have delineated different types of racism that negatively influence the lives of people of color in society (Bulhan, 1985; Carter, 2007; Clark, Anderson, Clark, & Williams, 1999; Essed, 1991; Harrell, 2000; Jones, 1997; Ridley, 2005; Rothenberg, 2007), and they include, but are not limited to, the following:

- *Systemic racism* is used to describe racism that has encompassed and permeates all major societal institutions. It functions as a deeply embedded system of social oppression but is also intensely contested (Feagin, 2006).
- *Institutional racism* refers to "patterns, procedures, practices, and policies that operate within social institutions so as to consistently penalize, disadvantage, and exploit individuals who are members of racial minority groups" (Better, 2007, p. 11).
- *Cultural racism* is a result of ethnocentrism and power. It refers to members of society favoring the values, beliefs, and norms of the dominant racial group over other racial populations. Through this process, the latter is constructed as racially inferior, thereby contributing to the oppression of these the racial minority groups (Jones, 1997).
- *Individual racism* refers to individual "beliefs, attitudes, and actions of individuals that support or perpetuate racism" (Wijeyesinghe, Griffin, & Love, 1997, p. 89).
- *Aversive racism* or *symbolic racism* have been used to describe the phenomenon of Whites endorsing egalitarian values and regard themselves as non-prejudiced, but discriminating against populations of color in subtle ways that are rationalized (Gaertner & Dovidio, 1986; Sears, 1988).
- *Vicarious racism* or *secondhand racism* refers to the process by which persons of color observe other people of color experiencing racism, reach the realization that they are also vulnerable to experiencing this racism, and experience negative consequences as a result of these observations and conclusions. People of color can either directly observe racist incidents or subsequently learn about such incidents through stories from family members, friends, community members, strangers, or people or messages in the media (Truong, McGuire, & Museus, 2011).
- *Internalized racism* is a term used to describe racially marginalized populations' acceptance of negative societal beliefs and stereotypes

about themselves that function to oppress them (Williams & Williams-Morris, 2000, p. 255). Through this process, marginalized racial groups adopt the dominant groups' version of reality and cease to define themselves and their reality independently (Bulhan, 1985).

Together, these definitions provide a more holistic understanding of the pervasive nature of racism in society and its various manifestations. Moreover, each type of racism that is delineated above can constitute a useful tool for understanding the certain aspects of the racial realities that Asian American students encounter in college life.

A few other important considerations related to these definitions are warranted. First, it is important to note that such definitions of racism or typologies of racism often imply that there is a racist system of power and privilege that advantages the dominant White majority and disadvantages people of color. According to these definitions, people of color are disempowered by systemic racism and cannot be the source of racism themselves. People of color can, however, commit acts of prejudice or prejudge people based on race and discriminate or differentially treat people on the basis of their racial backgrounds.

Another important consideration is the fact that racism can be either explicit and overt or subtle and covert. Given that racism has become less socially acceptable over time, it increasingly manifests in subtle ways (Sue, Bucceri, Lin, Nadal, & Torino, 2007). People who commit acts that perpetuate racism might believe that a particular racial minority population is inferior and express this in overt ways, or they can commit more subtle acts of racism by espousing liberal ideals while subconsciously believing that other racial groups are inferior and acting on those beliefs (Dovidio, Gaertner, Kawakami, & Hodson, 2002).

More subtle acts of racism are often called *racial microaggressions*, which can be defined as, "brief and commonplace daily verbal, behavioral, or environmental indignities, whether intentional or unintentional, that communicate hostile, derogatory, or negative racial slights and insults toward people of color" (Sue, Capodilupo, Torino, Bucceri, Holder, Nadal, & Esquilin, 2007, p. 271). There are three main types of racial microaggressions, and they include micro-assaults, micro-insults, and micro-invalidations. A micro-assault is the most like old-fashioned forms of racism in that it is an explicit verbal or nonverbal attack meant to degrade the intended target. A micro-insult is characterized by snubs, rudeness, or insensitivity and transmits demeaning messages about a person's racial heritage or identity. Finally, a micro-invalidation functions to "exclude, negate, or nullify the psychological thoughts, feelings, or experiential reality of a person of color" (Sue, Capodilupo, et al., 2007, p. 274).

There is evidence that Asian Americans experience unique racial microaggressions in everyday life and on college campuses in particular (Lewis, Chesler, & Forman, 2000; Museus, 2008a; Museus & Park, 2012). An example of a

13

micro-assault that is often experienced by Asian Americans in college is when someone calls an Asian American a "chink" or "gook" and engages in a physical bullying (e.g., Museus & Park, 2012; Sue, Bucceri, et al., 2007). An example of a micro-insult often experienced by Asian Americans might occur when people make racist jokes about Asian people having deficient English skills. Finally, micro-invalidations experienced by Asian American students in college can include incidents, for example, in which faculty members exclude Asian American perspectives and voices from the curriculum or ascribe intellectual superiority upon these students and convey that they should not require support. Whether these acts are intentional or unintentional, they can have significant cumulative negative academic, psychological, and social consequences for Asian American and other racial and ethnic minority undergraduates.

It is also important to acknowledge that racism is a stressor and exhibits significant negative physical, physiological, psychological, and social effects on victims of racial oppression (Bryant-Davis, 2007; Bryant-Davis & Ocampo, 2005; Carter, 2007; Carter & Forsyth, 2009; Carter, Forsyth, Mazzula, & Williams, 2005; Clark et al., 1999; Harrell, 2000). Indeed, people of color who experience racism in many forms and from many directions can experience racism-related stress. These consequences of racism-related stress may include, but are not limited to, experiencing headaches, anxiety, low self-esteem, humiliation, night-mares, anger and frustration, difficulty concentrating, lack of productivity and motivation, and depression. Symptoms of racism-related stress can also manifest in somatic form and include sleep deprivation, upset stomach, chest pains, tunnel vision, ulcers, back pains, loss of appetite, nausea, shortness of breath, weeping, vomiting, fatigue, increased heart rate, and hypertension (Bryant-Davis, 2007; Bryant-Davis & Ocampo, 2005; Carter, 2007; Carter & Forsyth, 2009; Clark et al., 1999; Harrell, 2000; Smith, Allen, & Danley, 2007; Solórzano, Ceja, & Yosso, 2000; Sue, Bucceri, et al., 2007).

Finally, it is important to note that, while subtle forms of racism are difficult to detect, evidence suggests that they might be just as harmful to the individuals who are victimized by them as more explicit manifestations of racism. In fact, scholars who study racial microaggressions have asserted that this form of racism is not trivial and may even be more problematic and psychologically damaging to individuals than more explicit forms because they have cumulative effects, their subtle nature makes them difficult to confront, and they can lead to victims investing psychological energy to figure out whether the experience was a manifestation of racism or an over-reaction to a benign incident on their part (Constantine & Sue, 2007; Perry, 2008; Perry & Robyn, 2005; Pierce, 1995; Solórzano et al., 2000; Sue, 2003; Sue, Capodilupo, & Holder, 2008). As a result, experiencing racial microaggressions has been associated with negative physical and psychological consequences such as increased discouragement, fatigue, and frustration (Solórzano et al., 2000). With this context of racism in mind, I now

14

turn to the ways that Asian Americans have historically been excluded from discourse around the role of racism in American society.

THE BLACK–WHITE PARADIGM IN AMERICAN SOCIETY

Before discussing the ways in which racism shapes the lives of Asian Americans in more depth, it is important to acknowledge the Black–White nature of racial discourse in the United States and the problematic implications of this binary. Asian Americans can and do experience all of the aforementioned forms of racism, but their racialized experiences are rarely at the center of racial discourse in American society. Indeed, several scholars have noted that racial discourse in America is characterized by a Black–White paradigm, which centers discussions of racism on the experiences and material conditions of Blacks and Whites, while excluding other racial groups (Espinoza & Harris, 1997; Gee, 1999; C. J. Kim, 1999). Moreover, the Black–White racial paradigm is readily apparent in both scholarly circles and mainstream media.

This often Black–White nature of racial discourse in American society is problematic for multiple reasons. First, while there is much about race and racism that can be learned from the experiences of Blacks and Whites, there is also much that is rendered invisible in discourse that excludes Asian Americans and other racial groups (Espinoza & Harris, 1997). For example, within the Black–White binary, immigration and language issues have been given insufficient attention (R. S. Chang, 1993). In addition, the Black–White paradigm precludes critical analyses of the relations between different groups of color. Most importantly, the Black–White paradigm impedes the development of more holistic understanding of the ways that race and racism shape the lives of all people within American society (Johnson, 1997). Therefore, it can be argued that moving beyond the Black–White paradigm is critical for developing more comprehensive understandings of racial issues in American society in general. In the context of higher education, the illumination of the racial realities of Asian American students can demonstrate some of the ways in which the inclusion of Asian Americans in racial discourse can inform larger discussions of race, culture, diversity, and equity in postsecondary education.

In the rare cases in which Asian Americans *are* brought to the foreground of racial discourse in the United States, they are often racialized in relation to their Black and White counterparts (C. J. Kim, 1999). Indeed, scholars have written about how Asian Americans have been racialized as relatively better than Blacks in the racial hierarchy or as relatively superior racial minorities who almost, but never quite fully, achieve White status (C. J. Kim, 1999; Wu, 1995). Of course, this conferral of honorary White status to Asian Americans reinforces existing racial paradigms that privilege Whiteness and position both Asian Americans and other groups of color as inferior to Whites in the racial hierarchy. Thus, there is a significant need for research and discourse that generates an authentic understanding of racism and the Asian American experience, particularly in the context of higher education.

THE RACIALIZATION OF ASIANS IN AMERICAN SOCIETY

In this section, I turn to focusing on the most common dominant racist constructions of Asian Americans in society. These racist constructions constitute pervasive racial stereotypes that illuminate the most salient ways in which American society racializes Asian Americans. Specifically, there are four stereotypes that permeate society's racialization of the general Asian American population, and they include stereotypes of this group as model minorities, deviant minorities, perpetual foreigners, and yellow perils (Chon, 1995; Eng, 2001; Espiritu, 2008; Lowe, 1996; Museus & Kiang, 2009; Saito, 1997a; Sue, Bucceri, et al., 2007; Yu, 2006). Asian Americans are also racialized by gender-specific stereotypes of Asian American men and women that have also persisted through many generations and permeate society. This section provides a brief overview of these stereotypes and their relevance to higher education.

The intent of this section is not to engage in a reductionist way of thinking about how race and racism impacts the lives of Asian American students, or suggest that knowledge of the stereotypes discussed herein is sufficient for understanding this impact. In fact, the current volume in its entirety paints a much more complex picture regarding the ways that race and racism, as well as ethnicity and culture, shape the experiences of this population. Rather, the current section is designed to briefly highlight some of the most salient ways that the Asian American population is racially constructed in and by American society.

THE MODEL MINORITY AND DEVIANT MINORITY MYTHS

The *model minority myth* is arguably the most pervasive racial stereotype of Asian Americans, and it casts Asian Americans as a monolithic group of people who achieve universal and unparalleled academic and occupational success (Li & Wang, 2008; Museus & Kiang, 2009; Sue, Bucceri, et al., 2007; Suzuki, 1977, 2002; Uyematsu, 1971; Yu, 2006). Although it can be viewed as seemingly benign or even positive, the model minority stereotype is problematic for many reasons. For example, the myth masks the vast diversity and disparities that exist within the Asian American population (e.g. Chew, 1994; Museus & Kiang, 2009). Moreover, the myth contributes to the invisibility of Asian Americans in higher education research, policy, and practice because it perpetuates misconceptions that Asian Americans are problem-free and do not require resources and support in college (Museus & Chang, 2009; Museus & Kiang, 2009). Furthermore, by casting all Asian Americans as model minorities in relation to other racial minority groups, society frames Asian Americans as the model to which other groups should aspire. This comparison can pit Asian Americans against other groups of color (M. J. Matsuda, 1996; Yu, 2006). Finally, the model minority myth can be used to dismiss the role of race and racism in creating challenges for populations of color.

It is important to note that, in the context of discourse about Asian American educational and occupational success, Southeast Asian Americans are racialized in unique ways. Specifically, Southeast Asian Americans are lumped into the same category as other Asian Americans and racialized as model minorities in some contexts, while they are racialized as deviant minorities in other settings. The *deviant minority myth* characterizes Southeast Asian Americans as academically inferior dropouts, welfare sponges, and gang members (Chhuon & Hudley, 2008; S. J. Lee, 1994; Museus, in press-b; Museus, antonio, & Kiang, 2012; Museus & Park, 2012; Museus, Vue, Nguyen, & Yeung, 2013; Ngo & Lee, 2007). Thus, Southeast Asian American experiences are shaped, in part, by these polarized extremes, depending on the environmental context. For example, Southeast Asian American college students experience both pressures to conform to the model minority archetype in some contexts, and are stereotyped as incapable of being academically successful in other environments (Museus & Park, 2012).

THE FOREVER FOREIGNER AND YELLOW PERIL MYTHS

The *forever foreigner myth* also permeates societal views toward Asian Americans, and refers to the exclusion of Asian Americans from the conceptualizations of what is American (Chon, 1995; C. J. Kim, 1999; Lowe, 1996; Saito, 1997b; Sue, Bucceri, et al., 2007; Volpp, 2001). The forever foreigner stereotype manifests in assumptions that all Asian Americans are foreign-born (Sue, Bucceri, et al., 2007). This myth also suggests that Asian Americans who are in the United States are incapable of assimilation and full integration into American society. At its extreme, the forever foreigner stereotype also manifests in Asian Americans being framed in opposition to what is considered American, with each of these constructions helping define what the other is not.

Closely related to the forever foreigner myth is the *yellow peril myth*, or the stereotype that Asian Americans are a threat to the United States (Espiritu, 2008; Lowe, 1996). Sometimes, yellow peril myths are gendered and have historically depicted Asian American men as hypermasculine sexual threats (e.g., Fu Manchu) or Asian American women as vicious and untrustworthy sexual deviants (e.g., dragon ladies) (Eng, 2001; Espiritu, 2008). This yellow peril myth led to military fears, such as the anti-Japanese American discourse that emerged during World War II or anti-Islamic people of color discourse that surfaced after Islamic extremists' attacks on the World Trade Center on September 11th of 2001. The yellow peril stereotype can also lead to economic concerns and anxieties, such as the fears over competition with Japanese automobile companies during the 1970s and 1980s.

In higher education, the notion of the forever foreigner and yellow peril myths can become intertwined with the model minority myth and lead to fears of hyper-successful foreigners taking over American education (Saito, 1997a; Takaki, 1998). One salient example of the model minority and the yellow peril myths is the *Maclean's* article discussed at the opening of this chapter, which was initially titled "Too Asian?" and perpetuated fears that over-achieving foreign Asian students are taking over top Canadian universities (Findlay & Kohler, 2010).

EMASCULATION AND EXOTICIZATION

Although Asian American men and women are often depicted as a yellow peril threat, they are also racialized as the opposite extreme (Eng, 2001; Espiritu, 2008; Prasso, 2005; Shek, 2006; Sue, Bucceri, et al., 2007). Asian American men are often portrayed as very unthreatening, asexual, effeminate, and socially awkward nerds. Historically, by utilizing these stereotypes to emasculate Asian American men, the dominant majority was able to address fears that Asian American men would "steal" White women and diminish the likelihood of these interracial unions (Eng, 2001). These emasculating stereotypes continue to manifest in contemporary society in a variety of forms today, as evidenced in the very rare casting of Asian American people who do not conform to this stereotype in Hollywood roles. This emasculation can have such a profound impact on the identities and experiences of Asian American men that it has been called a form of racial castration (Eng, 2001).

For Asian American women, the intersections of race and gender can produce stereotypes of hypersexual and submissive sex objects (Cho, 2003; Prasso, 2005). These stereotypes manifest in images of lotus blossoms, geishas, and prostitutes. These stereotypes also often depict Asian American women as the trophies of White men, with the former's purpose being to please the latter. Today, these emasculating and sexually objectifying stereotypes of Asian American men and women are pervasive in American society and the media continues to perpetuate them (Shek, 2006).

In the context of postsecondary education, Asian American men and women in college are likely to encounter these racial stereotypes on a regular basis, and experience negative consequences as a result. For Asian American men in college, emasculating stereotypes can perpetuate beliefs that they are easy targets for bullying. In addition, being continuously confronted with emasculating stereotypes can challenge their masculinity and lead Asian American men in college to overcompensate by engaging in hypermasculine or aggressive behavior, including adopting a "tough guy" persona and engaging in harmful behavior such as hazing or physical violence (Liu, 2002; Tran & Chang, 2013). For Asian American women in college, exoticizing stereotypes that depict them as submissive sex objects can be similarly damaging by making them more vulnerable to sexual harassment and violence (Cho, 2003). Perhaps one of the most gruesome examples of this is the 2000 abduction presented at the beginning of this chapter, and this is not an isolated assault.

Given that these racist constructions can play a profound role in the experiences of Asian American men and women in college, it is critical that higher education scholars, policymakers, and practitioners understand these racial constructions. It is equally important for college educators to engage in practice that can diminish the negative effects of such racial constructions on Asian American college students. Scholars have offered useful conceptual lenses to use in generating such understandings, and it is to these frameworks that I now turn.

AN ASIAN CRITICAL (ASIANCRIT) PERSPECTIVE

In this section, I provide an overview of an emergent Asian Critical (AsianCrit) Theory perspective that can be used as a conceptual lens for understanding the ways in which race and racism shape the lives of Asian Americans in society. Before presenting the AsianCrit perspective, a few caveats are in order. First, the origins and core tenets of Critical Race Theory (CRT), which, together with the literature discussed above, provide the conceptual foundation for the AsianCrit perspective. Then, I outline the tenets of the emergent AsianCrit framework. The AsianCrit perspective can be viewed as a tool for understanding the racial realities and racialized experiences of Asian Americans, as well as a conceptual lens through which the experiences of Asian American college students can be interpreted.

Critical Race Theory

CRT has garnered a significant amount of attention in higher education circles and has been utilized as a conceptual lens to study how dominant systems of racial oppression shape the lives of Asian Americans and other people of color. CRT is a critical theoretical framework that originally emerged in the field of legal studies in the 1970s (Delgado & Stefancic, 2001). Critical legal scholars created CRT in reaction to the unwillingness of the legal field to meaningfully critique and respond to the role of race and racism in the legal system and to give voice to people of color who experience racism within legal institutions. Put another way, CRT is a consequence of a racist legal system and was created to challenge dominant systems of racial oppression. Since its genesis, however, CRT has been adopted by scholars outside of the legal field and utilized as a critical lens to

19

analyze dominant systems of racial oppression in other spheres, such as higher education.

Different scholars have identified and framed the core tenets of CRT in disparate ways, and I discuss two of those framings in this section. For example, Delgado and Stefancic (2001) identified several core tenets of CRT, which include but are not limited to the following:

1. *Social constructionism* is the principle that there is no biological foundation for racial categories and race is instead a socially constructed phenomenon (Delgado & Stefancic, 2001).

2. *Racism as normal* suggests that racism is a normal and pervasive aspect of society (Delgado & Stefancic, 2001). Put another way, racism is a natural and normal part of everyday life and a permanent fixture in American society.

3. *Revisionist history* encompasses the reality that critical race scholars can expose the ways that race and racism permeate society and function to oppress people of color by re-analyzing and re-writing historical events through a critical race lens (Delgado & Stefancic, 2001).

4. *Differential racialization* refers to the notion that different racial groups are racialized in disparate ways, and the same racial group can be racialized differently depending on the time and circumstances (Delgado & Stefancic, 2001).

5. *Interest convergence* is the tenet that suggests that Whites who hold decision-making power in society will only support laws, policies, or programs that benefit people of color when they benefit Whites as well (Bell, 1980).

6. *Anti-essentialism* encompasses the notion that there is no essential experience or attribute that defines any group of people (Grillo, 1995; Harris, 2003). For example, there is no singular "Asian American experience."

7. *Intersectionality* refers to the reality that race intersects with class, gender, sexuality, ability, and other social axes to shape systemic forms of oppression and individual experiences (Crenshaw, 1993).

8. *Storytelling* is a tenet that is grounded in CRT scholars' belief that oppressed people have stories that can constitute valuable knowledge and can counter dominant hegemonic narratives (Chon, 1995; Delgado, 1989).

As mentioned, while CRT originated in the field of law, scholars in higher education have adopted CRT frameworks as a useful tool to challenge color-blindness and analyze the ways that race and racism function to oppress people of color in postsecondary education systems (e.g., Buenavista & Chen, 2013;

20

Buenavista, Jayakumar, & Misa-Escalante, 2009; Delgado, 1989; Jayakumar, 2012; Harper, Patton, & Wooden, 2009; Museus, Ravello, & Vega, 2012; Poon, 2013; Solórzano, 1998; Solórzano et al., 2000; Solórzano, Villalpando, & Oseguera, 2005; Solórzano & Yosso, 2002; Villalpando, 2004; Yosso, Smith, Ceja, & Solórzano, 2009). These researchers, for example, have used CRT to shed light on how seemingly neutral higher education policies and practices can contribute to the oppression of people of color and utilized this framework to provide a space for the excavation and centering of the voices of people of color in post-secondary education discourse.

Solórzano (1998) also offered a set of five major themes in CRT in the field of education. These tenets are slightly different from those outlined above and they include the following:

1. *The intercentricity of race and racism*, which suggests that race and racism are a central factor in the experiences of people of color, but they intersect with other forms of subordination, such as gender and class (Crenshaw, 1989, 1993; Russell, 1992).

2. *Challenge to the dominant ideology*, which refers to reality that CRT challenges dominant beliefs or meritocracy, colorblindness, race neutrality, and equal opportunity (Calmore, 1992; Crenshaw, Gotanda, Peller, & Thomas, 1996).

3. *Interdisciplinary perspective*, which suggests that CRT in education employs transdisciplinary knowledge from history, ethnic studies, women's studies, sociology, law, and other fields to better understand racism, sexism, and classism in education. It is important to underscore that CRT challenges ahistoricism and analyzes racism in both historical and contemporary contexts (Delgado, 1984, 1992; Garcia, 1995).

4. *Commitment to social justice*, which includes the commitment to struggle for the elimination of racism and other forms of oppression (Matsuda, 1991).

5. *Centrality of experiential knowledge*, which is the notion that the experiential knowledge of people of color provides legitimate and valuable tools for analyzing racial oppression and subordination (Bell, 1987; Delgado, 1989).

Higher education researchers have utilized the aforementioned tenets to analyze the experiences of Asian Americans in higher education (e.g., Buenavista & Chen, 2013; Buenavista et al., 2009). In addition, these core tenets of CRT, and the knowledgebase from which they emerged, have also provided the foundation for the generation of additional critical perspectives that are more tailored to the voices and concerns of various groups of color.

Indeed, although CRT is a critical framework that can be used to analyze how race functions in society in general and influences the lives of all people within it, scholars who utilize CRT have branched off to generate critical race perspectives and bodies of literature that focus on analyzing and understanding specific racial and ethnic groups (Brayboy, 2005; R. S. Chang, 1993; Delgado Bernal, 2002; Museus & Iftikar, 2013; Solórzano & Yosso, 2001; Valdez, 2000–2001; Villalpando, 2004; Wright & Balutski, 2013). For example, at a colloquium on Latina and Latino issues and CRT that was held in 1995, a group of Latina and Latino scholars conducted a critical assessment of CRT and created Latina and Latino Critical Theory (LatCrit) (Valdez, 2013). LatCrit was conceived as a close cousin to CRT and espouses the anti-subordination foundation of CRT, but is focused on highlighting the voices and addressing the concerns of Latinas and Latinos in discourse and policy.

A decade after the emergence of LatCrit, slightly deviating from the approach taken by LatCrit scholars who have utilized the core tenets of CRT to analyze the voices and concerns Latinas and Latinos in society (e.g., Solórzano & Yosso, 2001), Brayboy (2005) utilized CRT as a framework to create and propose a distinct Tribal Critical Theory (TribalCrit) perspective that highlights the voices and concerns of Indigenous peoples in America (Brayboy, 2005; Wright & Balutski, 2013). Brayboy's (2005) TribalCrit perspective shares many similarities with CRT, but also some differences. His perspective, for example, highlights the endemic nature of colonization, the reality that U.S. policies toward indigenous people are rooted in imperialism, the problematic nature of assimilation, the central role of sovereignty and self-determination, and the importance of understanding tribal philosophies, beliefs, customs, and traditions in under-standing the realities of indigenous people and communities. Much like CRT has constituted the groundwork for the emergence of LatCrit and TribalCrit, critical race scholars have also aimed to utilize CRT as a foundation for the analysis and understanding of Asian American experiences. It is to this literature that I now turn.

The Asian Critical (AsianCrit) Framework

Scholars who study CRT and Asian Americans have taken multiple approaches to applying critical race frameworks to the analysis of Asian American experiences. For example, many scholars have utilized core tenets of CRT to analyze experiences within this population (e.g., Buenavista & Chen, 2013; Buenavista, et al., 2009; Gee, 1999; Liu, 2009). Other scholars have argued for the need for a new AsianCrit perspective that more specifically addresses the needs and concerns of Asian Americans (R. S. Chang, 1993; Liu, 2009). These scholars have demonstrated the utility of using CRT as a conceptual lens to better understand the ways that racial oppression affects Asian American peoples and communities.

In recognition of the need for a conceptual framework that centers racial realities that are at the core of Asian American experiences, Museus and Iftikar (2013) have offered an AsianCrit perspective that outlines a unique set of tenets that are designed to provide a useful analytic framework for examining and understanding the ways that racism affects Asian Americans in the United States.[1] Before discussing the perspective, a few caveats are warranted. First, like LatCrit and TribalCrit, the AsianCrit framework is not intended to replace the tenets of CRT. Rather, AsianCrit utilizes both CRT and already-existing knowledge about Asian American experiences to offer a refined set of uniquely tailored tenets that can further advance critical analyses of racism and Asian American lives. Second, while the AsianCrit tenets are focused primarily on illuminating the ways that racism impacts Asian Americans, the framework also includes concepts that can be useful in understanding the experiences of other communities of color and can contribute to larger discussions regarding how racism functions in society. Third, these AsianCrit tenets are not intended to be a permanent or definitive framework, but are aimed at providing a conceptual foundation for scholarly discourse on racism and Asian Americans.

The AsianCrit perspective consists of seven interconnected tenets. The first four tenets build upon prior CRT tenets but incorporate additional knowledge of Asian American racial realities, while the last three tenets are combinations or reiterations of original CRT tenets that are critical in the examination of Asian American issues and experiences:

1. *Asianization* refers to the reality that racism and nativistic racism are pervasive aspects of American society, and society racializes Asian Americans in distinct ways. Whereas original CRT tenets clarify that racism is a normal aspect of society, Asianization focuses attention on the ways in which society lumps all Asian Americans into a monolithic group and racializes them as overachieving model minorities, perpetual foreigners, and threatening yellow perils (Chon, 1995; Espiritu, 2008; Lowe, 1996; Museus & Kiang, 2009; Saito, 1997a; Sue, Bucceri, et al., 2007; Yu, 2006). In addition, society also racializes Asian American men as emasculated beings and Asian American women as hypersexual and submissive objects (Cho, 2003; Eng, 2001; Prasso, 2005). This racial Asianization is a common mechanism through which society racially oppresses Asian Americans.

    It is important to note that the tenet of Asianization highlights the ways in which such racialization operates to (re)shape laws and policies that affect Asian Americans and influence Asian American identities and experiences. For example, the construction of Asian Americans as monolithic model minorities has served as one of the major organizing principles for policies, legislation, and resource distribution in the United States. The model minority stereotype has also profoundly impacted the individual identities and experiences of Asian Americans in society. One example of the ways in which racial constructions of Asian Americans as model minorities has impacted national policy and individual experiences is the model minority stereotype's contribution to constructions of Asian Americans as "honorary Whites" within Affirmative Action discourse. Such honorary White status has framed Asian Americans as victims of race-conscious policies, and this discourse influences both societal perspectives and decisions about Affirmative Action policies and programs (Wu, 1995).

It is also important to note that Asianization often manifests itself in polarized extremes. Asian Americans being racialized as honorary White model minorities or yellow peril threats depending on the current interests of the White majority (for more in-depth discussion, see Chapter 2). The gendered racialization of Asian Americans can also manifest in polarized extremes, with Asian Americans being racially emasculated in some contexts and portrayed as hypermasculine in others. In addition, these binaries illuminate the fluid nature of the racialization of Asian Americans in society.

2. *Transnational Contexts* highlights the importance of historical and contemporary national and international contexts for Asian Americans. As such, an understanding of how racism shapes Asian American experiences is informed by a critical analysis of the ways that historical and current economic, political, and social processes within the United States shape the conditions of Asian Americans. While CRT also acknowledges the importance of historical and contemporary national context, AsianCrit analyses foreground transnational contexts because a comprehensive understanding of how racism impacts Asian American lives is also informed by knowledge of how historical and current processes that extend beyond national borders—such as imperialism, the emergence of global economies, international war, and migration—shape the conditions of Asian American people and communities (Choy, 2000; Museus, antonio, & Kiang, 2012; Takaki, 1998).

There are many examples of how transnational contexts shape the lives of Asian Americans in the United States. For example, one of the government's intentions with the 1965 changes in immigration laws was to bring highly educated immigrants, such as South Asians, into the United States to meet that nation's job market and technological needs (Chan, 1991; Takaki, 1998). Additionally, U.S. colonial and post-colonial contexts and relationships have significantly shaped the cultures, economic and political positions, and citizenship status of Filipinos in the U.S. Finally, U.S. military intervention in Southeast Asia contributed to the displacement of many Cambodian, Hmong, Laotian, and Vietnamese refugees (Portes & Rumbaut, 1996; Takaki, 1998). It is important to note that knowledge of how these transnational contexts impact the lives of Asian Americans can contribute to better understandings of larger processes of how racism operates.

3. *(Re)Constructive History* underscores the importance of (re)constructing an historical Asian American narrative. First, similar to CRT's tenet of revisionist history, (re)constructive history emphasizes re-analyzing history to expose racism toward Asian Americans. Second, however, this tenet goes beyond re-examination to emphasize that Asian Americans have been racially excluded from American history and advocate for transcending this invisibility and silence to construct a collective Asian American historical narrative that includes the voices and contributions of Asian Americans in the United States (e.g., Chan, 1991; Takaki, 1998; Tamura, 2001, 2003; Umemoto, 1989). Moreover, history is critical to developing a collective pan-ethnic identity and consciousness. Indeed, (re)constructing an historical Asian American narrative can shed light on shared struggles and contribute to the development of a common Asian American culture, thereby contributing to the creation of conditions that are necessary to foster stronger Asian American identity and consciousness.

   In addition, (re)constructive history highlights the ways in which such histories not only add to or correct the historical record, but also function to provide critical insights on the present and inform a progressive future for Asian Americans (and other groups of color). As I demonstrate in the following chapters, an analysis of Asian American history can inform understandings of the current conditions of Asian American communities and help comprehend how education can be (re)shaped to better engage and foster success among Asian American students in higher education. For instance, an understanding of the historical struggles of Southeast Asian Americans can be utilized to inform understandings of the current conditions of these communities and the construction of progressive educational programs and practices that can foster the identity development and success of Southeast Asian American college students.

4. *Strategic (Anti)Essentialism* is based on the assumption that race is a socially constructed phenomenon that can be shaped and reshaped by economic, political, and social forces. Building on the CRT tenet of

25

anti-essentialism and the notion of strategic essentialism (Spivak, 1987), strategic (anti)essentialism acknowledges that dominant oppressive economic, political, and social forces impact the ways in which Asian Americans are racially categorized and racialized in society, but also highlights the reality that Asian Americans can and do engage in actions that affect these processes as well. For example, Asian American researchers and activists can and do engage in coalition building and (re)define racial categories to garner political power and influence in advocacy against racial oppression (Coloma, 2006; Umemoto, 1989). In the context of higher education, Asian American researchers and activists construct coalitions and collective voice to engage in anti-essentialist activities and reveal the diversity, inequity, struggle, and voices within their communities (Museus & Griffin, 2011).

Strategic (anti)essentialism, however, also recognizes that complete rejection of racial categorization and uncritical reification of racial categories can both yield undesirable outcomes. Moreover, the tenet acknowledges the potential complex and contradictory effects of engaging in important Asian American advocacy activities, such as coalition building for social justice, which can simultaneously advance the well-being of Asian American communities and reinforce racial categorizations and constructions of this population. Strategic (anti)essentialism suggests that effective research and activism should generate an understanding of Asian American communities as a whole and build on the possibilities for unity provided by the larger racial category while recognizing and developing intricate knowledge of the diversity and complexity that exists within these populations. Strategic (anti)essentialism also underscores the importance of researchers who study Asian Americans and activists who advocate for Asian American communities making purposeful decisions about which Asian American groups to include in their analysis (i.e., which Asian American groups to aggregate and disaggregate) toward the end of generating the most useful understandings of this population to advocate for the well-being of all of those within these communities.

5. *Intersectionality* is based on the notion that racism and other systems of oppression (e.g., sexism, heterosexism, ableism, etc.) intersect to mutually shape the conditions within which Asian Americans exist (Crenshaw, 1993). As a result of these systemic intersections, racial identity and other social identities (e.g., gender, sexual orientation, and class identities) mutually shape Asian American experiences.

This AsianCrit intersectionality tenet mirrors the original core CRT intersectionality tenet, acknowledges the omnipresent and intersecting nature of systems of social oppression, and rejects the notion that any one form of oppression is more salient than others. However, AsianCrit recognizes that, for analytical purposes, certain systems must be selected as the focus of investigation that most effectively shed light on the phenomenon under investigation. This tenet underscores the importance of those conducting intersectional examinations to be purposeful in making assessments of which systems and identities can provide crucial insights about the environments, curriculum, policies, programs, practices, processes, or issues that affect Asian Americans within the given situation (e.g., issue, time, space, and actors involved). The purposeful application of intersectionality can help facilitate deeper and more complex multilayered analyses of the ways in which social structures, political processes, and identities intersect to create certain conditions, realities, and experiences than what already exists.

6. *Story, Theory, and Praxis* underscores the notion that counterstories, theoretical work, and practice are important inextricably intertwined elements in the analysis of Asian American experiences and advocacy for Asian American people and communities. Building on the work of CRT scholars who underscore the value of stories (e.g., Yamamoto, 1997) and TribalCrit scholars who assert the connections between story and theory or theory and practice (Brayboy, 2005), AsianCrit analyses assert that stories inform theory and practice, theory guides practice, and practice can excavate stories and utilize theory for positive transformative purposes.

   Story, theory, and praxis also recognizes the relevance of imperial scholarship, or the notion that the voices of people of color and work of intellectuals of color have been historically marginalized in academia (Delgado, 1984, 1992). AsianCrit advocates against imperialism in the scholarly arena and centers the voices of Asian Americans and work of Asian American scholars. AsianCrit also suggests that the voices of Asian Americans and work of Asian American intellectuals can and should inform theory, and that knowledge in all of these forms can and should inform practice.

7. *Commitment to Social Justice* highlights the notion that critical theory is dedicated to advocating for the end of all forms of oppression (M. J. Matsuda, 1991). As such, AsianCrit is aimed at advocating for the elimination of racism. And, recognizing the intersections between racism and other systems of subordination, AsianCrit also advocates for the eradication of sexism, heterosexism, capitalism, and other forms of oppression.

27

This AsianCrit perspective can provide a useful tool for understanding and analyzing the conditions and experiences of Asian American people and communities in the United States. It can also constitute a valuable lens for understanding many of the Asian American undergraduate experiences synthesized in the following chapters.

IMPLICATIONS FOR INSTITUTIONAL POLICY AND PRACTICE

The racial context within which Asian American students exist has many implications geared toward higher education policy and practice that is designed to foster the learning and development of this population. First and foremost, college educators should make an effort to teach students that racism inevitably affects their lives. More specifically, institutional policymakers and practitioners in higher education should fund, create, and support programs and practices that foster racial awareness among Asian American students. Such efforts affect Asian American and other students in college. Given the reality that colorblind and post-racial ideologies are becoming increasingly prominent in public discourse and society, many Asian American students are likely to enter college without an understanding of racism and how it influences their lives. But, such understandings are critical for students to comprehend the conditions of their communities, the perspectives of their families, and themselves.

Moreover, institutional policymakers and practitioners who are interested in serving Asian American students in higher education can and should employ AsianCrit frameworks to inform the development of programs and practices that are specifically designed to serve this population. For example, the utilization of AsianCrit as a conceptual lens for the formation of institutional policies, programs, and practices could lead to institutional policymakers and practitioners developing programs that focus on deconstructing racial constructions of Asian Americans in society, linking transnational contexts to Asian American college students' experiences, teaching Asian Americans the importance of both the deconstruction of racial categories and pan-ethnic coalitions, and extracting counterstories from Asian American students that reflect Asian American communities, empower Asian Americans in college, inform the development of scholarly theories, and transform college and university cultures and climates.

I conclude this chapter with a word about the utility of this framework for readers who hope to develop a more holistic and complex understanding of Asian American students' experiences in higher education. The presentation of the AsianCrit framework herein is intended to permit readers to utilize this perspective in multiple ways as they move forward and navigate subsequent chapters of the volume. First, the AsianCrit perspective provides a conceptual lens for interpreting and understanding many of the contextual realities and individual experiences that are discussed in greater detail throughout the current volume. Second, the AsianCrit framework provides a holistic perspective that can help clarify how race and racism influence the critical contexts and lived realities of Asian American college student. With this framework in mind, I turn to the following chapters to unpack the historical contexts within which Asian American communities and Asian American college students exist.

NOTE

1   Several scholars with expertise in the area of race, ethnicity, and education were asked to review this framework, and their feedback was incorporated into the version presented herein. Tracy Lachica Buenavista, Nolan L. Cabrera, Kevin K. Kumashiro, Maria C. Ledesma, Julie J. Park, Lori D. Patton, Oiyan A. Poon.

Chapter 2

Critical Historical Contexts

"Neither the life of an individual nor the history of a society can be understood without understanding both."

C. Wright Mills

"What happens when someone with the authority of a teacher describes our society, and you are not in it? Such an experience can be disorienting—a moment of psychic disequilibrium, as if you looked into a mirror and saw nothing."

Adrienne Rich

"The notion of progress suffuses [history] textbook treatments of black–white relations, implying that race relations have somehow steadily improved on their own. This cheery optimism only compounds the problem, because whites can infer that racism is over."

James W. Lowen

Four years ago, I was asked to participate on a panel at Harvard University. The panel was focused on critical issues in the Asian American community. During the panel discussion, an Asian American graduate student from Harvard raised his hand and asked the question, "if the challenges that Black people have faced are so much worse than those of Asian Americans, why should anyone care?" Not wanting the conversation to evolve into a an Oppression Olympics contest, or competition over what groups are more or less disadvantaged by racism, I responded by saying that one of the most salient differences between the historical struggles of Black Americans and historical challenges faced by Asian Americans is that the latter are never discussed.

Of course, my response was not intended to suggest that the historical oppressions of Black and Asian American people are not markedly different. These two groups are racialized in different ways and oppressed through disparate mechanisms (C. J. Kim, 1999). And, my comment was not intended to imply that Black Americans have adequate voice or that they are represented positively or fairly in history books. On the contrary, many would argue that too few Black voices and heroes are celebrated in American history, Black people are often viewed from a deficit perspective, and historical accounts of racism are not sufficiently critical to foster complexity in students' understandings of the role of societal racism in Black experiences. Rather, my response to the Harvard student was intended to underscore the problematic reality that Asian Americans are especially invisible in American and higher education history.

Indeed, a large proportion of society knows the names of Harriet Tubman, Booker T. Washington, W. E. B. Dubois, Rosa Parks, Martin Luther King Jr., and Malcolm X—or at least has heard and discussed them in school. But, unless individuals in society are among the small minority who have had Asian American Studies courses in college, few know of Vincent Chin—the Chinese autoworker who was beaten to death in Detroit, Michigan in 1982 by two White autoworkers who mistook him for a Japanese American during the heightened xenophobia toward the Japanese and fears that they would take over the American auto industry. Few know the name of Wen Ho Lee, the Taiwanese American scientist, who was arrested in 1999, indicted on more than 50 criminal charges, placed in solitary confinement for more than nine months, and later freed of all accusations except one count of mishandling sensitive documents. And, few have had the opportunity to learn about the heinous conditions of Asian American immigrant sugar plantation laborers in Hawaii or the racial violence targeted toward Chinese railroad workers in the West.

In sum, most people in society—Asian Americans and non-Asian Americans alike—are deprived of a history that includes voices and faces from Asian American communities. This invisibility of Asian Americans in history is highly problematic. For Asian American students in postsecondary education, such invisibility can hinder their abilities to comprehend the historical forces that cause the current conditions within their communities and families. This omission of Asian Americans from history can lead to Asian American students in college internalizing the belief that they have not contributed to and are not full members of society or higher education. This exclusion can diminish the relevance of history for these students. And, because history is critical to the development of culture and collective identity, the absence of Asian Americans in the history books can hinder the development of a collective Asian American consciousness.

In the context of higher education in particular, the absence of Asian Americans in history books also deprives postsecondary educators of the tools to develop a contextual understanding of the Asian American students whom they serve. Indeed, just as understanding the history of fighting for Democracy in America is integral to college educators' abilities to comprehend the backgrounds and worldviews of their American students or the history of slavery and the fight for Civil Rights are critical to understanding the identities of Black community members in the United States, an understanding of Asian American history is important in understanding the backgrounds, worldviews, and identities of this population.

Stories from Asian American history, such as those discussed above, are important because they honor Asian American contributions to society and make this population relevant. They excavate the realities of Asian American struggle and achievement. They shed light on the complexity of Asian American people and communities. And, they illuminate the common experiences with racism, and help foster a sense of collective struggle within the Asian American community, as well as among Asian Americans and other people of color.

Although Asian Americans have been virtually excluded from mainstream history books, Asian American Studies scholars have emphasized a common historical past among Asian Americans (Kibria, 1998). In the remainder of this chapter, I utilize this scholarship from Asian American Studies and literature from the field of education to discuss some critical historical contexts that help better understand the experiences of Asian American college students. First, I provide a brief overview of immigration trends of Asian Americans. This context is critical to understanding the current social and economic conditions that are discussed in the following chapter. Next, I discuss the importance of historical perpetual racism and transnational contexts in understanding Asian American lives. Then, I discuss five critical stories in the history of Asian Americans in higher education that underscore the struggles and strengths of this population in postsecondary education. The chapter concludes with some recommendations regarding the ways in which college educators can utilize this historical information to facilitate the engagement, learning, and development of Asian American students in college.

The current chapter is not intended to be a comprehensive source of Asian American history. However, it is aimed at starting a conversation about Asian American history in higher education. Moreover, this chapter is one small step in (re)constructing higher education history into one that is more inclusive of Asian American voices and stories.

THE MIGRATION OF ASIANS TO AMERICA IN HISTORY

Asian American Studies scholars have generated useful historical analyses of Asian American migration and experiences (e.g., Chan, 1991; Hune, 2002; Okihiro, 1995; Takaki, 1998; Tamura, 1993, 2001a, 2001b; Wei, 2004). The work of these scholars clarifies that Asian American migration to the United States can be separated into two major waves (Hune, 2002; Okihiro, 1995). Prior to the first wave of entry, in the late 1870s, some Filipino seamen immigrated into the United States and formed communities in Louisiana. In addition, some Asian Indians entered the country and served as household servants to sea captains in Massachusetts or as indentured servants and slaves in Pennsylvania. However, little is known about these pre-first wave immigrants.

The first major wave of Asian migration to the United States began in the 1840s and continued until the 1930s (Hune, 2002; Tamura, 2001a). Approximately 1 million Asian Americans who entered during this first wave of migration to America helped develop the western states (Chan, 1991). These included approximately 7,000 Asian Indians, 370,000 Chinese, 400,000 Japanese, 7,000 Koreans, and 180,000 Filipinos. Most of these first wave migrants were laborers, and some opened small businesses. This wave of migrants faced significant racial discrimination that resulted in economic exploitation and limited political and legal rights. During World War II, which included American intervention from 1941 to 1945, children of the first wave of Asian migrants to the United States were imprisoned in internment camps or joined military forces. Two decades later, in the1960s and 1970s, children of the second generation participated in the Civil Rights Movement and fought to transform higher education to better reflect and respond to the needs of diverse communities (Wei, 1993).

The second wave of Asian migrants to the United States began arriving after the passage of the 1965 Immigration Act (Chan, 1991). The 1965 Immigration Act and other laws that followed ended race-based immigration restrictions on Asians and facilitated family reunification. The Act gave preferences to both professionals (e.g., scientists, doctors, nurses) in short supply in the United States and unskilled workers who could fill jobs (e.g., garment workers) that were undesirable to American workers. Therefore, many Asian Indians, Chinese, Koreans, and Filipinos, who immigrated into the United States during this second wave of migration, sought jobs and worked in these areas.

During the second wave of migration, in addition to the groups discussed above, many Southeast Asian American refugees entered the United States (Chan, 1991). As a result of U.S. military intervention in Southeast Asia, the end of the Vietnam War, the 1975 Indochina Migration and Refugee Assistance Act, the 1980 Refugee Act, and the 1987 Amerasian Homecoming Act, approximately 1 million Cambodian, Hmong, Laotian, and Vietnamese refugees entered the United States. Moreover, from 1960 to 1994, the Asian American population grew drastically, from 1 million to 8.8 million people (Tamura, 2001a).

This second wave is characterized by increasing diversification within the Asian American community (Chan, 1991; Hune, 2002; Museus, in press-b: Museus et al., 2013). Southeast Asians were not previously significantly represented in the United States population, but this second wave brought a substantial number of Southeast Asian refugees who came from historical, geographic, and socioeconomic backgrounds that were distinct from their East and South Asian American counterparts. Although some of the early Vietnamese refugees came from privileged backgrounds and had support networks to facilitate their adjustment to the United States, the vast majority of Southeast Asian refugees came from agrarian backgrounds and had endured traumatic experiences, such as displacement by war, unsanitary living conditions in refugee camps, separation from family, rape, murder, and genocide (Abueg & Chun, 1996; Boehnlein & Kinzie, 1997; Kinzie, 1989).

It is important to acknowledge that the salient challenges and negative experiences that characterize the refugee experience have led to the emergence of cultures of silence in some Southeast Asian families and communities. These cultures of silence are characterized by refugee parents' unwillingness to divulge and resistance to sharing stories about family and community histories with their children (Lin, Suyemoto, & Kiang, 2009). This culture of silence is significant for multiple reasons. First, although parents often refuse to share family and community histories in order to protect their children, evidence suggests that this silence can have negative consequences, including the perpetuation of trauma, hindering of Asian American students' understanding of their families' dynamics, and challenges in the development of Asian American students' psychosocial well-being. Institutions of higher education can play a key role in breaking these cultures of silence.

THE SIGNIFICANCE OF PERPETUAL RACISM IN ASIAN AMERICAN HISTORY

Noteworthy is the fact that racism has been a perpetual defining aspect of the Asian American experience since the arrival of the first large wave of Asian migration to the United States and throughout history. Indeed, as I discuss herein, Asians have historically faced race-based exclusion from the United States and experienced xenophobia and racism after arrival.

The United States utilized national policy focused on race-based exclusion to control Asian immigration at several periods in history (Chan, 1991; Hune, 2002; Takaki, 1998; Tamura, 2001a, 2001b). The first influx of Chinese immigrants in the mid-1800s experienced xenophobia, anti-Chinese mob violence, and policies that circumscribed their opportunities through exclusion from various labor markets (Ogbar, 2001). And, in 1882, the Chinese Exclusion Act outlawed Chinese laborers from entering the country for ten years. Ten years later, in 1892, the Chinese Exclusion Act was extended another ten years and, in 1902, the government extended the Act indefinitely (Chan, 1991; Takaki, 1998; Tamura, 2001a, 2001b).

34

After an influx of Japanese Americans entered the United States, they faced xenophobic reactions and racism similar to their Chinese counterparts (Chan, 1991; Takaki, 1998; Tamura, 2001b). For example, in 1906, the San Francisco school board mandated that Japanese and Korean students attend a segregated Chinese school. Japan, which was a strong military power at that time, protested and led the United States government to negotiate the Gentlemen's Agreement of 1907–1908, which was an agreement that the San Francisco school board would terminate its segregation order and Japan would prohibit laborers from leaving for the United States. Under the agreement, however, non-laborers, former residents, and family members of current residents were allowed to immigrate. In 1907, Congress also passed a law that outlawed the entry of Japanese and Korean laborers. The Gentlemen's Agreement led to the arrival of a large number of Japanese wives and picture brides, who function to reunite families and bring stability to the immigrant Japanese American community. This influx of Japanese women, however, fueled anti-Japanese sentiment, and led to Congress passing the 1924 Immigration Act, which banned the entry of all Asian immigrants except Filipinos, who were American nationals.

Many Filipinos came to the United States from the Philippines, which had endured a history of Spanish and American colonization (Tamura, 1993). The Philippines were under the control of Spain for approximately three centuries until the Treaty of Paris in 1899, which led to American control of the Philippines from 1899 to 1946. After large numbers of Filipino immigrants entered the United States in the early 1900s, the American government passed the 1935 Tydings-McDuffie Act, which established sovereignty of the Philippines in 1946 and stopped the migration of Filipinos to the United States. Specifically, the law imposed an annual quota of 50 Filipino immigrants to the continental United States. The law, however, did not place the same restrictions on Filipino immigration to Hawaii, and many Filipinos continued to immigrate into Hawaii in order to meet labor shortages.

The aforementioned legislative acts that limited or barred Asian immigration into the United States not only affected those who could not gain entry into America, but also hindered the growth of Asian American communities within the United States national borders. Moreover, in addition to this political form of racism, Asian Americans experienced social forms of racism that subordinated Asians in the American racial order. This subordination has historically perpetuated, in part, through the racialization of Asian Americans as perpetual foreigners and yellow perils. Moreover, this racialization has led to racial oppression throughout history that has manifested in both systemic (e.g., the internment of Japanese Americans during World War II) and individual (e.g., racially motivated hate crimes) forms of discrimination against Asian Americans within the United States, which I discuss in more detail below.

THE SIGNIFICANCE OF TRANSNATIONAL CONTEXT IN ASIAN AMERICAN HISTORY

The experiences of college students are rarely contextualized with historical perspectives, but historical contexts are critical to acquiring a holistic understanding of these undergraduates' backgrounds and lives. Moreover, historical transnational contexts and the ways that they shape the contemporary conditions of Asian American people and communities are critical to understanding Asian American undergraduates' backgrounds and experiences. For example, the conditions that surround the migration of various Asian American communities to the United States can inform understandings of Asian American students and have implications for the delivery of education to effectively serve these populations.

The conditions that surround Asian American migration to the United States vary drastically across ethnic groups. Moreover, the conditions of migration vary across individuals within Asian American ethnic groups. In this section, I discuss three critical conditions of migration that vary across communities and individuals: cultures of origin, reasons for migration, and access to resources.

Varied Cultures of Origin

Those who have migrated from Asia to the United States have come from a wide array of different geographic regions with varied cultures. Moreover, the cultures from which Asian migrants come have varying levels of congruence to the dominant culture of American society, in terms of politics, language, economics, and many other cultural elements. For example, due to this history of Western influence and colonization, it could be argued that Filipino migrants who come from urban areas of the Philippines might be more likely to enter the United States speaking proficient English, while Hmong students who migrated to the United States from a rural area of Laos might be more likely to have less developed English skills. Similarly, a Japanese student migrating from Tokyo likely comes from an economy that is more congruent with the United States than someone from rural Cambodia.

In addition, across the aforementioned varied Asian cultures and communities exist different perspectives toward and beliefs about education, ranging from cultures that view formal education as critical to success and to agrarian cultures that do not emphasize competitive formal schooling as a means to achieve a successful life. Indeed, large portions of immigrants from East and South Asia originate from cultures and communities in which education is the primary means of social mobility, access to high-quality educational institutions is competitive, and families invest resources in supplementary education (Min, 2003; Zhou & Kim, 2006). And, those immigrants bring those values into the

United States. In contrast, Southeast Asian American refugees are more likely to come from agrarian communities that have communal orientations and see farming capacities as more critical to the sustenance and welfare of their communities than formal and competitive schooling.

Diverse Reasons for Migration

People who have migrated from Asia to America also vary in the factors that caused their migration to the United States, with some migrating to seek educational and occupational opportunity and others being forced out of their homelands as a result of war (Portes & Rumbaut, 1996). Although the reasons for Asian migration to America cannot be generalized to an entire ethnic group, in general, East and South Asian immigrants are more likely to have come to the United States to seek opportunity and improve the lives of their families, while, as mentioned, Southeast Asian American refugees are more likely to have been displaced by war and the threat of post-war political persecution.

Immigrants can share similarities with refugees, but they also exhibit important differences. Immigrants are likely to enter the United States with the expectation of necessary adaptation to succeed academically and professionally. In contrast, many refugees might be forced out of their homeland and primarily be concerned with survival. Thus, immigrants are more likely to be ready to assimilate into society and its educational and occupational structures.

Differential Access to Resources

Finally, those who have migrated from Asia to the United States have come from communities with varying levels of access to resources. Indeed, in contrast to their East and South Asian immigrant counterparts, Southeast Asian refugees are more likely to have come from under-resourced nations and communities in Asia. Compared with East and South Asian immigrants, Southeast Asian refugees are also more likely to settle and form communities in the United States that suffer from insufficient resources. As I demonstrate in Chapter 3 of the current volume, these disparities in resources across different Asian American ethnic groups are reflected in recent national data on resources within the Asian American community.

In sum, these variations in cultural academic orientations, causes of migration to the United States, and access to resources among Asian American students in higher education play a role in shaping these undergraduates' academic orientations and access to resources as they enter postsecondary education. As such, these factors provide important contextual knowledge regarding the nature of Asian American communities and the values and resources that Asian American students bring with them to college. In the final section of this chapter, I discuss how such realities have important implications for higher education policy and practice. However, before discussing these implications, in the next section, I focus on historical events in Asian American history that have transpired specifically in the context of higher education.

CRITICAL EVENTS AND PERIODS IN THE HISTORY OF ASIAN AMERICAN HIGHER EDUCATION

An historical Asian American narrative within the field of higher education specifically is virtually non-existent. Of course, the construction of such a narrative is far beyond the scope of the current chapter or book. Similarly, the in-depth analysis of historical events in the history of Asian American higher education in particular is beyond the scope of the current discussion. Rather, in this section, I provide a brief overview of six significant events in Asian American history in higher education as a building block for scholarly discourse about the formation of an historical narrative that includes the voices of this population.

The six events discussed herein illuminate struggles and strengths of Asian Americans in higher education history. These historical events are intended to provide the foundation for the future generation of literature that can contribute to the formation of the aforementioned historical Asian American narrative in postsecondary education. These six events include the internment of Japanese Americans during World War II, emergence of the model minority myth, the Yellow Power Movement, the San Francisco State College (SFSC) strike, the Don Nakanishi tenure case, and the racially motivated murder of Won-Joon Yoon.

The Japanese Internment: 1942 to 1945

On the morning of December 7th, 1941, in the middle of World War II, the Japanese military bombed Pearl Harbor on the Hawaiian island of Oahu. The Japanese military sunk more than 20 ships in the United States Pacific Fleet and destroyed or damaged hundreds of U.S. aircraft that were stationed at Pearl Harbor. The aftermath of the destructive attack on Pearl Harbor was characterized by shock and trauma, as well as America's entry into World War II against the axis powers of Italy, Germany, and Japan.

Approximately ten weeks after the attack on Pearl Harbor, President Franklin D. Roosevelt signed Executive Order 9066, which authorized the internment of more than 120,000 Japanese Americans (Nagata & Cheng, 2003). The Executive Order forced these Japanese Americans to leave their homes on the West Coast, give up their freedom, and relocate into internment camps. The order applied to all men, women, and children of Japanese ancestry. Those who were ordered to relocate into internment camps included Japanese American citizens who were born and raised in the United States, and may have espoused pure patriotic loyalty to America during this time. However, these individuals' American-ness mattered little, as they were racialized and otherized by the United States government and American society.

When the Japanese arrived at the internment camps, they were incarcerated behind barbed wire fences, watched by armed guards, and were forced to live in substandard living conditions (Nagata & Cheng, 2003). Of course, the internment disrupted the lives of Japanese Americans and stripped them of their freedom. In addition to this disruption, some researchers have asserted that the internment experience caused racism-based trauma among many within the Japanese American community (Loo, 1993; Nagata & Cheng, 2003).

Societal xenophobia and racism clearly provided the foundation for the Japanese internment. During the internment, General John L. DeWitt was quoted several times publicly expressing xenophobic views toward Japanese Americans during the War, and these quotations illuminate common racist perspectives about people of Japanese ancestry at the time. For example, he testified before the House Naval Affairs Subcommittee to investigate congested areas on April 13th, 1943, and was quoted sharing the following thoughts:

> I don't want any of them here. They are a dangerous element. There is no way to determine their loyalty. . . . It makes no difference whether he is an American citizen, he is still a Japanese. American citizenship does not necessarily determine loyalty. . . . But we must worry about the Japanese all the time until he is wiped off the map.
>
> *(Korematsu v. United States)*

While several Italian and German residents were interned, the vast majority of citizens of Italian and German descent remained free from confinement. Thus, only Japanese Americans were singled out for incarceration because of their racial background, providing a salient example of how racism powerfully shaped the lives of Japanese Americans—and probably a plethora of other Asian Americans who were mistaken for being Japanese American—and the ways in which racialized constructions of Asian Americans as a perpetually foreign yellow peril threat manifested in the mid-1900s.

Many Japanese Americans complied with the order and waited until the end of the war to regain their freedom, while others engaged in actions to reassert their American-ness and change societal perceptions of the Japanese American community (Austin, 2004). For example, several Japanese Americans joined the military to prove their allegiance to the United States and defend their country, and became members of the famous 442nd Japanese Regiment Combat Team comprised of Americans of Japanese ancestry. Members of the 442nd went on to receive several badges of honor and significant recognition for the role that they played in World War II.

39

In addition, just a few months after the signing of Executive Order 9066, War Relocation Authority (WRA) Director, Milton Eisenhower, facilitated the creation of the Japanese American Student Relocation Council, which was aimed at moving Japanese American students from the internment camps to college campuses (Austin, 2004). Working within the context of the aforementioned societal racism, barriers from several federal agencies, apathetic higher education leaders, and hostility toward the Japanese, the WRA worked with Japanese American college students to facilitate the relocation of approximately 4,000 Japanese Americans from their internment camps on the West Coast to hundreds of colleges in other parts of the country, and ensure their safe adjustment to their new locations. The Council stressed that Japanese American college student would serve as "ambassadors of good will" and, accordingly, some Japanese students assumed a responsibility to represent the Japanese community in desirable fashion and have a positive impact on society.

The stories of the Japanese Internment and ambassadors of goodwill constitute salient reminders of how Asian Americans can be subject to racially motivated subordination in society, particularly in the face of uncertain military, political, or economic pressures that induce fear and xenophobia. Interestingly, it has been noted that these ambassadors of goodwill might have had negative unintended consequences. Austin (2004), for example, clarified that their pressure to be ambassadors and strive for creating a positive representation of Japanese Americans might have fueled the model minority myth that rose to prominence in the following decades.

The Rise of the Model Minority Myth: 1960s to 1980s

For centuries, depending on the economic and political context of the time, racial constructions of Asian Americans have shifted back and forth, between the racialization of this population as a model minority or a yellow peril (Wu, 1995). During times of relative peace and stability, Asian Americans have been compared with other racial minorities and characterized as a model minority. In contrast, in times that were fraught with political anxieties and concerns over limited resources, Asian Americans have been viewed as a yellow threat to the well-being of American society. It could also be argued that these racial constructions interact with one another, and that the model minority image periodically fuels rising fear that Asian Americans are a threat to the welfare of American society (Wu, 1995). Moreover, the shift of dominant racial constructions of Asian Americans between the polarized extremes of model minority and national threat demonstrates the ways that economic and political forces shape the racialization of Asians in America (Omi & Winant, 2002).

As mentioned in Chapter 1 of this volume, the model minority myth is the overgeneralization that all Asian Americans achieve universal and unparalleled academic and occupational success (Museus, 2009a; Museus & Kiang, 2009; Suzuki, 1977, 2002). Historical manifestations of images of Asian Americans as model citizens and workers date back to the early 1800s (Wu, 1995). During the early 1800s, there were periods in which Chinese Americans were compared with their Black slave counterparts and lauded for their superior work ethic. Similarly, in the early 1900s, there is also some indication that, during some periods, Japanese Americans were viewed as model citizens. As discussed in the previous section, during the Japanese internment of the 1940s, Japanese American ambassadors were faced with pressure to be model citizens and this image began to emerge again in localized contexts in society.

Scholars, however, have argued that the model minority myth actually rose to prominence during the Civil Rights Movement of the 1960s and fight for equality (Suzuki, 1977; Uyematsu, 1971; Wu, 1995). In a defining historical moment in 1966, the *New York Times* published an article that was titled "Success Story, Japanese American Style" (Pettersen, 1966). This article characterized Japanese Americans as a minority group that had risen above the barriers of racial prejudice and discrimination to embody the ultimate American success story, and contrasted them with "problem minority" groups that have been unable to achieve the same success. The story suggested that, because Asian Americans could succeed despite racial prejudice and discrimination, so too should Blacks and Latinos be able to rise above such challenges. The *New York Times* article marks the beginning of the domination of the model minority image in the racial construction of Asians in America. Indeed, from the 1960s through the 1980s, images of Asian Americans in the media were almost uniformly congruent with the model minority image (Wu, 1995). During this period, Asian Americans were repeatedly portrayed as intellectually superior, hard-working, family-oriented, and law-abiding. While stories that counter the model minority image are increasingly emerging in academic literature and the media, the model minority stereotype persists and it continues to permeate national policy discussions and images in mainstream media (Museus, 2009a; Museus, antonio, & Kiang, 2012).

It is important to note that, when the model minority image emerged in the 1960s, conservatives utilized the myth to discount Civil Rights Activists' challenges to the racial order and fight for equality (Uyematsu, 1971). Since the 1960s, conservatives have continued to use this stereotype as a tool that is aligned with their political values and positions (Wu, 1995). The model minority myth supports general conservative ideologies by suggesting that Asian Americans achieve success by rejecting problem minorities' challenges to racial hierarchies. Therefore, the myth suggests that, for other racial minority groups to achieve success, they should reject efforts to challenge racial oppression as well, working to keep the racial order intact. Moreover, the model minority stereotype pits racial minority groups against one another by framing Asian Americans as honorary Whites who acquiesce to the superiority of Whites in return for being constructed as superior to other racial minority populations.

Although the perspectives of people throughout the United States are shaped by the model minority myth, many people in society have never heard this specific term, and few people are aware of the origins of the myth and the role that it played in discounting the fight for civil rights and equal opportunity. Nevertheless, the historical political realities that gave rise to the myth are critical to the development of more complex and holistic understandings of ways that the model minority stereotype continues to impact discussions of access, diversity, and equity in American higher education today. Indeed, the highly political nature of the formation of the model minority stereotype can help understand how the perpetuation of the myth today buttresses contemporary policy discussions in higher education. The model minority myth, for example, misleadingly reinforces conservative and colorblind perspectives that Asian Americans have universally overcome racial and cultural barriers to achieve unparalleled success and ignores the real challenges that this population faces in American society—and these messages discount the need for Affirmative Action policies and programs.

The Yellow Power Movement: 1966 to 1975

Another historical event that transpired in the 1960s was the emergence of the Yellow Power Movement. During the 1960s, Asian Americans organized a Movement that sought "freedom from racial oppression through the power of a consolidated yellow people" (Uyematsu, 1971, p. 12). In higher education, key characteristics of the Yellow Power Movement of the 1960s included the solidification of a pan-ethnic Asian American identity, the construction of pan-ethnic Asian American political coalitions, Asian American engagement in political and social activism, and the establishment of ethnic studies programs that serve Asian American communities and other communities of color.

It is important to note a few important contextual factors that catalyzed the emergence of the Yellow Power Movement. First, a common American experience among people of Asian descent provided the foundation for the movement. Indeed, prior to World War II, pan-ethnic Asian American coalitions were not possible because the Asian American community was largely comprised of immigrants who came from rival nations in Asia and did not share a common language (Espiritu, 1993). By the 1960s, however, many third-generation Asian Americans who were college-age had the shared experiences of racial oppression in the United States and a common language, which enabled the formation of a pan-ethnic Asian American identity and eventually pan-ethnic Asian American political coalitions (Espiritu, 1993; Umemoto, 1989).

A second contextual factor that led to the emergence of the Yellow Power Movement is the fact that, by the mid-1960s, the United States was heavily involved in the Vietnam War abroad and many American lives were being lost. These global political realities led to growing anti-war sentiment and discontent with imperialism affecting Third World countries (Tamura, 2001a; Umemoto, 1989). At the same time, people of color within the United States were still facing horrendous racism and there was an increase in anti-racism perspectives.

Third, during the 1960s, as the United States witnessed an increased awareness of oppression, violence and the repression of anti-war, racial minority, women's rights, and other social movements led to growing frustration and anger. Salient examples of this violence and repression in the 1960s include the assassinations of Martin Luther King, Jr. and Robert Kennedy (Umemoto, 1989). Other examples of this violence and repression during this era include police beatings of protesters at the Democratic National Convention and police violence against the Black Panther Party (BPP), attacks on Chicano youth, and a drunk officer's shooting of a Chinese woman in the eye. As a result of this suppression, many adopted the perspective that significant change had to be achieved through force. Within this turbulent political context, the Black Power Movement began to grow in size and influence, with more than 30 BPP chapters emerging across the country and thousands of Black people committing to the BPP's struggle against racial oppression. The convergence of growing social unrest with the inspiration of the Black Power Movement led to the emergence of the Yellow Power Movement in the late 1960s.

Recognizing that Asian Americans suffered from racism alongside other people of color and noticing the growth of the Black Power Movement, Asian American activists increasingly engaged in civil rights and anti-oppression activities (Ogbar, 2001). In October of 1967, Chinese students at SFSC formed the Intercollegiate Chinese for Social Action (ICSA), which was aimed at cultural and community activities, such as advocating against poverty and tutoring immigrant children in English. In the spring of 1968, the Philippine-American Collegiate Endeavor (PACE) was established and was aimed at fighting for the rights of Filipino youth. In the summer of 1968, the Asian American Political Alliance (AAPA) was also established at the University of California, Berkeley, and the AAPA constituted the first pan-ethnic Asian American political coalition and was a vehicle for sharing political concerns across ethnic groups and collective action. In 1968, all three of these organizations joined Black and Mexican American student organizations in the Third World Liberation Front (TWLF). The TWLF was aimed at combating institutionalized racism through increased consciousness and the elimination of racism (Umemoto, 1989).

During this era, Asian American activists fought to shed silence, form a new political consciousness, and determine their own futures. In addition, the Yellow Power Movement activists demanded more Asian American administrators and faculty at college campuses and a curriculum that was responsive to the needs of Asian American communities, rather than large corporations. Asian American

43

"activists positioned themselves as purveyors of a new ethnic consciousness and part of a new generation of progressive change" (Ogbar, 2001, p. 31). During this era, Asian American coalitions also worked in collaboration with Black, Chicano, Latino, and Native American activists to demand an end to the Vietnam War, police brutality, severe exploitation of farmworkers, and Eurocentric education (Ogbar, 2001; Umemoto, 1989).

Although the Yellow Power Movement is rarely included in history books, this historical enterprise provides context for understanding Asian American students in higher education. The movement offers a counternarrative to the pervasive racialized constructions of Asian Americans as a docile model minority that is unaffected by racism. Moreover, the Movement illuminates the reality that Asian Americans have been a part of the struggle for social equality in America.

The San Francisco State Strike: 1968 to 1969

The SFSC strike of 1968 was a microcosm of the larger social movements against racial oppression in the 1960s, and is another salient event in the history of Asian American students in higher education (Umemoto, 1989). Before discussing the SFSC strike, it is important to note that several environmental factors provide important context for the SFSC protest. For example, the Master Plan for Higher Education in California provides important context for understanding the strike. Projections indicated that the full-time student body would triple between 1958 and 1975, and the space race placed pressure on institutions of higher education to fuel American industries, particularly in math and science. The Master Plan was aimed at restructuring California education to meet the needs of rapidly growing student populations and the industry in the state. The Master Plan proposed to address these needs by restricting admissions to the top colleges in the state and divert students to junior colleges, which led to decreased access and a decline in underrepresented students of color at the most selective postsecondary institutions within the state system of higher education.

For Asian American activists, the convergence of Asian American community and student interests also provides important context because this merger created local conditions that engendered interests and engagement in the strike (Ogbar, 2001; Umemoto, 1989). In 1968, in the San Francisco area, there was an increasing awareness of the significant racial and social problems that existed in San Francisco's Chinatown (Umemoto, 1989). In addition, with their growing racial consciousness, Asian American students recognized that they were deprived an education that included their communities' historical legacies and contributed to positive social change within those communities. When TWLF demands for a Black Studies program at SFSC were met with resistance from administrators, who argued that they had a duty to keep subjectivity and politics out of the university, tensions escalated and led to the protest.

44

The SFSC administration's resistance to student demands led many students to conclude that the university's image of objectivity and neutrality was founded on racism and classism, as well as increasing frustration and anger among students (Umemoto, 1989). In May of 1968, TWLF students protested with a sit-in at the office of the President of SFSC. During this sit-in, the police used force to navigate the protest, and this violence led to 10 injuries and 26 arrests. The SFSC administration's resistance to student demands for culturally relevant education and its repression of student protests led activists to conclude that their demands constituted a fundamental challenge to the system and led to the increased mobilization of hundreds of students in advocacy of institutional transformation.

On November 5th of 1968, protesters held a meeting of more than 700 students and community supporters (Umemoto, 1989). On November 6th, several hundred student activists began the SFSC strike as they marched into classrooms, set trash cans on fire, disrupted campus activity, and marched to the President's office in support of TWLF's demands. On November 7th, 600 protesters marched to the SFSC administration building at SFSC, and by November 8th, the campus witnessed a 50 percent decrease in classroom attendance.

In 1968, a shift in the political climate led to the election of Ronald Reagan as California Governor in 1966, Richard Nixon as President in 1968, and Republican control of the California state legislature by 1968. Governor Reagan appointed a conservative Japanese American, named Samuel Ichiye Hayakawa, as President of SFSC. After his appointment, Hayakawa banned campus rallies. And, while students continued to protest, they were met with police violence and hundreds were arrested (Umemoto, 1989). During the first two weeks of the strike in early November, the police arrested 148 protestors. On December 2nd of 1968, 1,500 protestors gathered for a campus rally, police beat and arrested hundreds of them. On December 4th of 1968, approximately 6,000 protestors gathered and were met with police violence and arrests. On January 23rd of 1969, more than 500 protestors demonstrated on campus and, within minutes, police arrested more than 400 of them. Between November of 1968 and March of 1969, more than 900 faculty and student protestors were arrested at state college campuses in California (Dumke, 1969).

The SFSC strike underscores the reality that Asian Americans have a history of resistance in the United States that should be told. Umemoto (1989) asserts the following:

Asian American students played a significant role in student movements of the sixties, as clearly demonstrated by the San Francisco State Strike. . . . Their demand for a relevant and accessible education stemmed from the aspirations of peoples who had fought for justice and equality since their arrival in the

45

United States. And, in many ways, it was this legacy that steeled the movement and today frames the context for understanding the long-lasting significance of the strike.

(pp. 35–36)

Like the larger Yellow Power Movement, the strike provides a counternarrative to stereotypes of docile and complacent Asian Americans. In addition, the story highlights the significance pan-ethnic identity and coalitions in political movements. And, the legacy of the TWLF and the strike illuminates the common histories and struggles across communities of color.

The Nakanishi Tenure Battle: 1987 to 1990

Almost two decades after the San Francisco State strike of 1968, another historic battle that is relevant to the history of Asian American higher education occurred in Southern California: The fight for Dr. Don Nakanishi's tenure at the University of California, Los Angeles (UCLA). In the summer of 1987, Dr. Nakanishi was denied tenure at UCLA (Nakanishi, 1990). However, because promotion and tenure are synonymous with power and privilege in the academy, the denial of Nakanishi's tenure was symbolic of the reality that Asian Americans faced racial barriers. Nakanishi and his supporters decided to spend the next two years fighting the decision, and they launched a legal and political battle against the university for his tenure.

There were several reasons to suspect that the denial of Nakanishi's tenure was a result of subjectivity and discrimination (G. Matsuda, 1990; Nakanishi, 1990). First, prior to the decision, Nakanishi's scholarship on racist admissions and affirmative action led to a federal investigation and negative attention at UCLA (G. Matsuda, 1990). Second, many Asian Americans were aware that they faced a glass-ceiling because of racial prejudice and discrimination in the professions, and saw the tenure decision as another manifestation of this racial barrier (Nakanishi, 1990). Third, emergent evidence suggested that top officials in the tenure processes at UCLA exhibited racially prejudiced views of Nakanishi. Specifically, Nakanishi's colleagues reported that top administrators at UCLA had referred to Nakanishi as a "dumb Jap" or "fat Jap."

Although UCLA officials deliberately delayed the legal case over Nakanishi's tenure, perhaps in an effort to allow time for political support for Nakanishi's case to dissipate, multiple short-term victories had the opposite effect of increasing support for the challenge to the tenure decision (Nakanishi, 1990). Nakanishi's team won two grievances, which acknowledged procedural irregularities in the tenure review process and that the Dean of his college had deliberately attempted to deny him tenure. In addition to winning these two victories, Nakanishi's team garnered increased support from several different constituencies, including one critical source of support: Asian American college students (Chien, 1990; Katayama, 1990).

The advocates in support of Nakanishi's case understood that their ability to win the battle was dependent on their ability to apply political pressure to the university (Minami, 1990). And, Asian American college students played a key role in the battle for Nakanishi's tenure because they were able to lead a movement that applied significant political pressure (Chien, 1990; Katayama, 1990). First, UCLA students garnered support from 27 state legislators, community leaders, religious leaders, educators, and students on other college campuses. Second, UCLA students began discussions with key Asian American and Pacific Islander alumni about boycotting alumni donations to UCLA until the case was resolved. Third, UCLA students engaged in months of outreach and lobbied the UCLA Graduate Student Association and Undergraduate Student Association to declare a position on the case, resulting in the unification of the entire UCLA student body in support of a positive tenure decision. Finally, they fostered awareness of the case through leaflets, petitions, candlelight vigils, presentations, and a massive protest that included more than 8,000 students across several college campuses in California.

In May of 1989, Nakanishi was granted tenure by UCLA, resulting in the continuation of his very successful career at the university, which culminated in his retirement in 2009. For students who were involved in the battle for Nakanishi's tenure, however, it has been argued that the victory was a re-affirmation of the need for Asian American Studies, faculty of color, community-based research, and equal rights for due process (Katayama, 1990). Indeed, the Nakanishi tenure case can certainly been viewed as a victory that facilitated progress in each of these aforementioned areas. And, for those who read about Nakanishi's battle for tenure today, the battle might also represent an example of the power that Asian American student organizing can yield to create positive social transformation.

The Murder of Won-Joon Yoon: 1999

Even if they are not often included in history books, Asian American history in higher education is permeated with experiences of racial prejudice, racial discrimination, and racially motivated hate crimes on college campuses. While there are a plethora of stories that illuminate such incidents, in this section, I discuss one racially motivated hate crime that transpired over a decade ago. In July of 1999, at Indiana University in Bloomington, a White supremacist went on a killing spree and he shot and murdered a Korean American student, named Won-Joon Yoon.

Benjamin Smith was raised in the suburbs of Chicago. In college, Smith attended both the University of Illinois and Indiana University, where he emerged as a White supremacist and was known for passing out racist flyers and pamphlets on campus (The Brady Center to Prevent Gun Violence, 2009). After leaving Indiana University, Smith moved to Morton, Illinois, which was near the home base of Matthew Hale and his Word Church of the Creator, a White supremacist organization that advocated for White superiority over racial and religious minorities.

While living in Morton, Smith decided to launch a race-war (The Brady Center to Prevent Gun Violence, 2009). Because Smith had previously been accused of beating his girlfriend and possessing illegal contraband, he had a restraining order placed on him. While the restraining order prohibited Smith from purchasing firearms and he was unable to purchase a gun from a federally licensed weapons dealer, he did eventually acquire multiple firearms through classified advertisements.

Armed with two guns, Smith set out on a killing spree July 2nd (The Brady Center to Prevent Gun Violence, 2009). First, in Rodgers Park in Chicago, Smith shot six Orthodox Jews who were on their way home from their temple. Minutes later, in Skokie, Illinois, Smith shot and murdered Ricky Byrdsong, a Black basketball coach at Northwestern University. On July 3rd, Smith shot and wounded a pedestrian in Springfield, Illinois. Then, Smith drove to Decatur, Illinois and shot and wounded another victim. Next, Smith drove to Urbana, Illinois, where he fired upon, shot, and wounded Stephen Kuo, an Asian American college student from the University of Illinois.

On July 4th, the third day of the killing spree, Smith drove to Bloomington, Indiana. In Bloomington, a 26-year-old student at Indiana University named Won-Joon Yoon was standing on the sidewalk and preparing to enter Korean United Methodist Church (Burck, 1999). However, Smith opened fire on Yoon, hitting him in the back with two bullets and ending his life. After the shooting in Bloomington, police tracked Smith down and, as they were about to arrest him, witnessed him shoot himself in the chin and take his own life.

It is important to consider the aftermath of the shooting. Although such incidents can sometimes be mourned in fleeting ways and have little long-lasting impact, it can be argued that the Bloomington community reactions to the murder of Yoon reflect some commitment to diversity and tolerance. First, on July 7th, the Common Council of the City of Bloomington passed a resolution to honor the life of Yoon and "emphatically reaffirm our pledge that we as a community will never succumb to the seeds of hatred and violence" (Cole, 1999, p. 1). Then, on July 12th, almost 3,000 people gathered at Indiana University's Musical Arts Center to celebrate the life of Won-Joon Yoon and mourn their loss. The auditorium was filled to capacity and overflowed with attendees, and a message from President Bill Clinton was read, urging passage of the Hate Crimes Prevention Act, which expanded protection from hate crimes when it was eventually signed into law by President Barack Obama in 2009 (Matz, 1999).

Finally, after Yoon's death in 1999, Indiana University established a scholarship in Yoon's memory, which is designed to provide financial support for students who exemplify and advocate for racial and religious understanding and tolerance (Indiana University Newsroom, 2013).

Won-Joon Yoon's murder was a tragedy. However, this historic incident can also teach us important lessons about the present. For example, Smith's shooting spree illuminates parallels in the ways that racism can shape the experiences of Asian Americans and other communities of color. Indeed, in illuminating how Yoon and Byrdsong both became victims in the same racially motivated rampage, this story can provide a basis for the analysis of commons struggles between Asian Americans and other people of color. In addition, the Bloomington community's reaction to Yoon's death underscores how the tragic incident led to a renewed commitment to diversity and tolerance. The intent here is not to argue that Indiana University did everything that it could to turn Yoon's death into an educationally valuable historic moment, but it made an effort to utilize the incident as a catalyst for difficult dialogue and positive change. The importance of this effort is reflected in the comments of Pam Freeman, the University's Associate Dean of Students and Director of Student Ethics and Anti-Harassment Programs, who asserted that, "it's important that we not forget history and that we just continue to be strong in our resolve to help people understand that we all are entitled to live in safety and peace and we don't all have to be alike to do that" (Amato, 2009).

IMPLICATIONS FOR INSTITUTIONAL POLICY AND PRACTICE

As mentioned above, this chapter was not intended to provide any in-depth analysis of Asian American history in higher education. Nevertheless, the preceding trends and events that provide the historical context for contemporary Asian American communities and the lives of Asian American students in higher education have significant implications for institutional policy and practice on college and university campuses. I conclude this chapter with a discussion of just a few of these implications herein. These implications include understanding and engaging historical context to inform the co-curriculum on college campuses, using history to foster critical thinking about Asian American and other college students, generating more contextual and complex understandings of contemporary phenomena, and to provide the foundation for critical dialogues about Asian Americans in postsecondary education.

Understanding and Engaging Historical Community Contexts

It is important that educators understand the historical context of Asian American communities' pre-migration cultural origins, reasons for their migration to the

United States, their migration experiences, and their experiences as immigrants and refugees in America. Indeed, having knowledge of various Asian American communities' pre-migration, migration, and post-migration experiences can help educators better understand their students' lives and how to effectively structure curricular and co-curricular programs and activities in ways that best serve these individuals. In addition, even with an understanding of historical Asian American community contexts, the ways in which this knowledge is incorporated into the co-curriculum might vary between Asian American students whose families have been in the United States for generations and those whose families have recently migrated to and settled in America. Thus, the application of historical community contexts into the curriculum might be uniquely tailored to various subpopulations within the Asian American category.

Scholars have provided one example of how they have incorporated knowledge of Southeast Asian American historical community contexts into the curriculum to most effectively serve Cambodian and Vietnamese students. They have, for example, highlighted how college educators' understandings of Southeast Asian American cultures and communities, these communities' displacement from their homelands, and these communities' struggles in escaping political persecution and migrating to the United States can inform the development of curriculum that can simultaneously foster learning, facilitate intergenerational communication, and constitute a source of healing for these students and their families (e.g., Kiang, 2002, 2009; Lin et al., 2009). This is just one salient example of how such contextual knowledge can constitute and invaluable tool in the planning and delivery of educational programming and practice to serve Asian American students in college.

Using History to Foster Critical Thinking

Historical trends and stories, such as those shared discussed above, can be used to construct activities and discussions that can facilitate critical thinking and promote positive developmental outcomes among Asian American college students. Indeed, rather than offering mere summary accounts of factual data and historical events, the historical contexts and events described above include critical and controversial issues that can challenge commonly held assumptions about the political and social realities of Asian American students' lives. Thinking about history in this way can permit bringing Asian American history to life by connecting it to the lived realities of Asian American college students today.

There are many ways to utilize the historical contexts above to facilitate the development of critical thinking skills amongst Asian American and other students in postsecondary education. The Japanese internment story can spark healthy debates between Asian American students and their peers about whether it was acceptable for the federal government to order the incarceration of Japanese

Americans, while also underscoring the potentially deterministic nature of racism in American society. The story of the Yellow Power Movement can provide the basis for critical discussions regarding the reasons why public discourse around the Civil Rights Movement excludes the stories of Asian Americans in this era. The historical endurance and the model minority myth and the political context around its rise to prominence in the 1960s can provide educators with a basis for posing critical questions about whether and how this racial stereotype might serve the purposes of various political parties, whether a juxtaposition of model minority imagery with stereotypes of Blacks and Latinos as intellectually inferior might lead to discounting these latter populations' race-related challenges, or what other negative consequences might result from the model minority construction.

Generating More Complex Understandings of Contemporary Social Phenomena

In addition to helping college educators better understand Asian American students and how to effectively serve them, the historical contexts discussed above can help institutional policymakers and practitioners better comprehend phenomena that are often seen as benign social conditions but are actually politicized and harmful realities that shape the experiences of Asian Americans in higher education. In particular, a historical perspective of the political dynamics that gave rise to salient stereotypes of Asian Americans and how the White majority utilized those overgeneralizations to achieve political ends can help postsecondary policymakers and practitioners better understand the damage that can be done by further perpetuating such stereotypes in higher education discourse.

The Pew Research Center's (2012) national report on the rise of Asian Americans in the United States is one recent development that can be used as an example to underscore how some of the aforementioned historical contexts can inform understandings of contemporary social phenomena and corresponding policy discourse. The Pew Center's report highlighted recent national statistics that demonstrated that Asian Americans have surpassed Latinos as the largest group of new immigrants and that they are more educated than other groups. In doing so, the report failed to paint a more authentic and complex picture of the Asian American population. Had the Pew Center understood the ways that the model minority myth had been initially constructed and utilized as a political tool to reinforce conservative political perspectives around civil rights and the reality that the myth is still being used as a political tool by conservatives in debates about Affirmative Action today, it might have chosen to construct a more complex narrative about Asian American immigrants in the United States.

51

Providing a Foundation for Critical Dialogues and Collective Consciousness

Finally, postsecondary educators can utilize specific historical accounts, such as the stories discussed above, to provide a foundation for dialogues about Asian American college student experiences. As mentioned above, the incorporation of these histories into curricular and co-curricular activities can provide a solid foundation for faculty and staff to more effectively understand the complexities of Asian American experiences, teach Asian American students how their communities have contributed to American history, engage Asian American students by giving them voice and visibility in the curriculum, and empower Asian Americans in college by exposing them to the potential influence that they can have on education and social justice.

Equally important is the fact that, through the incorporation of these histories into the curriculum and co-curriculum, college educators can create a foundation of common historical knowledgebase about Asian American history and, in doing so, contribute to the further development of a collective Asian American consciousness. Of course, Asian American Studies programs have been utilizing Asian American history to foster such collective consciousness for decades. However, as the Asian American population grows and an increasingly number of Asian Americans enter other academic disciplines and professional fields, it is important to develop an historical narrative and collective consciousness in these other areas, because they are critical to ensuring that Asian American people and communities become an authentic element of the historical and cultural fabric of these arenas.

Chapter 3

Critical Demographic Contexts

"The power of visibility can never be underestimated."

Margaret Cho

"We all should know that diversity makes for a rich tapestry, and . . . all the threads of the tapestry are equal in value no matter what their color."

Maya Angelou

"There should exist among the citizens neither extreme poverty nor, again, excessive wealth, for both are productive of great evil."

Plato

"Poverty is the worst form of violence."

Mahatma Gandhi

Today, the Asian American community is so vast and diverse that it is difficult to identify characteristics that describe the entire population. However, national data suggest that there are at least three salient features of the Asian American community: rapid growth, diversity, and inequality (Museus, 2013). First, according to 2010 Census statistics, Asian Americans are the fastest growing racial group and are becoming increasingly visible in the United States (U.S. Census Bureau, 2011). Second, the Asian American population includes individuals who represent diverse nations, generations, cultures, communities, languages, and other characteristics that contribute to the rich tapestry of diversity within the United States. And, third, the Asian American community encompasses drastic inequalities. Indeed, within the Asian American population exist some of the most affluent ethnic populations in the United States, as well as some of the most under-resourced and underserved communities in the nation.

In this chapter, I delve more deeply into these three characteristics of the Asian American community. However, before proceeding with this discussion, it is important to note a few caveats. First, it is important to acknowledge that the racial and historical contexts that are discussed in the previous two chapters of this volume are inextricably intertwined with the contemporary social and economic conditions that characterize Asian American communities in the United States. Indeed, upon critical examination of recent national data, it is readily apparent that those Asian American communities that migrated to America as a result of United States imperialism and military intervention, that originated from primarily agrarian communities, and that are the most recent communities to establish themselves within national borders are those that suffer from the greatest socioeconomic disparities.

Also noteworthy is the fact that the demographics of the Asian American community vary drastically between and across geographic regions of the United States (Museus, 2013). For example, Asian Americans are concentrated and enjoy a noticeable level of visibility and voice in some states and localities, while they are few in number and virtually invisible and voiceless in other regions. In addition, Asian Americans are growing rapidly in certain geographic areas and relatively slower in other locations of the United States. Moreover, the ethnic and socioeconomic composition of Asian American communities also varies significantly from one region to another across the nation. And, in some cases, the same Asian American ethnic subpopulation exhibits relatively high levels of educational attainment and affluence in one geographic area and faces drastic educational and socioeconomic inequalities in other regions of the country, such as in the case of Filipinos who are relatively education and affluent in Southern California but face educational and socioeconomic disparities in Hawaii.

As mentioned, the Asian American community is characterized by rapid growth, diversity, and inequality (Museus, 2013). In the following sections, I utilize data from the U.S. Census, the Integrated Postsecondary Education Data Systems (IPEDS), and the American Community Survey to analyze these three characteristics of the Asian American population in greater detail. The chapter concludes with implications for institutional policy and practice.

RAPID GROWTH

As mentioned, the Asian American population is rapidly growing (Museus, 2013). In fact, 2010 Census statistics indicate that Asian Americans are the fastest growing racial group in the nation (U.S. Census Bureau, 2011). Specifically, between the years 2000 and 2010, the Asian American population grew at a rate of 43 percent, which was four times faster than the growth rate of the total population. With regard to their share of the total national population, AAPIs represented approximately 4.5 percent of the nation in 2000 and that percentage grew to 6 percent in 2010.

When national population projections are examined, it is clear that the Asian American community will continue to grow, both in raw numbers and in their percentage of the total U.S. population. For example, in raw numbers, the Asian American population is projected to increase from 14.7 million in 2010 to approximately 33 million in 2050 (Figure 3.1). In addition, population projections indicate that approximately 8 percent of U.S. citizens will be of Asian descent by the year 2050 (Figure 3.2). It is important to note that these projections are conservative estimates because they only include individuals who identified as "Asian alone" on census forms and do not include the substantial portion of the Asian American population that identifies with two or more racial categories. This multiracial Asian American population represented approximately 15 percent of the total Asian American community. Thus, if this multiracial segment of the community were incorporated into the analysis, it would significantly increase the current and projected representation of Asian Americans in the national population.

The growth of the larger Asian American community is mirrored by the increase in Asian Americans entering American postsecondary education (Museus, 2013). Figure 3.3 shows actual Asian American undergraduate and graduate student enrollments in postsecondary institutions between 1999 and 2009 and projected enrollments of this population in higher education to 2019. As the figure suggests, between 1999 and 2009, the number of Asian American undergraduate and graduate students enrolled in institutions of higher education increased by about 430,000 students, from approximately 0.91 million to about 1.34 million, during this time period. Moving forward, undergraduate and graduate Asian

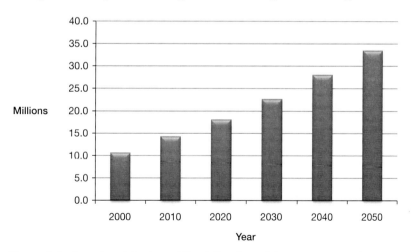

Figure 3.1 Actual and Projected Total Number of Asian American Citizens in the United States, 2000–2050.

Data Source: U.S. Census (2004). Figures expressed in millions. Museus (2013) © 2013 Stylus Publishing, LLC.

55

American student enrollments are projected to increase from 1.34 million students in 2009 to approximately 1.7 million in 2019, which is an estimated increase of about 395,000 undergraduate and graduate students or growth rate of approximately 30 percent.

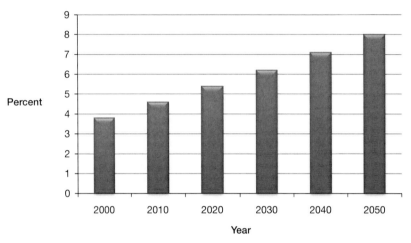

Figure 3.2 Actual and Projected Proportions of United States Population that Identifies as Asian American, 2000–2050.

Data Source: U.S. Census (2004). Museus (2013) © 2013 Stylus Publishing, LLC.

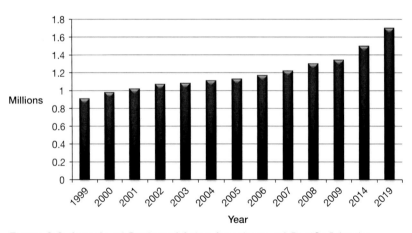

Figure 3.3 Actual and Projected Asian American and Pacific Islander Undergraduate and Graduate Enrollment in Postsecondary Institutions.

Data Source: Integrated Postsecondary Education Data System (IPEDS), 1999–2000. Figures are expressed in millions. Museus (2013) © 2013 Stylus Publishing, LLC.

These national statistics reinforce the reality that the Asian American community is rapidly growing. Given the significant and growing presence of Asian Americans in the United States in general and higher education in particular, an increasing number of postsecondary institutions will have the moral responsibility of implementing institutional policies and programs that are designed to most effectively serve and foster success among this population. Institutions of higher education also have a responsibility to understand the nature of the Asian American segments of their student populations. Such an understanding includes a comprehension of the diversity that exists within the Asian American community and their socioeconomic conditions, which I discuss in the following sections of this chapter.

DIVERSITY

Another characteristic that describes the Asian American population is the vast diversity that exists within it (Museus, 2013). The 2010 Census has identified twenty-five distinct Asian American ethnic groups. The ten largest ethnic groups comprised the vast majority of the total Asian American population in 2010 (Figure 3.4). Chinese Americans were the largest Asian American ethnic group in 2010 and comprised 22 percent of the Asian American community, followed by Filipino (20 percent), Asian Indian (18 percent), Vietnamese (10 percent), Korean (10 percent), Japanese (8 percent), Pakistani (2 percent), Cambodian (2 percent), Hmong (2 percent), and Thai (1 percent) Americans. In addition to ethnic diversity, several scholars have underscored that Asian Americans represent a wide range of national origins, cultures, generational statuses, languages, religions, socioeconomic statuses, poverty rates, education attainment levels, professional occupations, political orientations, and other salient community characteristics (M. J. Chang, Park, Lin, Poon, & Nakanishi, 2007; Hune, 2002; Lee & Kumashiro, 2005; Museus, 2009a).

Figures 3.5 through 3.7 display the nativity and citizenship characteristics of Asian Americans in the United States. In these figures, Asian Americans under the age of 25 and those 25 years of age and over are disaggregated. Disaggregating these statistics by age permits a more complex understanding of the characteristics of the segment of the Asian American population that is most likely to be entering or currently enrolled in institutions of higher education in the United States (those under 25 years old). As shown in Figure 3.5, the Asian American population includes a significant representation of both U.S.-born and foreign-born individuals, and there are noticeable differences in the nativity of those under 25 and those who are 25 years of age or over. Specifically, only approximately 20 percent of those who are age 25 and over were born in the U.S., while that figure is 76 percent for those under 25 years old. In contrast, 48 percent of Asian American residents aged 25 and over have been naturalized

57

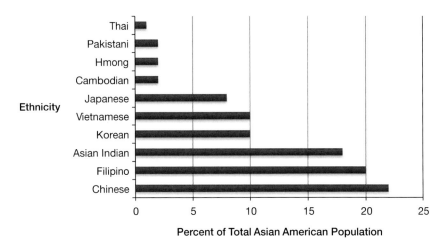

Figure 3.4 Ten Largest Asian American Ethnic Groups and their Share of the Total Asian American Population.

Data Source: U.S. Census (2011). Museus (2013) © 2013 Stylus Publishing, LLC.

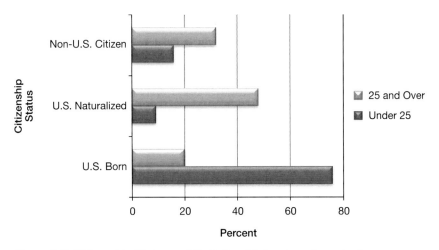

Figure 3.5 Citizenship Status and Nativity of Asian Americans by Age.

Data Source: Public Use Microdata Sample (PUMS): 2006–2010, 5-year estimates. Appropriate sample weights were applied.

as citizens, while only 9 percent of those under 25 received citizenship through naturalization. And, 32 percent of those aged 25 and over are non-citizens, compared with only 16 percent of those under 25.

With regard to language, the statistics in Figure 3.6 illustrate generational disparities in English speaking ability. Among Asian Americans who are ages 25 and over, 24 percent do not speak English at all or do not speak it well, while

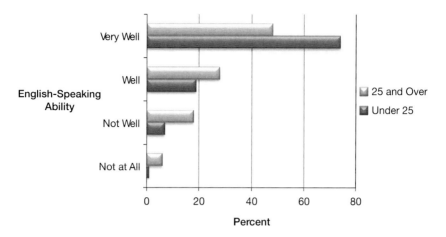

Figure 3.6 English-Speaking Ability of Asian Americans by Age.

Data Source: Public Use Microdata Sample (PUMS): 2006–2010, 5-year estimates. Appropriate sample weights were applied.

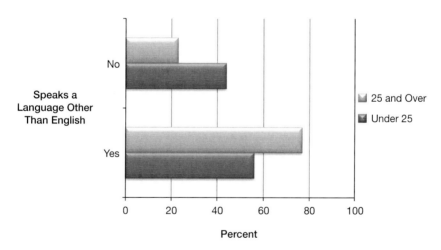

Figure 3.7 Multilingualism of Asian Americans by Age.

Data Source: Public Use Microdata Sample (PUMS): 2006–2010, 5-year estimates. Appropriate sample weights were applied.

that figure is only 8 percent for those under the age of 25. In contrast, approximately half (48 percent) of Asian Americans who are ages 25 and over report speaking English very well, and three-quarters (74 percent) of those who are under the age of 25 report speaking the English language very well. It is reasonable to hypothesize that English speaking ability is related to the extent to which Asian Americans speak a language other than English, and this is supported

59

by the statistics in Figure 3.7. It shows that older Asian Americans, who are less likely to speak English well, are more likely to speak another language. Approximately 77 percent of Asian Americans who are ages 25 and over speak a language other than English, while that figure is 56 percent for those under age 25. It is important to acknowledge that these statistics indicate that most Asian Americans speak English well or very well, and a majority of them speak another language, suggesting high levels of bilingualism among this population.

Vast religious diversity also exists within the Asian American community. In 2012, the Pew Research Center conducted a nationally representative survey of the religious affiliations of 3,511 Asian American adults who were ages 18 and over in the United States and one of their key findings is displayed in Figure 3.8. The Pew Center found that significant religious diversity exists among Asian Americans, with Christians (42 percent) making up the largest religious segment of the population, followed by religiously unaffiliated (26 percent), Buddhist (14 percent), Hindu (10 percent), Muslim (4 percent), and Sikh (1 percent) Asian Americans.

With regard to socioeconomic status, contrary to model minority misconceptions of universal educational and occupational success, a significant portion of the Asian American population earns modest wages. Figure 3.9 illustrates that approximately half of Asian Americans, ages 25 and over, make $20,000 or less annually. And, about 80 percent make $60,000 or less in annual wages. It is important to note that Asian Americans also disproportionately live in regions of the United States with higher costs of living.

Also contrary to the model minority myth is the reality that Asian Americans do not universally reach the highest levels of education. In fact, as Figure 3.10

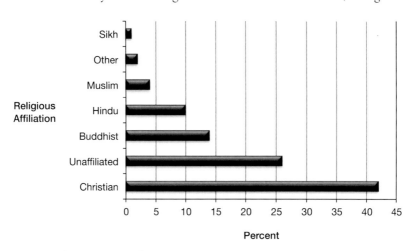

Figure 3.8 Religious Affiliation of Asian Americans.

Data Source: Pew Research Center (2012).

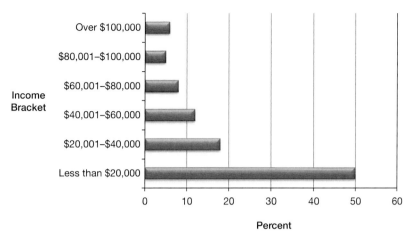

Figure 3.9 Income Levels of Asian Americans.

Data Source: Public Use Microdata Sample (PUMS): 2006–2010, 5-year estimates. Appropriate sample weights were applied.

shows, 14 percent of Asian Americans who are ages 25 and over have not earned a high school diploma, 17 percent graduated from high school, 13 percent attended college but received no degree, 7 percent attained an associate's degree, 30 percent attained a bachelor's degree, and approximately 20 percent received a graduate or professional degree. As I discuss in the next section, however, some ethnic subpopulations, particularly Southeast Asian Americans, are overrepresented among those who have not received a college degree and have much lower rates of college degree attainment.

These aforementioned national statistics begin to illuminate the reality that Asian Americans are not a homogenous population that enjoys universal success, but instead are a community with significant disparities in educational and socioeconomic statuses. I discuss these social inequalities in greater detail in the next section.

INEQUALITY

The third and final characteristic that describes the Asian American community and is discussed herein is inequality (Museus, 2013). Typically, conversations that are about inequalities and invoke Asian Americans portray this population as doing very well relative to other racial groups, but fail to engage in more complex analyses of the disparities that exist *within* the Asian American population (Museus, 2009a; Museus & Kiang, 2009). However, as I discuss below, recent national statistics reveal drastic ethnic disparities in educational attainment, occupational attainment, and socioeconomic status within the Asian American

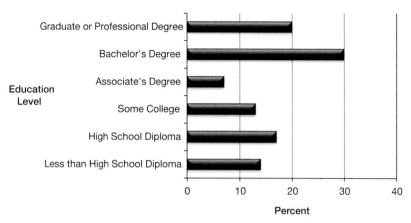

Figure 3.10 Educational Attainment Levels of Asian Americans.

Data Source: Public Use Microdata Sample (PUMS): 2006–2010, 5-year estimates. Appropriate sample weights were applied.

population. They also reveal that some Asian American ethnic subgroups suffer from relatively low rates of educational and occupational attainment and comparatively poor socioeconomic conditions relative to the overall national population within the United States.

The Asian American population includes ethnic groups that exhibit both extremely high rates and very low rates of educational attainment. Figures 3.11 and 3.12 display data on the percentage of Asian Americans, 25 years of age and over, who have not earned a high school diploma and who have completed a bachelor's degree by ethnic background. Several ethnic groups displayed in the graph are more likely to have earned a high school diploma than the national population, while Hmong (39 percent), Cambodian (38 percent), Laotian (33 percent), and Vietnamese (29 percent) Americans are more than twice as likely than the national average (15 percent) and as much as five times as likely than other Asian American ethnic groups (e.g., Taiwanese) to have dropped out before graduating from school. Asian American bachelor's degree completion rates also reveal significant ethnic disparities (Figure 3.12). While Asian Indian (76 percent) and Taiwanese (72 percent) Americans hold bachelor's degrees at more than twice the rate of the nation, those identifying as Hmong (14 percent), Cambodian (13 percent), and Laotian (12 percent) Americans hold baccalaureate degrees at less than half the total national average (28 percent).

Similar to the aforementioned ethnic inequalities in educational attainment that exist within the Asian American population, disaggregated analyses reveal that ethnic disparities in occupational attainment also permeate the Asian American community. For example, Figure 3.13 shows that though some Asian American ethnic groups have unemployment rates much lower than the total national average (7.9 percent), Cambodian (8 percent), Hmong (9 percent), and Laotian (9 percent) Americans have higher rates of unemployment than other Asian American subgroups and the total national population. National data also indicate that ethnic groups have differential access to professional careers. As shown in Figure 3.14, East and South Asian American groups appear to be well-represented in business and management fields and health and science professions, while Southeast Asian Americans are underrepresented in these White collar spheres. Indeed, 23 percent of Taiwanese and 22 percent of Japanese Americans work in business and management, while that figure is less than 8 percent among Cambodian, Hmong, and Laotian Americans. On a similar note, more than 20 percent of Japanese and Filipino Americans have attained careers in the health and science professions, and that figure is less than 7 percent for their Cambodian, Laotian, and Hmong American counterparts. These Southeast Asian Americans are overrepresented in production and transportation, with 46 percent of Laotian, 43 percent of Hmong, and 38 percent of Cambodian Americans having jobs in this arena.

It is reasonable to hypothesize that the aforementioned ethnic disparities in educational and occupational attainment could be, at least in part, a function of disparities in socioeconomic status. And, evidence indicates that Southeast Asian Americans, who the preceding statistics suggest have lower rates of educational and occupational attainment, are more likely to come from under-resourced

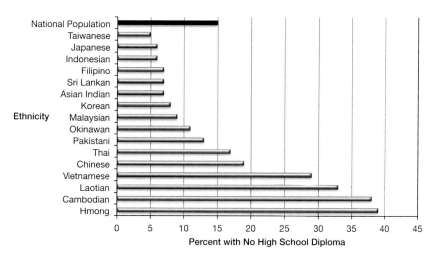

Figure 3.11 Percent of Asian Americans Without High School Diploma by Ethnicity.

Data Source: Public Use Microdata Sample (PUMS): 2006–2010, 5-year estimates. Appropriate sample weights were applied, and individuals 25 and over were included in the analysis. Museus (2013) © 2013 Stylus Publishing, LLC.

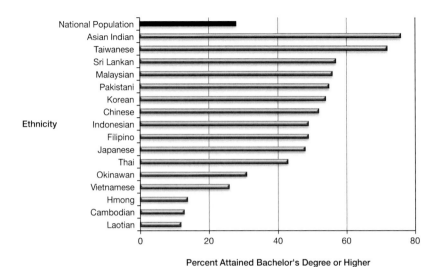

Figure 3.12 Percent of Asian Americans with Bachelor's Degree by Ethnicity.

Data Source: Public Use Microdata Sample (PUMS): 2006–2010, 5-year estimates. Appropriate sample weights were applied, and individuals 25 and over were included in the analysis. Museus (2013) © 2013 Stylus Publishing, LLC.

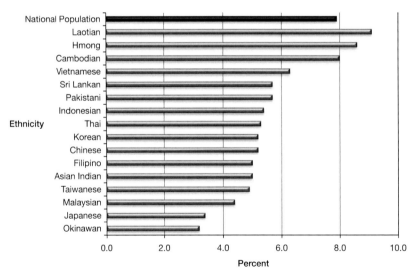

Figure 3.13 Unemployment Among Asian Americans by Ethnicity.

Data Source: Public Use Microdata Sample (PUMS): 2006–2010, 5-year estimates. Appropriate sample weights were applied, and individuals 25 years of age and over were included in the analysis. Museus (2013) © 2013 Stylus Publishing, LLC.

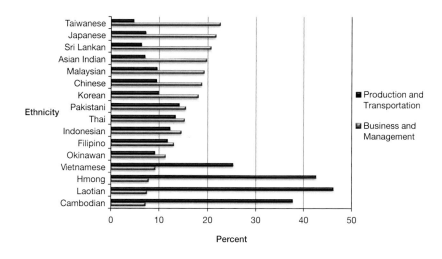

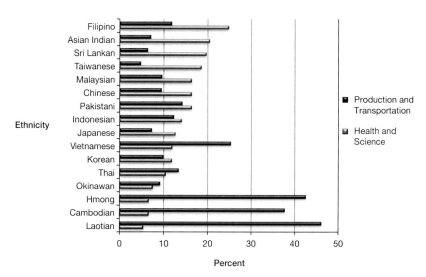

Figure 3.14 Concentration of Asian Americans in Professional Fields by Ethnicity.

Data Source: Public Use Microdata Sample (PUMS): 2006–2010, 5-year estimates. Appropriate sample weights were applied, and individuals 25 years of age and over were included in the analysis. Museus (2013) © 2013 Stylus Publishing, LLC.

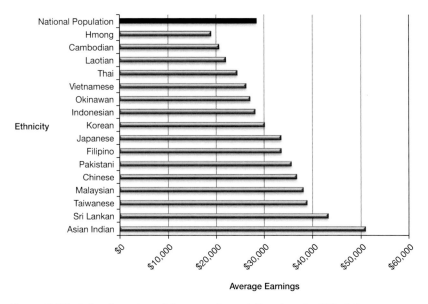

Figure 3.15 Asian Americans' Average Annual Earnings by Ethnicity.

Data Source: Public Use Microdata Sample (PUMS): 2006–2010, 5-year estimates. Appropriate sample weights were applied. Appropriate sample weights were applied, and individuals 25 and over were included in the analysis. Earnings were adjusted for inflation and are expressed in 2010 dollars. Museus (2013) © 2013 Stylus Publishing, LLC.

ethnic communities (Figure 3.15). Indeed, on average, Asian Indians ($50,988) and Sri Lankans ($43,283) report earnings that are approximately $22,000 and $15,000 above the national average ($28,452), respectively. In contrast, Hmong ($19,053), Cambodian ($20,737), Laotian ($22,111), Thai ($24,509), Vietnamese ($26,352), Okinawan ($27,162), and Indonesian ($28,251) Americans all have average annual earnings that are below the national average. Moreover, these disparities are quite substantial for some groups. For example, Hmong and Cambodian Americans report average annual earnings of approximately $19,000 (67% of the national average) and $21,000 (73% of the national average), respectively.

IMPLICATIONS FOR INSTITUTIONAL POLICY AND PRACTICE

The demographic realities discussed herein have many implications for institutional policy and practice. I conclude this chapter with a discussion of five major implications: using complex data to debunk misconceptions and develop more authentic understandings of Asian American students; identifying and serving underrepresented and underserved ethnic groups; parsing and understanding diverse groups within the Asian American student population; linking historical context and socioeconomic conditions to generate more holistic understandings of Asian American students' community contexts; and developing programs and practices that target underserved Asian American student populations.

Using Disaggregated Data Analyses to Debunk Misconceptions

First, this chapter underscores the utility of using such disaggregated data to develop more intricate and accurate understandings of Asian American populations in higher education. Such disaggregation is not a new phenomenon. Indeed, several researchers have conducted prior analyses that offer examples of the utility of the disaggregated examination of both quantitative and qualitative data on Asian Americans in postsecondary education (see, for example, M. J. Chang et al., 2007; GAO, 2007; Hune, 2002; Museus, 2009a, 2011b, 2013; Museus & Truong, 2009; Teranishi, 2007). While these analyses have increased current levels of understanding regarding the complexity and diversity of the Asian American community, it is important to note that individual institutions of higher education have unique Asian American student bodies that might not necessarily reflect the characteristics of the national population. Therefore, it is important for colleges and universities to develop their own systems to collect and analyze data that permit more complex understandings of their unique Asian American student bodies.

Given the realities mentioned above, in addition to collecting data on race, the institutional research and student affairs assessment offices on college and university campuses should ensure that both their quantitative and qualitative collection of data on Asian American and other students include the acquisition of other demographic information, such as data on ethnicity and socioeconomic status. This information is critical to postsecondary institutions' abilities to develop more accurate understandings of the experiences of their students. Moreover, they are essential in the formation of data-driven programs and practices that will actually respond to the needs of their student bodies in meaningful ways.

Identifying and Serving Underrepresented and Underserved Ethnic Groups

Asian Americans are not often included in the underrepresented and underserved categories, which are often reserved for all other communities of color. However, disaggregated data analyses reveal that, in specific contexts, certain ethnic groups within the Asian American population can certainly be considered underrepresented and underserved. The preceding analysis, for example, shows that several Asian American ethnic groups are underrepresented and underserved within specific disciplines.

It is imperative that college educators adopt more complex perspectives around the identification and support of underrepresented and underserved students. In fields where specific Asian American ethnic groups face disparities, they should be included in the underrepresented and underserved category, so they are eligible for access to targeted financial and academic support. In most cases, Southeast Asian Americans do face inequities and can be included in underrepresented and underserved categories. Given the clear, consistent, and overwhelming evidence that now clarifies and reaffirms the reality that Southeast Asian Americans face similar economic and educational disparities as other underrepresented and underserved communities of color (e.g., Black, Latino, Native American, and Pacific Islander populations), it is no longer acceptable for national governmental and policy organizations or postsecondary institutions to exclude this population from the underrepresented and underserved label or from conversations about access, diversity, and equity in higher education.

Understanding the Diversity within Asian America

College educators should make efforts to truly understand the diversity that exists within their Asian American college student populations, and the implications of this diversity for their abilities to serve these students. Indeed, diversity has become a buzzword in postsecondary education and in discourse around Asian Americans. However, institutional policymakers and practitioners should be grappling with the task of understanding what this diversity means for their ability to serve their Asian American populations.

Different forms of diversity within the Asian American college student population raise distinctive issues and pose varied implications for postsecondary educators. Ethnic diversity can underscore the importance of understanding historical transnational contexts and community cultures of students. Socioeconomic diversity can highlight the need for college educators to understand how the socioeconomic conditions of Asian American college students' communities impact their experiences. Generational and linguistic diversity might reinforce the value of multilingualism in the dissemination of information and design of educational programming. These are just a few of the many ways in which the purposeful consideration of diversity in the construction of campus spaces, curricula, policies, programs, and practices can enhance college educators' abilities to effectively serve their students.

Linking Historical Contexts and Social Conditions

It is also important that educators consider and comprehend both the historical context of Asian American communities and the socioeconomic conditions that characterize them today. The consideration of both historical and social contexts underscores the fact that these factors are associated with educational and occupational outcomes. Underscoring this point is not only important in acknowledging the limitations of meritocratic perspectives in explaining Asian American success, but it also paints a more holistic picture of the contextual realities that shape the lives of Asian American students on college and university campuses.

Indeed, historical and socioeconomic contexts can be critical influences on the development of curricular and co-curricular programming, particularly for Southeast Asian American populations. Considering both the historical and socioeconomic contexts of Southeast Asian American communities, for example, curricular and co-curricular programming that is designed to be responsive to the realities of these communities should both engage the historical refugee and contemporary socioeconomic realities of Southeast Asian American communities by fostering Southeast Asian American college students' awareness of how larger social forces have created the inequitable conditions of their communities and engaging them in efforts to positively transform their very underresourced and underserved communities.

Targeting Resources for Underserved Asian American Students

It is debatable whether Asian Americans are an underserved student population. On one hand, some assume that Asian Americans are not underserved because, in the aggregate, they have higher educational attainment rates than other racial and ethnic groups. On the other hand, it could be argued that all Asian Americans are underserved in postsecondary education because they have been historically ignored in higher education policy and practice. What is certain is that Southeast Asian Americans and low-income Asian Americans are underserved because they face drastic inequalities in educational attainment.

Despite the fact that Southeast and low-income Asian Americans are underserved and face salient challenges because of their race, ethnicity, and socioeconomic status, they continue to be ignored in policy and practice in postsecondary education. Indeed, financial resources that are dedicated to projects and scholarships for underserved communities often exclude Southeast Asian Americans and low-income Asian Americans. Similarly, some targeted support programs do not target Southeast Asian Americans and low-income Asian Americans in the design and delivery of their services. Indeed, considering the stark socioeconomic realities faced by these populations, institutions of higher education that serve Southeast and low-income Asian Americans have a moral responsibility to offer targeted support for these students.

Chapter 4

Asian American Identity in College

"Ever since I was a child I have had this instinctive urge for expansion and growth. To me, the function and duty of a quality human being is the sincere and honest development of one's potential."

Bruce Lee

"My identity might begin with the fact of my race, but it didn't, couldn't end there.

At least that's what I would choose to believe."

Barack Obama

"Washing one's hands of the conflict between the powerful and the powerless means to side with the powerful, not to be neutral."

Paulo Freire

Asian American identity is complex. For some Asian Americans, a pan-ethnic Asian American consciousness might be their most salient form of identification, while others might primarily identify with their own ethnic group. For some people who identify as Asian American, being Asian American might mean identifying with a pan-ethnic population of people who have similar struggles and experiences in the United States, while others might view it primarily as a political tactic that is designed to help them garner greater voice in advocacy for their own ethnic group. For some Asian Americans, the act of identifying as Asian American might cause internal conflict because they feel connected to, but marginalized and voiceless within, this population.

It is difficult to find comprehensive syntheses of knowledge related to Asian American identity. In the current chapter, I seek to provide the most comprehensive synthesis of Asian American identity to date, and unpack some of the aforementioned complexities of Asian American identity development processes.

First, I offer a discussion of the concepts of oppression and resistance to contextualize the discussion of Asian American identity. Second, I provide a brief overview of key concepts and definitions related to Asian American identity development. Third, I delineate critical elements of Asian American identity in college. Fourth, I outline the various theories of Asian American identity that have been proposed in existing literature. The chapter concludes with implications for policy and practice.

OPPRESSION AND ASIAN AMERICAN IDENTITY

Racial identity development can be seen as a process of adaption, but more specifically, racial identity development can be viewed as a process of adjustment to systems of racial and other forms of oppression. Racial oppression leads to the racial subjugation and marginalization of people of color, creating psychological and social challenges for them and making it difficult for them to develop a positive cultural identity or sense of self (Birman, 1994). It is this marginalization and the challenges that result from it that provide the critical contexts for understanding racial identity development processes. Therefore, any understanding of racial identity development must begin with a comprehension of how racial oppression functions in American society (Torres, Howard-Hamilton, & Cooper, 2003).

Racism and other forms of oppression, such as sexism and heterosexism, are central to the fabric of American society. In the current synthesis, I focus on racial oppression, but I acknowledge that these other forms of oppression shape the lives of Asian Americans as well, and I invoke them at various points in the discussion. For the system of racial oppression to be eradicated, it must first be acknowledged that the White majority has historically possessed disproportionate power and privilege in American society, and the White population has racially subjugated racial minority groups through processes of racialization, racial stereotyping, racial prejudice, and racial discrimination, in order to maintain their power and privilege (Helms, 1994). This disproportionate power and privilege has resulted in a racial hierarchy, with Whites at the top and people of color in subordinated positions below them. For society to eradicate racial oppression, if possible, the White majority must lose some of its power and privilege and this racial hierarchy must be uprooted and transformed into a more equitable power structure.

In his seminal work, *Pedagogy of the Oppressed*, Freire (1970b) asserted that oppression is a process of dehumanization and a form of overwhelming control of the oppressor over the dehumanized and oppressed. Freire argued that oppressors see themselves as human beings and other people as objects, a view that justifies the fact that their right to live in peace takes precedent over the lives and

71

rights of the oppressed. In contrast, oppressed peoples have no power, voice, or ability to determine their destinies. Eventually, the oppressed internalize the perspectives of their oppressors, which function to reinforce the oppression and subjugate them. As such, oppressed people's thoughts are influenced and determined by their oppressors, resulting in the oppressor controlling the future of the oppressed.

The Elements of Oppression

Scholars have outlined valuable frameworks for understanding processes of oppression that can be used to shed light on how racial oppression operates (Bell, 1997; Freire, 1970b; Hardiman & Jackson, 1997), and I review two of them herein. Bell (1997) has argued that there are six interrelated characteristics of oppression. He argued that oppression is pervasive, restricting, hierarchical, complex, internalized, and enacted through isms:

1. *Pervasive*: Oppression consists of pervasive social inequalities that are embedded in social institutions and individual consciousness throughout society.
2. *Restricting*: Systems of oppression entail structural and material constraints that shape individuals' opportunities and sense of possibilities.
3. *Hierarchical*: The existence of oppression denotes hierarchical relationships that permit groups with power and privilege to benefit from the subjugation of subordinated groups.
4. *Complex*: Power and privilege are relative because individuals hold multiple interconnected social group memberships.
5. *Internalized*: Systems of oppression lead to both empowered and disempowered groups within the system internalizing oppressive beliefs that reinforce the oppressive system and hierarchical relationships that define it.
6. *Enacted through "Isms"*: Oppression manifests in racism, sexism, classism, heterosexism, ableism, and other forms of oppression, and these "isms" form an interconnected overarching system of domination.

The Matrix of Oppression

Alternatively, Hardiman and Jackson (1997) have offered a social oppression matrix perspective that explains how oppression occurs when one social group, either consciously or subconsciously, disparages another group for its own benefit. The authors outline four key elements of social oppression within social systems:

1. *Imposed Realities*: The group with power and privilege has the power to define reality and determine what is normal, real, or true.
2. *Institutionalization*: Prejudice, discrimination, harassment, exploitation, marginalization, and other forms of differential treatment that lead to inequities and inequalities are institutionalized and systematic. Because these actions permeate social institutions and systems, they do not require the conscious thought or effort of those in positions of power and privilege, but become a part of normalized behavior.
3. *Colonized Minds*: Colonization of the minds of subordinated groups occurs through socializing the oppressed individuals and their internalization of oppressive beliefs, which reinforce the oppressive ideology and system.
4. *Cultural Extermination*: The oppressed group's history, language, and culture are distorted, discounted, or exterminated, and the dominant group's culture is imposed upon these populations.

Hardiman and Jackson's (1997) oppression matrix suggests that oppression occurs at cultural (e.g., societal values, norms, and codes), institutional (e.g., oppressive rules, regulations, and structures), and individual (e.g., conscious or unconscious decisions to act in ways that reinforce systems of oppression) levels. And, at these different levels, the oppression matrix implies that social oppression manifests in various contexts, psychological processes, and applications.

The Resistance of Oppression

It is also important to note that, while Asian American identities exist within and are shaped by social oppression, Asian Americans also possess agency to resist those systems of oppression in a variety of ways. Solórzano and Delgado Bernal (2001) proposed a model that outlines four main types of behavior in which people of color engage in opposition to social oppression. First, *reactionary behavior* is not a form of resistance, but indicates situations in which an individual espouses neither a critique of social oppression nor social justice values. An example of reactionary behavior is when someone acts out simply for purposes of disruption or the agitation of people around them. Second, *self-defeating resistance* refers to cases in which an individual might have developed a critique of social oppression, but is not motivated to act in ways that contribute to social justice, social transformation, and eradication of oppression. These individuals may act in self-destructive manners, such as dropping out of school in response to their critique of the education system. Third, *conformist resistance* is characterized by situations in which people espouse social justice values, but might not critique the social structures that are responsible for creating inequities and inequalities in society. For these individuals, dominant liberal values and expectations shape

73

their behavior and, while they might want their own life or the lives of oppressed people to improve, they often blame themselves or oppressed communities for their conditions. Finally, *transformative resistance* occurs when individuals both critique social structures of oppression and are at least somewhat motivated to engage in social justice behaviors. Transformative resistance can occur when individuals confront oppression, are driven to navigate and survive in systems of oppression, and demand social change.

Although it is difficult to find empirical research that examines whether and how Asian American college students engage in various forms of resistance, there is some indication that Asian American college students do engage in conformist and transformative resistance behaviors (Poon, 2013). Moreover, some evidence suggests that the availability of campus social spaces and networks that foster the development of critical consciousness and critique of oppression appear to be important in cultivating Asian American transformative resisters in college. In particular, Asian American or other ethnic student organizations can constitute safe spaces or critical counter-spaces, in which Asian American college students can grapple with critical social questions and develop transformative resistance strategies.

Oppression Theory and Asian American Identity

This discussion of oppression provides important context for understanding Asian American identity. First, oppression theory reminds us that Asian Americans are historical subjects and their lives are shaped by history (Bell, 1997). As discussed in previous chapters within this volume, American society has historically racialized and oppressed Asian Americans through processes of Asianization and consequent systems of legal, political, and social subordination. This critical historical context can inform knowledge of how racial oppression continues to impact the lives of Asian Americans today.

Second, the theories of social oppression remind us that Asian American identity formation is not independent of social context, but instead, Asian American identities are shaped by and develop within larger social systems. Indeed, because social systems are one salient influence on Asian American identity, understanding and acknowledging the significance of contemporary societal racism is necessary to fully understanding how Asian Americans negotiate their environments and define themselves within those environmental contexts.

Finally, these oppression theories can aid us in understanding the nature of the processes by which Asian Americans respond to their social context and undergo identity transformation. For example, some of the Asian American identity theories outlined in the following discussion are based on the notions that systemic racism imposes White majority perspectives and beliefs about reality upon Asian Americans and this racism functions to subordinate, denigrate, and eradicate elements of Asian cultures within society. In addition, some Asian American identity theories are based on the assumption that Asian Americans undergo processes of internalization and externalization of racism. Indeed, they suggest that, at some point in their lives, Asian Americans undergo a process of internalizing negative views of their own cultures and community, which work to reinforce beliefs of White superiority and systems of racial oppression. The theories also suggest that Asian Americans can eventually go through a process of externalizing racism, through which they become increasingly conscious of how they are racially oppressed and this oppression has shaped their belief systems.

The concept of resistance is also relevant to discussions of Asian American identity for several reasons. First, it is reasonable to assume that Asian Americans who are unaware of racial oppression or do not fully understand it and have not developed an Asian American consciousness are less likely to engage in acts of resistance. Second, even in cases in which Asian Americans develop an understanding of racism and an Asian American identity and consciousness, it could be argued that they are likely to respond in ways that resemble self-defeating or conformist resistance, unless their Asian American identity formation and emerging consciousness is accompanied by an understanding of productive transformative resistance.

ASIAN AMERICAN IDENTITY DEVELOPMENT MODELS

Racial and ethnic identity development is a component of people's self-concept that is based on how an individual defines oneself in relation to particular racial or ethnic groups. Uba (1994) posited that ethnic identity also functions as (1) a schema that generates knowledge, beliefs, and expectations about the ethnic groups to which people belong; (2) a cognitive framework for people to view and interpret objects, situations, events, and other people; and (3) a basis for individual behavior. Therefore, it can be argued that racial and ethnic identity plays a central role in the educational experiences of Asian American students in higher education.

Several different types of Asian American identity models have been proposed, and I delineate some of them in this section. Before doing so, however, it can be useful to highlight a few key themes in the scholarship on Asian American identity to contextualize the discussion of these specific models. First, while it can be argued that some Asian American identity models are more focused on race and others are focused more on ethnicity and culture, it can also be argued that all of these models are based on the assumption that Asian Americans grow up navigating multiple cultures, which include the culture of the dominant majority and their Asian ethnic heritage. Therefore, Asian American identity models both partially explain how Asian Americans navigate these multiple cultural contexts and how these contexts shape individual Asian Americans' worldviews and sense of self.

Second, it can be argued that Asian American identity is not static and is always in flux. Indeed, while many existing Asian American identity models outline various stages through which individuals progress as their identity develops, evidence suggests that Asian American college students' identities are constantly changing (Wong, 2013). Indeed, environmental context, individual assumptions, relationships, and interactions influence Asian American students' constant (re)shaping and (re)definition of their own identities.

Third, Asian American identity frameworks suggest that Asian American identity is complex and can be based on an individuals' identification with several different social groups. For example, a consideration of previous scholarship suggests that Asian Americans identities are comprised of their association with some combination of six different race-, ethnicity-, and culture-based social groups (Helms, 1994; Kiang, 2002; Museus, Vue, et al., 2013; Yinger, 1994):

- *Racial Minorities*: Asian Americans can develop a sense of collective identification that is based on an individual's perceived shared experience with other people of color. Such experiences can include, but are not limited to, racial prejudice and discrimination, racial exclusion and isolation, and race-related disenfranchisement.
- *Asian Americans*: Asian Americans can cultivate a sense of collective identity that is based on their shared experiences with members of their own racial group (i.e., other Asian Americans).
- *Ethnic Groups*: Asian Americans can develop a sense of collective identification that is based on an individual's shared common national origin, history, culture, and language with a specific cultural group (e.g., Chinese, Hmong, Indian, Filipino, etc.).
- *Immigrant Groups*: Some Asian Americans can identify with other people who entered the United States after birth and have had to or must adjust to the new culture, lifestyle, and status within society.
- *Refugee Groups*: Certain Asian Americans, many Southeast Asian Americans in particular, can identify with other people who were displaced from their home countries and migrated to the United States. These individuals might have experienced stress and trauma as a result of fear of political persecution, loss of family and friends, murder and genocide, refugee camps with poor living conditions, and uncertainty about their future.
- *Indigenous Groups*: Specific Asian American groups can foster a sense of collective identity with members of indigenous populations. This is not to be mistaken with the identity of populations that are indigenous to the United States (i.e., Native Americans and Hawaiians), is most

relevant for select Asian American ethnic groups (e.g., Filipino, Indian, and Okinawan Americans), and refers to individual identification based on a shared experienced of colonization of their homelands.

The various combinations of these social groups and Asian Americans' associations with them mutually shape Asian Americans' complex racial and ethnic identities. Moreover, these intricate racial and ethnic identities interact with Asian Americans' gender, sexual orientation, religious, and other identities to mutually shape the experiences, worldviews, and lives of Asian American people (Museus & Park, 2012; Park, 2009c, 2012b; Pepin & Talbot, 2013).

Finally, although Asian American identity models typically do not focus on environmental context or space, it is important to underscore the role of space in Asian American identity development processes. Although many physical spaces on campus might serve as sites for identity exploration and development, scholars have specifically underscored how campus spaces, such as ethnic studies courses and ethnic student organizations, can be useful sites for Asian American identity exploration and development (Kiang, 2002, 2009; Museus, 2008b; Museus, Lam, Huang, Kem, & Tan, 2012; Rhoads, Lee, & Yamada, 2002; Vue, 2013). Indeed, such sites can serve as spaces in which Asian American students can collectively learn about their Asian American histories and cultures, thereby experiencing identity development and the acquisition of a sense of purpose. This is a particularly important point for educators who are interested in shaping educational environments that might facilitate identity development among their Asian American students in higher education.

In the remainder of this section, I delineate several Asian American identity models. I begin by discussing Kodama, McEwen, Liang, and Lee's (2002) Asian American psychosocial identity model. Then, I provide an overview of models that focus on the identities of racial and ethnic Asian American populations. It is to these models that I now turn.

Asian American Psychosocial Development Model

Building on the work of Chickering (1969), Kodama, McEwen, Liang, and Lee (2002) generated a model of Asian American psychosocial development. Chickering identified seven vectors along which individuals develop and that comprise their psychosocial identity development, including establishing identity, developing purpose, developing competence, developing integrity, moving through autonomy toward interdependence, managing emotions, and developing mature interpersonal relationships. However, the authors noted that Chickering's identity theory is acultural, and they underscored the importance of understanding the impact that culture has on Asian Americans' psychosocial identity.

77

In proposing their Asian American psychosocial identity model, Kodama et al. (2002) highlighted the importance of acknowledging the ways in which the *dominant culture* in society and traditional *Asian cultural values* interact to influence Asian American identity. Regarding the influence of the dominant culture, Kodama et al. emphasized the impact of racism and racial stereotypes on Asian American psychosocial development. They explained that these environmental factors function to perpetuate psychosocial dominance over Asian Americans by fostering negative sense of self among these individuals (Hamamoto, 1994).

Kodama et al. (2002) also emphasized the impact of traditional Asian cultural values, which often contradict values in dominant Western society, on Asian American psychosocial development. Specifically, the authors underscored the impact that Asian cultural values of collectivism, interdependence, prioritization of family needs above one's own, interpersonal harmony, and deference to authority can have on Asian American individuals' psychosocial development (B. S. K. Kim, Atkinson, and Yang, 1999). They explained that the differences between Western societal values and Asian cultural values could pose challenges for Asian American students. For example, while Western cultures view identity formation as including the development of autonomy and independence, Asian families might place greater value on collectivism and welfare of the family unit. Consequently, Kodama et al. argued that psychosocial development theory should acknowledge that Asian Americans might be required to negotiate these differences—a negotiation that will shape their psychosocial state.

The Kodama et al. (2002) psychosocial identity model places *identity* and *purpose* in concentric circles at the center of an axis, and the model indicates that individuals' identity and purpose are closely connected to the development of *competence*, development of *integrity*, achievement of *interdependence*, ability to manage *emotions*, and ability to maintain harmonious *relationships*. In addition, the psychosocial identity model suggests that the aforementioned dominant cultural factors and traditional Asian cultural values shape Asian American identity and purpose. The model also posits that the relationship between the self and the two external cultural domains can facilitate Asian Americans' development of identity and purpose. Finally, Asian Americans' establishment of identity and development of purpose, in turn, influence their abilities to acquire competence, develop integrity, achieve interdependence, manage their emotions, and maintain harmonious interpersonal relationships.

In addition to offering an Asian American psychosocial development perspective, Kodama et al. underscored the problematic acultural nature of dominant identity theories. Kodama et al. also demonstrated how these traditional theories could be modified and enhanced by the incorporation of a consideration of cultural influences. In addition to the aforementioned Asian American identity models, scholars have generated a handful of useful theories that shed light on the intersection between Asian American identity and other social identities that some Asian Americans espouse (e.g., other racial, gender, sexual orientation identities). Kodama et al.'s model helped advance discourse around Asian American psychosocial development. However, it is important to note that it has been argued that revising foundational student development theories that are based on European American values and assumptions to fit the experiences of students of color might be a less than ideal method to develop perspectives that explain the experiences of this population (McEwen, Roper, Bryant, & Langa, 1990). Rather, creating new and independent theories derived directly from the voices of students of color might be more desirable.

Asian American Identity Development Model

More than three decades ago, J. Kim (1981) developed the first Asian American identity development model. Kim (1981) based her model on data that were collected from a sample of Japanese women. However, the model is often cited as being applicable to the entire Asian population (Torres, Howard-Hamilton, & Cooper, 2003). The Asian American identity development model consists of five progressive stages that include the following:

1. *Ethnic awareness* refers to the stage in which family members serve as significant influences on individuals' lives. Depending on the amount of exposure to the Asian heritage, children develop neutral or positive views toward their ethnic origins.

2. *White identification* often begins when individuals enter the schooling system and are exposed to environments that convey racial prejudice to them. Due to the recognition of differences between White people and themselves and the racial prejudice that they experience, the individual can experience self-blame, internalize White values, and attempt to eliminate their Asian American selves.

   This stage can be experienced in two ways. First, active White identification occurs when Asian Americans considers themselves to be similar to their White peers, do not acknowledge differences between them and their White counterparts, and attempt to eliminate their Asian selves. In passive White identification, Asian Americans do not consider themselves to be White or distance themselves from Asians, but they accept White values, beliefs, and standards.

3. *Awakening to social political consciousness* refers to the stage in which individuals acknowledge that they are a racial minority and their identification with White society diminishes. In this stage, individuals experience an increasing awareness of racial oppression and their political consciousness and Asian American self-concept becomes more positive.

79

4. *Redirection to Asian American consciousness* constitutes the stage in which individuals develop a renewed connection with and embrace their Asian American heritage and culture. In this stage, individuals also often realize that White oppression is the cause of many negative experiences of Asian American youth, and they might also develop anger toward the White majority and a stronger sense of pride in their ethnic heritage.

5. *Incorporation* is the final stage of the Asian American identity model and, in this phase, the individual learns how to balance their own identity and appreciation for others. As a result, identification with or against White culture is no longer a salient consideration or issue.

It is important to note that this last stage of Kim's model can be controversial. Although it might be argued that these stages are not intended to be linear, the placement of the incorporation stage as the final phase in the identity development model might suggest to some people that the highest form of identity evolution is one characterized by racial harmony. It could be argued that individuals who espouse this incorporation perspective are no more "developed" than those who espouse worldviews that are congruent with the reduction stage because the major difference between the two stages is that the former has adopted a colorblind perspective and the latter has an espoused commitment to social justice and resistance to racial oppression. Accordingly, not all models outlined herein suggest that comfort and racial harmony are the indicators of the most developed Asian American identities.

Multiracial Asian American Identity Typology

Several mixed-race identity models and typologies have been proposed and can aid in understanding the identity of multiracial Asian Americans (e.g., Poston, 1990; Renn, 2000, 2003, 2004, 2008; Root, 1990, 1998; Wijeyesinghe, 2001). Although a comprehensive review of existing perspectives of multiracial identity is beyond the scope of the current chapter, I review one multiracial identity typology perspective herein to shed light on mixed-race identity and highlight the complexity and fluidity with which mixed-race Asian Americans shape and reshape their identities. Renn (2000), for example, developed a typology of multiracial college students' identity, which clarifies that these students exhibit five different identity patterns, including holding a *monoracial* identity (i.e., identifying with one single racial group), multiple monoracial identities (i.e., identifying with more than one racial group), a multiracial identity (i.e., identifying with a distinct "multiracial" group rather than any one heritage), an extraracial identity (i.e., opting out of identifying with a racial group), or a situational identity (i.e., changing the way they identify in different contexts).

80

Renn's (2000) typology and other models of multiracial identity can add to the discourse around Asian American identity in many ways, but I highlight three contributions of Renn's typology herein. First, the typology offers a perspective that acknowledges that mixed-race Asian Americans can identify with more than one racial group. Second, the situational ways in which many mixed-race students identify according to her typology underscore the fluid nature of multiracial Asian American identity. And, third, the perspective recognizes that the environments between and among which students move play a significant role in shaping their identity choices. Given that the mixed-race segment of the Asian American population is growing rapidly, perspectives such as Renn's are useful and will become even more critical for understanding the complexity of Asian American identity in the years to come.

South Asian Immigrant Identity Model

Recognizing that identity development theorists' and researchers' homogenization of Asian American ethnic subpopulations can mask important differences across these groups, Ibrahim, Ohnishi, and Sandhu (1997) developed a model that is specific to South Asian immigrants. The authors highlighted the fact that South Asian immigrants come from colonized nations and, therefore, view and understand White values, beliefs, and assumptions through colonized people's eyes. In addition, South Asian immigrants have strong ethnic pride in their home countries and they do not feel pressured to deny their ethnic heritage.

Due to the history of colonization and strong ethnic pride among South Asian immigrants, Ibrahim et al. (1997) assert that South Asian immigrants do not experience a pre-encounter or conformity stage. They argue that South Asian immigrants accept cultural differences as a reality of life and believe that they have been brought into the United States, where hard work can help them achieve the American dream. Therefore, Ibrahim et al. argue that the stage of *conformity* does not apply to South Asian immigrants, because those individuals view distance between the dominant culture and their traditional culture as a way of life. It is this foundation upon which Ibrahim et al. base their South Asian immigrant identity model. They outlined four stages as an explanatory model of South Asian immigrant identity:

1. *Dissonance* is the stage in which South Asian immigrants realize that cultural differences cannot be overcome, mainstream America's acceptance of ethnic minorities does not necessarily occur, and hard work is not sufficient.
2. *Resistance and immersion* refers to the stage in which South Asian immigrants suffer a crisis, reject mainstream cultural values and beliefs, and revert to their ethnic heritage. In this stage, they develop a

81

recommitment to and identification with South Asian culture and can engage in a reaffirmation of their ethnic identity.

3. *Introspection* refers to the stage of identity development in which South Asian immigrants become secure about their ethnic identity. At this point, they seek individuality as a member of the South Asian immigrant population while also recognizing some positive elements of the dominant culture.

4. *Synergistic articulation and awareness* occurs when South Asian immigrants are able to objectively accept or reject cultural values and beliefs of both the dominant majority and ethnic minority groups. At this stage, South Asian immigrants have achieved individuality and a sense of self-worth, and they recognize that identifying with their own ethnic group can coincide with other groups' positive attributes.

In addition to offering an ethnic-specific model of South Asian immigrant identity, an important contribution of Ibrahim et al.'s perspective is that it underscored the importance of considering the historical contexts of colonialism and immigration, and the worldviews that result from these historical realities, in the understanding of Asian American ethnic group identity.

Filipino American Identity Development Model

Like Ibrahim et al. (1997), Nadal (2004) recognized that pan-ethnic Asian American identity models could mask important unique attributes of specific ethnic groups within the Asian American population. Building on previous identity development literature (e.g., J. Kim, 1981; Suinn, Ahuna, & Khoo, 1992), Nadal argued that there are significant social, cultural, economic, and psychological differences between Filipino and other Asian Americans that warrant an ethnic specific identity model for Filipino Americans. Nadal's Filipino American identity model consists of the following six stages:

1. *Ethnic awareness* is the stage in which children are raised in Filipino culture by their families and develop positive or neutral attitudes toward themselves and their Filipino heritage, Filipino Americans, and White Americans, while having neutral attitudes toward Asian Americans and other racial and ethnic minorities.

2. *Assimilation* refers to the stage in which Filipinos highly value White society. In this stage, they repress Filipino culture, lifestyle, and value systems. Moreover, the continued realization of White dominance in society pressures Filipinos to seek Whiteness and assimilation into dominant culture.

82

3. *Social political* awakening refers to the stage where experiences with racial prejudice and discrimination lead to the realization that the individual cannot achieve Whiteness. In this stage, the individual becomes aware of social and political injustice, which results in their abandonment of White societal values and an increased understanding of oppressed groups.

4. *Pan-ethnic Asian American consciousness* is the fourth stage of Filipino American identity development. In this stage, Filipinos are socialized to accept their identity as Asian American. In this stage, they can seek power in numbers *vis à vis* membership and coalitions in the larger Asian American community.

5. *Ethnocentric realization* is characterized by a realization that Filipinos have been unjustly classified as Asian American and an increased awareness of the marginalization of Filipinos within the Asian American community.

6. *Incorporation*: Similar to Kim's (1981) highest level of identity development, this stage is characterized by an ethnocentric consciousness that is defined as "a sense of one's personal collective identity, centered on a specific concern for the issues and situations of one's specific ethnic group" (Nadal, 2004, p. 59). At this stage, Filipinos balance their ethnocentric consciousness with an appreciation for other cultures.

In addition to offering an identity model that is uniquely tailored to the Filipino population, Nadal's model highlighted the importance of culture and underscored the intertwined and interactive nature of racial and ethnic identity for Filipino Americans, although it could be argued that this interconnectedness could be applied to other Asian American ethnic groups.

Southeast Asian American Identity Model

Building on the work of these previously discussed scholars (Ibrahim et al., 1997; J. Kim, 1981; Nadal, 2004), Museus, Vue, et al. (2013) considered historical refugee contexts, the role of culture, and the interconnectedness of multiple elements of identity to construct a Southeast Asian American identity model. Unlike previous racial and ethnic identity models, however, Museus, Vue, et al. proposed a model that was not stage-like, but instead outlined a set of distinct and interconnected processes that all inform Southeast Asian American identity formation. The authors, however, do note that these processes could apply to other racial and ethnic groups as well.

The Southeast Asian American identity model consists of five interconnected processes. First, *enculturation to ethnic cultures* refers to the process of Southeast Asian Americans being socialized into and participating in the maintenance of

83

various elements of their traditional Cambodian, Hmong, Mien, Lao, or Vietnamese cultural heritages. These elements include, but are not limited to, cultural values, ideals, norms, customs, food, and language.

The second process of Southeast Asian American identity formation is *acculturation to the dominant culture*. This refers to the process of Southeast Asian Americans adapting to dominant White society and culture. In previous models, this process of acculturation is associated with assimilation into White society, identification with Whiteness, and dis-identification with individuals' ethnic heritage. However, the Southeast Asian American identity model assumes that individuals can be socialized into multiple cultures simultaneously. Therefore, this process of acculturation can take place throughout the lifespan, even when people are engaged in processes of enculturation and learning about their own ethnic heritage.

The third process, which focuses on developing an *awareness of oppression*, is similar to the social and political awakening that occurs in earlier models (e.g., Kim, 1981; Nadal, 2004). However, the Southeast Asian American identity model suggests that this awakening process can be multidimensional and include an increased awareness of the oppression of several different groups to which an individual belongs, including (1) people of color, (2) Asian Americans, (3) their specific ethnic group, and (4) immigrant and refugee populations. This awakening can be accompanied by increased interest in eliminating oppression and advancing social justice.

The fourth Southeast Asian American identity process is the *redirection of salience*, which refers to Southeast Asian Americans' situational redirection of salience to various identities in a given context. This process suggests that, depending on the time and space, Southeast Asian Americans redirect salience to a particular identity that coincides with their experience in that context. For example, a Vietnamese American's identity of primary salience might be their ethnic identification with Vietnamese American culture and community when they are surrounded by Vietnamese family at home, but they might shift primary salience to their identity as a person of color when they transition to other spaces (e.g., a workshop on racism).

The final Southeast Asian American identity process that Museus, Vue, et al. outlined is the *integration of dispositions*. They assert that Southeast Asian Americans engage in a process of integration, through which they construct a holistic identity by "finding comfort as members of various identity groups to which they belong, developing a critical appreciation for aspects of the majority culture, and establishing an awareness around and sense of responsibility to combat the oppression and inequalities faced by their own and other communities" (p. 59).

Museus, Vue, et al. provided a useful model for understanding Southeast Asian American identity. They also, however, challenged existing and usual conceptualizations of racial and ethnic identity development. Specifically, their model departs from the stage-like approach of many earlier perspectives, and offers a more fluid approach to understanding identity development among Asian Americans. The model also challenges the notion that a particular process defines a given stage of development (e.g., assimilation defines White identification), and offers a more complex perspective that is based on multiple processes that can take place simultaneously and become integrated into one's identity throughout the lifespan.

Asian American Identity Consciousness Model

Accapadi (2012) underscored the importance of moving beyond stage models of Asian American identity and creating Asian American identity models that take into account the contextual, complex, multidimensional, continuous, fluid, and dynamic nature of Asian American identity processes. She proposed a Point of Entry (POE) Model of Asian American Identity Consciousness. The POE Model delineates the different factors that can provide a point of entry into an individual's Asian American identity journey. Specifically, Accapadi identifies six different environmental and individual factors that can catalyze Asian American's journeys to find their identity: immigration history, ethnic attachment, familial influences, external influence, self as other (i.e., physical appearance), and other social identities.

The POE Model posits that four environmental factors constitute points of entry into an Asian American identity journey. First, *immigration histories*, as well as how close or far removed Asian Americans are from those histories, shape their Asian American consciousness. Second, *ethnic attachment* refers to the notion that Asian Americans' attachment to their ethnicity, such as cultural norms and language, influence one's Asian American consciousness. Third, *familial influences* refer to the ways that family send messages to Asian Americans that shape their sense of self. Finally, *external influences* refer to the environmental racial realities of Asian Americans' lives, which include racism and racial climates.

In the POE Model, two individual factors also help shape Asian American consciousness. First, *self as other* (i.e., physical appearance) can, at least in part, define their Asian American race-consciousness, as Asian Americans are forced to navigate the ways in which people within their surrounding environment categorize and treat them as a result of their phenotypic features. In addition, Asian Americans' *other social identities* (e.g., class, gender, sexual orientation, religion, ability, etc.) can provide a point of entry into the Asian American cons-ciousness developmental journey because they interact with racial and ethnic factors to mutually shape Asian Americans' experiences and (re)shape Asian Americans' worldviews and sense of self.

Although Accapadi's (2012) POE model might contribute to the discussion about Asian American identity and consciousness, especially important is how the model promotes a reconsideration of the ways in which higher education researchers and practitioners conceptualize identity development processes. Factor models, such as the POE Model, can make unique contributions to our understanding of Asian American identity, above and beyond other existing models, by encouraging educators to view Asian American identity development processes through a different but equally useful conceptual lens—a lens that is not primarily focused on the type of transitions that students might undergo, but is instead aimed at understanding various catalysts of identity development. Specifically, models that delineate the various factors that influence Asian American consciousness can provide significant contributions to identity discourse by generating an understanding of the different points of leverage that college educators can use to nurture Asian American students' movement and progress along trajectories of Asian American identity development.

IDENTITY INTERSECTIONS AND ASIAN AMERICAN COLLEGE STUDENTS

It is important to acknowledge that Asian American college students' experiences are mutually shaped by their multiple social identities. Indeed, existing research clarifies how race and ethnicity interact with gender, sexual orientation, socioeconomic status, immigration status, religion, and other social identities to influence the nature of Asian American students' experiences in higher education (Buenavista et al., 2009; Buenavista & Chen, 2013; Tran & Chang, 2013; Museus, 2011b, in press-b; Museus & Griffin, 2011; Museus & Truong, in press; Narui, 2011; Pepin & Talbot, 2013; Park, 2008, 2009a, 2009b, 2009c, 2012b; Park, Lew, & Chiang, 2013). Although this research has begun to shed valuable light on the ways that intersecting identities impact Asian American contexts, identities, and experiences in higher education, this scholarship is still in its infancy and more theoretical and conceptual frameworks that help understanding how these social identities interact to determine the nature of Asian American experiences in college are warranted.

IMPLICATIONS FOR INSTITUTIONAL POLICY AND PRACTICE

The theories outlined in this chapter have several implications for institutional policy and practice in higher education. Before discussing some of these implications, it is important to acknowledge that no one theory is sufficient for explaining all of the situations and experiences of Asian American students (Evans,

86

Forney, Guido, Patton, & Renn, 2009). Rather, the combination of afore-mentioned theories provide a toolkit for college educators to understand the various ways that racial and ethnic influences might shape the challenges faced by and worldviews of the students with whom they work.

Providing Space for Culture and Identity Exploration

The aforementioned identity theories imply that Asian American students in higher education must inevitably navigate and negotiate multiple cultures. Indeed, these theoretical perspectives acknowledge that dominant society and the racism that it perpetuates pressures Asian American students to dis-identify with their cultural heritage and assimilate into the dominant majority culture within society. Moreover, these theoretical frameworks suggest that Asian American students are influenced by their traditional cultures, and likely face pressure from their families and communities to learn and maintain aspects of these cultural heritages.

These contradictory cultural pressures can cause significant internal conflict and challenges for Asian American students in higher education. Although some colleges and universities do construct spaces for Asian American students to explore this cultural conflict and the challenges that result from it (Kiang, 2002, 2009; Museus, 2008a; Museus, antonio, & Kiang, 2012; Park, 2009c, 2012b; Ryoo & Ho, 2013; Vue, 2013), these spaces are often difficult to find and reach too few Asian American students, such as in the case of Asian American Studies programs and courses, or they are not purposefully structured to facilitate Asian American identity development, like in the case of ethnic student organizations that primarily serve as networks of social support. Thus, postsecondary educators can and should create spaces for Asian American college students to engage in critical dialogue about and explore these tensions, as well as develop a better understanding about how to navigate them. Such spaces can take the form of guest speakers who present on racism and Asian Americans, dialogues that allow students to discuss their common struggles, programming that allows students to share their stories with peers through presentations, digital stories, spoken word poetry, blogs, and other outlets.

Creating Cognitive Dissonance and Disequilibrium

If college educators are interested in nurturing the identity development of their Asian American students, they should consider the importance of exposing these students to new information that can create cognitive dissonance. Such dissonance causes cognitive disequilibrium that requires Asian American students in college to reconcile their previously held beliefs and redefine their identity as an Asian American.

In cases in which Asian American college students do not encounter salient events that cause such dissonance (e.g., a hate crime) or spaces that will catalyze such dissonance (e.g., ethnic studies courses), these students might be less likely to experience significant cognitive disequilibrium, become comfortable with the reality that they are inevitably marginalized within society, and subsequently experience an increased Asian American racial or ethnic consciousness. However, through curriculum and student affairs programming, faculty and student affairs educators can expose these students to information that can facilitate such dissonance and disequilibrium. As a result, these educators can utilize tools, such as literature, videos, and storytelling, to facilitate Asian American students' development of more complex understandings of their social contexts and themselves.

Fostering Social and Political Consciousness and Agency

The aforementioned identity theories suggest that Asian American students can go through a process of increased awareness of social oppression. However, sometimes this increased awareness of the ways in which systems of social oppression harm Asian American communities and other oppressed populations is not accompanied by a better understanding of Asian Americans' agency to combat this subordination.

When the awakening to social oppression is not accompanied by an understanding of how to productively cope with and resist these forms of subjugation, it can result in despair, negative psychosocial consequences, and unproductive forms of resistance. Case in point: Several years ago, I was speaking about racism and Asian Americans in the Northeast and a student in the audience asked if I had ever experienced the racism that I was discussing in my own life and how I coped with it. I responded by saying "you are looking at it," and explaining how my work was both a coping mechanism and method of promoting positive social change. I later discovered that the student, who had been experiencing racist incidents in his dorm room, subsequently told an administrator on his campus that he no longer had to set his dorm room on fire because the discussion allowed him to see that there were more productive ways of coping.

Given the aforementioned realities, college educators have a moral responsibility to not only foster Asian American students' awareness of social oppression, but also cultivate those students' understandings of vehicles for transformative resistance. Knowledge of ways to engage in transformative resistance can both enhance students' ability to navigate the psychological consequences of experienced racism, but also enable them to contribute to social justice efforts to combat social oppression in society. Some ways that educators can and do teach students about transformative resistance is by role modeling social justice through their own work, bringing in guest speakers who might engage in different kinds of social justice but can also serve as model transformative resisters, and create curricular and co-curricular opportunities for students to engage in research and serve activities that can empower oppressed communities.

Offering Culturally Relevant Advising and Counseling

Finally, institutions of higher education should consider the importance of culturally relevant advising and counseling for Asian American students. Such consideration, however, is a necessary but not sufficient condition for effectively serving Asian American students. Rather, proactive efforts must also be made to either (1) hire Asian American advisors and counselors or (2) hire advisors and counselors who have sufficient knowledge of Asian American cultures and ensure that Asian American students on campus are aware that these advisors and counselors will be sensitive to their situations and needs.

At institutions where hiring new advisors and counselors is not an option and current advisors and counselors do not have a working knowledge of Asian American cultures, colleges and universities can and should leverage available resources to educate these professionals about issues specific to Asian American students and train them to effectively serve this population. Efforts to leverage available resources could include engaging Asian American faculty in constructing culturally relevant advising and counseling training workshops, bringing in experts on the experiences of Asian American students to conduct trainings about culturally relevant advising and counseling, engaging Asian American students in dialogues that can help educate advisors and counselors about Asian American experiences and issues, and utilizing available literature on Asian American students as a basis for such discussions.

Considering the Multifaceted Nature of Asian American Identity

It is important for college educators to acknowledge the various elements that comprise students' Asian American identities. Although educators might sometimes view Asian American identity as a unidimensional racial identity, the discussion above clarifies that Asian American consciousness can be comprised of a students' association with several different social groups, including people of color, Asian Americans, their own ethnic group(s), immigrants, refugees, and indigenous populations. Consideration of these different aspects of Asian American identity is critical for educators to develop a more holistic understanding of the worldviews and experiences of the Asian American students whom they serve.

In light of the multifaceted nature of Asian American identity, educators who develop curricular and co-curricular programming with the goal of fostering

Asian American identity development should consider all of these facets. Such deliberate attention to the multiple dimensions of Asian American identity can enable educators to develop programming that allows unique voices within the Asian American student population to be heard and validated, while being able to identify themes across these unique experiences to foster greater awareness of common struggles and a greater Asian American consciousness.

Chapter 5

Asian American Race Relations in College

One spring afternoon in 2010, I entered a subway car in downtown Boston on my way to the University of Massachusetts Boston campus. At the next subway stop, two White and two Asian American youths, who appeared to be around traditional college age, entered the subway car together and sat across from me. As the doors closed and the train proceeded to its next stop, the teens started joking and shortly thereafter their humor became racialized. I sat and observed as the two White youths began spouting racial jokes about their Asian American peers' chinky eyes and inferior language speaking abilities. I observed the Asian American boys become visibly embarrassed, look seemingly ashamed, and struggle for words to respond.

As I observed this racial joking incident on the subway, I became upset, but I continued to watch the interactions but refrained from intervening. Days later, I reflected on the episode and questioned why I had not reacted and engaged the students in a conversation. Several times before, when I had heard racist insults in public spheres, I did say something to the perpetrators to let them know that their actions were inappropriate, but for some reason, this time was different.

A few days later, after some critical reflection, I concluded that one reason that I did not intervene was because the White youths on the subway were supposedly friends of their Asian American peers. As a result, I did not know whether the White youths were intending to cause harm with their words. I did not get involved because the youths were not engaging in a racially motivated hate crime or explicit heinous act of discrimination, but they instead were committing a racial microaggression, which can erroneously seem harmless on the surface but send subtle messages of inferiority to Asian Americans. I did not respond to the incident for the same reason that the two Asian American youths probably did not confront their White peers about their racial jokes on the subway. And, I did not react to the White teens for the same reason that probably I had not confronted my White friends in elementary school, who used racial slurs and jokes in their daily language and humor—words that are now permanently seared into my brain and constitute some of my most salient childhood memories.

This opening vignette is the true account of an exchange that I witnessed a few years ago. I share this story because it underscores the complexity of race-relations in the United States. For example, the vignette highlights the increasingly covert and subtle ways that racism manifests in modern daily life in America. The story conveys complexity in the ways in which racism operates in contemporary society, which can be transmitted intentionally or unintentionally, to its victims. The account illuminates the reality that family, friends, or anyone else can be the vehicle through which racism is perpetuated and communicated to a given individual. It provides an example of how words that are seemingly benign on the surface might be wounding the psyche. Perhaps most importantly, the story excavates the reality that, in environments that are not purposefully structured to facilitate meaningful and productive interracial interactions, the cross-racial exchanges that transpire can be negative in both nature and consequence.

For more than three decades, the topic of interracial interactions and their consequences has had significant implications for major higher education policy issues, such as Affirmative Action and race-conscious college admissions policies. Affirmative Action in college admissions first received the attention of the Supreme Court in 1978, when the High Court heard *Regents of the University of California v. Bakke*. In the *Bakke* case, a student challenged the race-conscious admissions policies of the medical school of the University of California, Davis. After hearing the *Bakke* case, the Supreme Court upheld the legality of race-conscious admissions. Justice Lewis Powell, who wrote the High Court's majority opinion in the *Bakke* decision, underscored the notion that the ability of institutions of higher education to admit diverse student bodies is critical to creating robust learning environments and preparing college students to function effectively in an increasingly diverse and global society. The idea is that diverse learning environments can provide educational spaces in which students can develop the knowledge and skills to contribute to a diverse democracy and workforce. It is largely for these reasons that the Supreme Court concluded that diversity is a compelling state interest and provided a rationale for the justification of race-conscious college admissions policies.

Debates around race-conscious admissions and the importance of diversity have continued. In 2003, two students legally challenged the University of Michigan's race-conscious admissions policies in *Gratz v. Bollinger* and *Grutter v. Bollinger*, and the High Court reaffirmed the legality of race-conscious admissions policies and Justice Powell's diversity rationale. Finally, last year, the Supreme Court heard the case of *Fisher v. University of Texas*, through which Abigail Fisher challenged the race-conscious admissions policy at the University of Texas at Austin. The outcome of the *Fisher* case is still uncertain, but the diversity rationale will likely be a significant consideration in the deliberations and eventual conclusion of the case.

92

As a result of the diversity rationale, the 35 years that have passed since the *Bakke* decision have witnessed the emergence of a substantial body of scholarship on the educational benefits of diversity in higher education. This significant and growing body of higher education research illuminates the ways in which student interactions with people, who are from different racial and ethnic backgrounds than their own, can facilitate a wide array of critical cognitive and civic outcomes. However, postsecondary education scholars have noted that institutions of higher education have disproportionately focused on admitting racially diverse student bodies, while assuming that meaningful interracial interactions will organically occur among these diverse student populations and neglecting to give sufficient attention to the need to purposefully structure educational environments in ways that will promote meaningful and fruitful interracial interactions (M. J. Chang, Chang, & Ledesma, 2005).

Given the realities above, it is imperative that postsecondary educators better understand how different racial groups experience both negative and positive race relations in college and make more substantial efforts to invest energy and resources into purposefully constructing campus spaces and opportunities for students to engage in meaningful interactions across racial lines. The current chapter is aimed at generating a more holistic understanding of Asian American students' experiences engaging in interracial interactions in college, which can both contribute to a more holistic understanding of Asian American experiences in college and contribute to larger national discourse about diversity in higher education. First, I present a model that elucidates the nature of students' interracial interactions in college. Second, I discuss research that examines each of the key elements of this model in greater detail and in the context of Asian American college students' experiences specifically. The chapter concludes with some implications of this discussion for institutional policy and practice.

A MODEL OF INTERRACIAL INTERACTIONS IN COLLEGE

The model in Figure 5.1 builds upon the work of prior researchers (e.g., Milem, Chang, & antonio, 2005; Museus, Ravello, & Vega, 2012; Robinson, 2012), and provides a framework for understanding Asian American students' interracial interactions in college. First, the model indicates that prior interracial interactions (e.g., pre-college) shape the nature of future interaction experiences in higher education. Second, the model suggests that the larger campus racial environments of postsecondary institutions and the availability of purposefully structured diverse learning opportunities are correlated, and both of these factors influence the nature of interracial interactions in college. That is, campus racial environments determine the likelihood that students will have access to diverse learning opportunities, and the availability of diverse learning opportunities influences the ways in which students experience their institutions' racial environments.

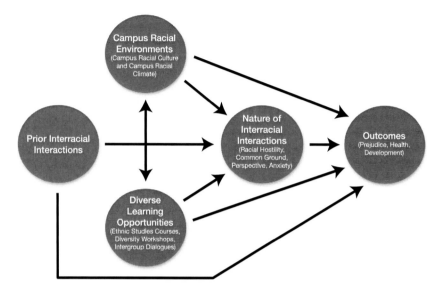

Figure 5.1 A Model of Interracial Interactions in College.

Finally, the aforementioned campus racial environments, availability of purposefully structured diverse learning opportunities, and the nature of students' interracial interactions all interact to determine the outcomes of the interracial interactions.

I discuss each of the components of this conceptual model in greater detail in the sections that follow, but a few caveats are warranted before proceeding. First, the model is based heavily on literature from psychology and higher education. Second, it is important to acknowledge that the model does not propose to include an exhaustive list of variables that affect race relations in college. Rather, it is intended to highlight key aspects of those interactions in higher education, illuminate how these key components of interracial interactions are related to one another, and offer a conceptual framework around which the current chapter is organized.

PRIOR INTERRACIAL INTERACTIONS

Research suggests that Asian American students' exposure to diversity and interracial interactions prior to entering college influences both the extent to which they will engage in such interactions in postsecondary education and their experience interacting with people of different racial groups in college (Robinson, 2012; Sáenz et al., 2007). Indeed, there is some indication that Asian American students' pre-college interactions can send students on an interracial interaction trajectory as they transition to the college environment (Robinson, 2012). Specifically, Asian American students who experience negative interracial interactions in their neighborhoods and K-12 schools might be less likely to seek out or might even avoid such interactions in college, while those who experience positive pre-college interracial interactions might be more likely to pursue such experiences in postsecondary education.

It should be noted, however, that the aforementioned interracial interaction trajectories are not necessarily deterministic. Specifically, the nature of the campus racial environments in higher education can make Asian American students who are on negative interracial interaction trajectories encounter experiences that make them more likely to engage in such relations or make those who are on a positive trajectory less likely to engage in interactions across racial lines (Robinson, 2012). Thus, while it is important to take pre-college experiences into account when designing and constructing campus environments, programs, and practices that are conducive to positive interracial interactions, educators should consider the reality that those Asian American students who experience both negative and positive pre-college interactions across race can be engaged in meaningful interracial interactions in college.

CAMPUS RACIAL ENVIRONMENTS

The environments of college and university campuses are comprised of many different elements, but two aspects of postsecondary institutional environments that comprise the overall campus racial environment of institutions and play an especially key role in shaping the race-related experiences of Asian American and other college students are: the campus racial culture and campus racial climate. Before discussing campus racial culture and campus racial climate in depth, it is useful to define and differentiate between the two terms. Although there is overlap between these two campus environmental concepts, they both provide distinct and useful conceptual tools for analyzing, interpreting, and understanding Asian American college students' racialized experiences within postsecondary education institutions.

The campus racial culture refers to the deeply embedded and pervasive aspects of postsecondary institutions, such as cultural values, beliefs, assumptions, and norms. The concept of the campus racial climate suggests that, while these interconnected cultural elements are often discussed in de-racialized ways in higher education, they are not necessarily race-neutral. The *campus racial culture* can be defined in the following way:

> the collective patterns of tacit values, beliefs, assumptions, and norms that evolve from an institution's history and are manifest in its mission, traditions, language, interactions, artifacts, physical structures, and other symbols, which

> differentially shape the experiences of various racial and ethnic groups and can . . . oppress racial minority populations within a particular institution.
>
> (Museus, Ravello, & Vega, 2012, p. 32)

In addition, it is also important to note the mechanisms by which the campus racial culture can and does often contribute to the oppression of people of color at postsecondary institutions:

> The campus racial culture is disproportionately shaped over time by the racial majority at a given college or university and consequently is congruent with, engages, reflects, and validates the values of the cultures from which the individuals from the racial majority come. At the same time, that culture is often less congruent with, engaging of, reflective of, and validating of the cultural backgrounds of racial and ethnic minority populations.
>
> (Museus, Ravello, & Vega, 2012, p. 32)

Therefore, the campus racial culture not only underscores the salience of various elements of a college or university's culture in shaping the experiences of those within it, but also suggests that postsecondary institutions develop a cultural fabric over time that is comprised of values, beliefs, assumptions, norms, and other cultural elements functions to validate the majority and contribute to the oppression of racial and ethnic minority populations on these campuses.

In contrast to the concept of campus racial culture, in higher education scholarship, the *campus racial climate* can be conceptualized as current "overall racial environment" of a college or university (Solórzano et al., 2000, p. 62). Higher education scholars have delineated one contextual factor that influences and five components that comprise the campus racial climate in a *campus climate for diversity* framework (Hurtado, Milem, Clayton-Pedersen, & Allen, 1998; Milem et al., 2005). The *external forces* are the contextual influences that impact the campus racial climate and include historical forces (e.g., events in American history that shape the way society views diversity issues) and governmental policies, programs, and initiatives (e.g., Affirmative Action). The *historical legacy of inclusion and exclusion* at an institution refers to the vestiges of a history of racial segregation in colleges and universities (e.g., the continued differential distribution of benefits on campuses). The *compositional diversity* of institutions refers to the numerical representation of racial and ethnic groups on campus. The *organizational or structural* dimension of the climate refers to how different groups become embedded within the organizational and structural processes (e.g., the curriculum) of postsecondary institutions. The *behavioral climate* has to do with the nature of interracial interactions that occur on college and university campuses. The *psychological climate* encompasses the perceptions of prejudice, discrimination, and racial conflict on campus.

96

There are at least a few noteworthy distinctions between the campus racial culture and campus racial climate in higher education literature. Whereas the campus culture is deeply embedded in the cultural values, beliefs, assumptions, and norms that permeate the institution, it has been argued that the campus climate refers to more current environmental patterns and perceptions (Peterson & Spencer, 1990). In addition, it has been asserted that the institutional culture is more difficult to change due to its deeply embedded nature, while the campus climate is relatively malleable. Moreover, whereas the campus racial culture is a concept that can be used to examine how seemingly objective dominant cultural value and belief systems within an institution can function to subtly marginalize the values, perspectives, and voices of people of color, thereby contributing to their oppression (Museus, Ravello, & Vega, 2012), most existing research that examines the nature and impact of the campus racial climate aims to unpack the ways in which racial prejudice and discrimination shape the experiences of various racial and ethnic groups within the environments of their respective campuses (see Harper & Hurtado, 2007). However, it is important to acknowledge that the more holistic campus climate for diversity framework that is discussed above encompasses elements of institutional culture and blurs the lines between the two concepts of the campus racial culture and campus racial climate.

Elements of Campus Racial Environments

It is important to note that Asian American students in higher education are significantly less likely than White peers to be satisfied with the environments on their respective campuses and with the overall college experience (Harper & Hurtado, 2007; Kuh, 2005). These lower levels of satisfaction may be a result of the nature of the campus racial environments that Asian Americans experience in higher education. I discuss the various racialized aspects of college and university environments that mutually influence the experiences of Asian American students in college. The extent to which Asian American students experience these elements of their campus racial environments largely determines the level of hostility that they experience when they interact with people from other racial groups.

Cultural Dissonance. Asian American students can experience significant levels of cultural dissonance as they adjust to and navigate institutions of higher education. The term *cultural dissonance* refers to the tensions that Asian American students might experience as a consequence of the incongruence that exists between students' cultural meaning-making systems, which are a reflection of the cultures from which they come, and the new cultural information that they encounter in their college environment (Museus, 2008a). Thus, many Asian American students who attend predominantly White institutions (PWIs) with cultures that reflect the cultural values, beliefs, and perspectives of the White

97

majority are likely to encounter dominant cultures that differ substantially from the cultures found within their Asian American communities and experience significant levels of cultural dissonance in college. Moreover, the levels of cultural dissonance that Asian American students experience within their respective institutional environments is associated with greater levels of cultural stress and likelihood of subsequent disengagement from the predominantly White dominant cultures of their respective campuses and classrooms (Museus, 2008a; Museus & Park, 2012; Museus & Quaye, 2009).

Contradictory Cultural Pressures. Campus racial cultures and climates also cause contradictory pressures for Asian American students in higher education. On one hand, Asian American college students have reported experiencing significant pressures to assimilate into the cultures of their respective campuses (Duster, 1991; Lewis et al., 2000; Museus & Park, 2012). On the other hand, Asian American students report experiencing substantial pressures to conform to stereotypes that categorize and otherize them as different from members of the mainstream culture of their respective college and university campuses. Indeed, like other students of color at PWIs, Asian American students in college "feel they are required to 'blend in' on predominantly White campuses while at the same time the application of academic and behavioral stereotypes emphasizes their group characteristics and difference" (Lewis et al., 2000, p. 79). Moreover these conflicting messages can lead to Asian American students experiencing internal conflict about whether they should conform to the dominant cultures of their respective campuses or resist them.

Cultural Marginalization and Isolation. Asian American students can also experience cultural isolation within the cultures of their respective campuses (Lewis et al., 2000; Museus & Park, 2012; Park, 2008). First, within the larger campus environment, Asian American students sometimes report feeling like they are the only Asian Americans on their respective campuses. Second, Asian American college students report feeling isolated within salient subcultures to which they belong within the larger environment of the campus, such as Greek life (Park, 2008). Third, even at institutions that have large numbers of Asian American students in the aggregate, Asian American students can feel isolated because they are one of few students from their own ethnic group on campus (Museus & Park, 2012; Vue, 2013). Moreover, it is important to note that, while Asian American college students are sometimes blamed for their own "self-segregation," evidence indicates that Asian Americans often report wanting to connect with different communities of color throughout their campuses, but that their self-segregation is in reaction to unwelcoming and sometimes hostile campus racial environments outside of predominantly Asian American spaces at their institutions (Museus & Park, 2012).

Racial Discrimination. In addition to the aforementioned cultural factors, Asian American college students experience explicit and implicit forms of racial discrimination. Regarding overt forms of discrimination, evidence indicates that Asian American students are more likely to encounter racial harassment in college than their White counterparts (Ancis, Sedlacek, & Mohr, 2000; Cress & Ikeda, 2003; Y. K. Kim, Chang, & Park, 2009; Kotori & Malaney, 2003; Museus & Park, 2012; Museus & Truong, 2009; Park, 2009a). Such harassment can manifest in the form of racial profiling from police, racial slurs, and racial bullying. Moreover, it is important to note that, compared with White students, Asian Americans are more likely to experience racial harassment from both faculty and peers on their college campuses (Ancis et al., 2000; Y. K. Kim et al., 2009; Kotori & Malaney, 2003).

As for more covert forms of racial discrimination, Asian Americans encounter racial microaggressions, which are subtle environmentally or individually conveyed racial slights or insults that can send negative messages to Asian American students and reinforce racist ideologies about this population, on their respective college or university campuses (Sue, Bucceri, et al., 2007). It is important to acknowledge that faculty and peers can commit racial microaggressions toward Asian American students in college either intentionally or unintentionally, making it difficult for Asian American college students to assess whether and how to respond to racially microaggressive acts. Two of the main ways that faculty and peers commit racial microaggressions toward Asian American students is by dismissing the reality that racism influences Asian American experiences and by reinforcing racialized stereotypes of these students.

Model Minority Stereotype. Stereotypes of Asian Americans can constitute one salient form of cultural assumptions that permeate society and the environments of specific institutions in higher education. Indeed, Asian American students in college report experiencing several different stereotypes (Chou & Feagin, 2008; Lewis et al., 2000; Museus, 2007, 2008b; Museus & Park, 2012). Existing research indicates that Asian American college students' experiences are significantly shaped by the model minority stereotype (Cheryan & Bodenhausen, 2000; Lewis et al., 2000; Museus, 2007, 2008b; Museus & Kiang, 2009). While the model minority myth has been part of the dominant narrative in American society for decades and can seem harmless, this stereotype can negatively affect Asian American students' college experiences on a daily basis.

Although the model minority stereotype is often perceived as a positive depiction of Asian Americans because it portrays their entire racial group as intellectually superior, it is also coupled with assumptions that Asian Americans spend all of their time studying and frames them as socially awkward, only interested in math, and nerdy (Museus & Park, 2012). These negative social aspects of the model minority stereotype have significant implications for Asian American college students' experiences and interactions with members of different racial groups who might make such racialized overgeneralizations about them and see them as socially inferior.

99

The model minority myth has several other negative ramifications. For instance, this stereotype can mask the challenges that Asian Americans face in higher education, making it easy for educators to dismiss the needs of these students (Museus & Kiang, 2009; Suzuki, 2002). The model minority myth can also place immense pressures on Asian American college students or contribute to the existence and perpetuation of unreasonable expectations of academic perfection. The heightened pressures and level of expectations can lead Asian American students to disengage from college classrooms or opt out of seeking support to avoid disconfirming the stereotype, disappointing others, and not being seen as a "real Asian" (Lewis et al., 2000; Museus, 2007, 2008b; Museus & Park, 2012). These pressures and expectations can also lead to anxiety and "choking" under pressure on examinations (Cheryan & Bodenhausen, 2000).

Deviant Minority Stereotype. Cultural stereotypes of Southeast Asian American students take on a distinct form (Ngo & Lee, 2007). As discussed in previous chapters, many Southeast Asian Americans who migrated to the United States were displaced from their nations of origin by war, entered the United States as refugees, and consequently face significant economic and educational disparities. Consequently, Southeast Asian Americans are racialized as model minorities who achieve universal and unparalleled academic and occupational success in some situations, and they are racialized as deviant minorities who are dropouts, gang members, and welfare sponges in other contexts. Therefore, Southeast Asian American experiences are mutually influenced by these polarized extreme stereotypes.

Unfortunately, little is known about how the model minority and deviant minority stereotypes interact to influence the experiences of Southeast Asian American college students. However, there is some indication that Southeast Asian American students report both stereotypes having an impact on people' perceptions of them (Museus & Park, 2012). It is possible that Southeast Asian American students both face the pressures of the model minority myth to achieve perfection and internalize messages that they are not capable of achieving such status, which could have negative academic, psychological, and social consequences.

Forever Foreigner Stereotype. Another stereotype that exists in college and university environments and influences Asian American students' daily lives is the forever foreigner stereotype (Museus & Park, 2012; Sue, Bucceri, et al., 2007). The forever foreigner myth refers to the ways in which Asian Americans are characterized as perpetual foreigners in the United States, despite the fact that they were born and raised in America or immigrated to the United States as young children. In some cases, faculty and peers can categorize Asian American students as foreigners based on their phenotype or physical appearance, and challenge their American-ness or presence in the United States (Museus & Park,

2012). Such actions can send messages to Asian Americans that they are outsiders and marginalize them within the campus environment.

Emasculating Stereotypes. It is also important to note that racism and sexism interact to mutually create racialized and sexualized stereotypes that, while rarely discussed in the experiences of Asian American college students, do have an impact on the campus environment and the experiences of these individuals (Cho, 2003; Museus & Truong, in press; Tran & Chang, 2013). For example, Asian American male college students' lives might be shaped by emasculating stereotypes of them as socially awkward and asexual or effeminate nerds (Museus & Truong, in press; Tran & Chang, 2013), and consequently act out in unproductive ways. These Asian American men, for example, can engage in hypermasculine activity, such as engaging in hazing of violence, which can lead to negative academic, psychological, and social consequences for Asian American students and their peers in college.

Sexually Objectifying Stereotypes. There is also evidence that racism and sexism interact to produce racialized and gendered stereotypes of Asian American women as exotic, hypersexual, and submissive sex objects in college (Cho, 2003; Museus & Truong, in press). These stereotypes can be harmful in many ways. In fact, these stereotypes of exoticization and sexual objectification can result in the differential treatment of Asian American female students, sexual harassment of Asian American women, and sometimes even motivate sexual assaults of Asian American female college students (Museus & Truong, in press).

It is important to acknowledge that racial stereotypes of both Asian American men and women can and are internalized by Asian Americans themselves, which can lead to these individuals developed stereotype-based perceptions of members of their own community (Museus & Truong, in press). Indeed, Asian American women can perpetuate emasculating stereotypes of Asian American men, and Asian American men can objectify Asian American women. Moreover, racialized and sexualized stereotypes of both Asian American men and women result in a negative sense of self among these individuals. Given the ways in which we know stereotypes impact individual perceptions, thoughts, and behavior, it is imperative that educators working with Asian American students understand the preceding stereotypes and the ways that they influence the identities and experiences of Asian American college students.

DIVERSE LEARNING OPPORTUNITIES

Although the overall racial environment of colleges and universities shapes the experiences of Asian American students, institutions (including faculty, administrators, staff, and students) of higher education can and sometimes do purposefully structure specific spaces within the larger campus racial culture and campus racial climate that can provide space for meaningful interracial interactions to occur. In this section, I discuss such spaces by providing a brief overview of the optimal conditions under which interracial contact should occur to produce positive outcomes, as well as the ways that such spaces manifest on college campuses.

While multiple frameworks for understanding the nature of interracial contact have been proposed and discussed (Aberson & Haag, 2007; Crisp & Turner, 2011), it could be argued that Allport's (1954) intergroup contact theory is the most frequently cited perspective in the literature on interracial interactions. Allport clarified that, if intergroup contact occurs under optimal environmental conditions, such interactions can be a viable mechanism for reducing prejudice. Allport outlined four main characteristics of optimal environmental context for intergroup contact: (1) *equal status* among interacting groups, (2) *common goals* among these participants, (3) *intergroup cooperation*, and (4) the *support* of laws, customs, or authorities within the setting. Allport's intergroup contact theory has provided the conceptual foundation for hundreds of analyses of the impact of interracial and other kinds of intergroup interactions on the reduction of racial and other forms of prejudice. As discussed below, Allport's intergroup contact theory does provide a useful framework for understanding the ways in which educators can utilize diversity to promote positive educational outcomes.

Colleges and universities, however, often fail to engage college students in purposefully structured interracial interactions that can promote positive outcomes in college (Harper & Hurtado, 2007). On college and university campuses, ethnic studies programs, other courses focused on fostering racial awareness, purposefully structured interracial dialogues, and diversity workshops do constitute spaces in which Asian American students can connect with people from other racial and ethnic groups, learn about other racial groups, and teach others about their experiences as an Asian American student (see, for example, antonio, 2001a, 2001b; Kiang, 2002, 2009; Loes, Pascarella, & Umbach, 2012). Moreover, if these campus spaces are characterized by the optimal conditions that Allport (1954) outlined, then their positive effects might be further enhanced (Pettigrew & Tropp, 2006). However, as mentioned, many Asian American and other college students will not be able to access and participate in such meaningfully activities and interactions unless they create such opportunities themselves or with their peers in higher education (Chang et al., 2005; Harper & Hurtado, 2007; Robinson, 2012).

NATURE OF INTERRACIAL INTERACTIONS

The aforementioned pre-college experiences and environmental influences impact the nature of Asian American and other college students' interracial interactions. Although the nature of interracial interactions can be characterized in many different ways, existing empirical literature underscores at least four salient factors that characterize the nature of such interactions. These four aspects of interracial interactions are racial hostility, perceived common ground, perspective taking, and level of interaction anxiety.

Racial Hostility

First, as previously mentioned, the campus racial environments that I discuss above determine the extent to which Asian American college students might perceive racial hostility, which can include racial prejudice and discrimination, originating from other racial groups within their campus racial environments. The extent to which Asian American students perceive hostility in their inter-actions with members of other racial groups on campus could make them more averse to engaging in interactions across racial lines and diminish the quality of such interactions (Museus & Park, 2012; Robinson, 2012). In contrast, Asian Americans who experience or perceive low levels of racial hostility in their interactions with members of other racial populations on their respective cam-puses will be more likely to seek out and have positive engagement interacting across racial lines in college.

Perceived Common Ground

Second, the extent to which Asian American students in higher education perceive common ground between themselves and those with whom they interact influences the likelihood of their engagement in such interactions and the nature of such interactions (Gomez, Dovidio, Huici, Gaertner, & Cuadrado, 2008; Robinson, 2012). Evidence suggests that Asian American college students, like members of other racial groups, are less likely to pursue or be comfortable in interactions with other-race peers on campus if they do not perceive common values, perspectives, or experiences. In contrast, when Asian American students perceive such common ground, they are more likely to seek out and find comfort engaging in such interactions in college.

Perspective Taking

Third, the concept of perspective taking refers to Asian American and other college students' abilities to understand and empathize with the perspectives of racially different others, which is associated with lower levels of racial prejudice (Aberson & Haag, 2007; Pettigrew & Tropp, 2008; Robinson, 2012). Existing empirical research suggests that the perspective taking abilities of Asian American college students and the different-race people with whom they interact in higher education is positively associated with these individuals' likelihood of seeking out additional interracial interactions or the satisfaction that they experience interacting across racial lines (Robinson, 2012).

Interaction Anxiety

Finally, perceived racial hostility, perceptions of common ground, and perspective taking abilities are all associated with Asian American and other college students' level of interracial interaction anxiety (Robinson, 2012). Moreover, interracial interaction anxiety can influence Asian American college students' interactions across racial lines in multiple ways. For example, other people can interpret the anxiety that Asian Americans experience during interracial interaction in negative ways (West, Pearson, Dovidio, Shelton, & Trail, 2009). These negative perceptions of anxiety can lead to other people experiencing decreased interest in interacting with Asian American students and function to reinforce the stereotypes of Asian Americans as socially awkward model minority nerds. In addition, existing research suggests that interracial interaction anxiety can lead to Asian American students withdrawing from interracial interactions and diminish the quality of those interactions (Littleford, O'Doherty Wright, & Sayoc-Parial, 2005; Robinson, 2012; Son & Shelton, 2011).

It is important to note that interaction anxiety is particularly salient in understanding Asian Americans' interracial interactions. First, societal stereotypes that Asian Americans are not really racial minorities who experience racism and that Asian Americans are submissive or passive can result in pervasive perceptions that it is acceptable to openly share prejudicial views against members of this racial group. Second, the high levels of prejudice encountered by Asian Americans could be associated with the fact that this population reports the highest levels of social anxiety among all racial groups (Park, Sulaiman, Schwartz, Kim, Ham, & Zamboanga, 2011). Third, evidence suggests that, compared with other racial groups, this anxiety is especially salient in Asian Americans' interracial interaction experiences.

OUTCOMES OF INTERRACIAL INTERACTIONS

As mentioned, Asian American students' race relations in college can generate both negative and positive outcomes. As I illuminate above, on one hand, significant racial hostility and anxiety can characterize Asian American students' interactions across racial lines in college (Chou & Feagin, 2008; Museus & Park, 2012; Sue, Bucceri, et al., 2007). Such negative interactions are less likely to generate benefits, and more likely to lead to negative outcomes. On the other hand, if and when Asian American students encounter and engage in educationally purposeful interracial interactions, these students and the different-race individuals with whom they interact can experience increased understanding across racial lines, reduced prejudice and discrimination, and lead to enhanced learning outcomes (Pettigrew & Tropp, 2006, 2008). In the remainder of the current section, I provide a brief overview of the negative and positive consequences of Asian American students' interracial interactions in college.

Negative Outcomes of Interracial Interactions

Both hostile campus racial environments and the interracial interactions that Asian American students encounter within them can lead to multiple negative outcomes, such as increased racial prejudice and negative health consequences for Asian American and other students in higher education. Indeed, although much of the literature examining interracial interactions focuses on prejudice reduction, it is possible for negative interracial interactions to lead to higher levels of subsequent racial prejudice (Allport, 1954). In particular, when the environmental context within which interactions take place does not include optimal interracial interaction conditions, such as equal status and common goals, it can lead to negative interactions that increase prejudice. And, when interracial interactions are characterized by high levels of racial hostility, low levels of perceived common ground, minimal perspective-taking, and high levels of interaction anxiety, these experiences can function to increase participants' prejudicial views toward racial others.

Regarding negative health consequences, racially hostile campus environments and the interracial interactions that students encounter within them can result in significant negative consequences for Asian American and other students' emotional, physical, and psychological health (Truong & Museus, 2012). In fact, evidence suggests that racist campus environments and interactions can lead to depression, headaches, anxiety, low self-esteem, humiliation, upset stomach, chest pains, tunnel vision, ulcers, back pains, nightmares, loss of appetite or overeating, nausea, shortness of breath, weeping, vomiting, fatigue, increased heart rate and hypertension, anger and frustration, difficulty concentrating, lack of productivity and motivation, sleep deprivation, and recounting specific racist situations days, weeks, months, and years after they occur (Bryant-Davis, 2007; Bryant-Davis & Ocampo, 2005; Carter, 2007; Carter & Forsyth, 2009; Carter et al., 2005; Clark et al., 1999; Harrell, 2000; Truong & Museus, 2012).

Positive Outcomes of Interracial Interactions

In contrast to the aforementioned negative outcomes, research suggests that meaningful interracial interactions can result in reduced prejudice and positive developmental outcomes among Asian Americans and other students in higher education. Regarding prejudice reduction, hundreds of existing empirical studies clarify that interracial interactions can lead to lower levels of racial prejudice among individuals who encounter and engage in such interactions (e.g., Bowman & Griffin, 2012; Denson, 2009). This literature also suggests that the optimal conditions that Allport (1954) outlined, while not necessary conditions for the interactions to reduce prejudice, do function to enhance the impact of interracial contact on racial prejudice reduction (Pettigrew & Tropp, 2006). In short, interracial interactions that occur when there is equal status, common goals, and intergroup cooperation among participants, as well as supportive authorities, are an effective means to reducing racial prejudice.

In addition to prejudice reduction, existing research suggests that interracial interactions can lead to positive developmental outcomes, including enhanced academic, diversity, and democratic outcomes. Regarding academic outcomes, research unequivocally indicates that interracial interactions lead to positive academic outcomes, such as knowledge acquisition, more complex and critical thinking skills, perspective-taking and pluralistic orientations, increased creativity and generation of original ideas, and more positive educational aspirations (antonio, 2001b, 2004; antonio, Chang, Hakuta, Kenny, Levin, & Milem, 2004; Chang, Astin, & Kim, 2004; Denson & Chang, 2009; Hurtado, 2005; Jayakumar, 2008; Locks, Hurtado, Bowman, & Oseguera, 2008). As for diversity outcomes, several studies clarify that interracial interactions are associated with a range of diversity-related outcomes, including greater recognition of the existence of racism and other social problems, increased appreciation for and openness to diversity, heightened commitment to racial understanding, increased ability to relate to people of other races, and greater competence in diversity issues (antonio, 2001b; Crisp & Turner, 2011; Denson & Zhang, 2010). Finally, interracial interactions have been associated with a wide range of democratic outcomes, which have to do with the ability and interest to be productive contributing members of a democratic society (antonio, 2001a; Bowman, Brandenberger, Hill, & Lapsley, 2011; Chang et al., 2004; Denson & Zhang, 2010; Gurin, Dey, Gurin, & Hurtado, 2003; Gurin, Nagda, & Lopez, 2004; Hurtado, 2005; Jayakumar, 2008). These democratic outcomes include, but are not limited to, improved leadership skills, greater engagement in volunteer work, increased commitment to civic activity, engagement in politics, increased problem-solving abilities, and enhanced abilities to work productively with other people.

The current synthesis is not intended to provide an exhaustive list of the outcomes that Asian American college students experience from interracial interactions. It is intended, however, to illuminate the ways in which interracial interactions, as well as the environmental contexts within which they occur, can lead to both very negative or positive outcomes. In doing so, the discussion underscores the severity of educators' responsibility to construct environments in ways that facilitate interracial interactions that minimize the potential negative outcomes and maximize the positive consequences of interracial contact.

IMPLICATIONS FOR INSTITUTIONAL POLICY AND PRACTICE

The preceding discussion highlights the ways in which institutions of higher education can and sometimes do construct campus racial environments that promote educationally enriching interracial interactions through various mechanisms, including ethnic studies programs, diversity courses, diversity workshops, and interracial dialogues. The above synthesis also underscores the ways that college educators can incorporate optimal conditions (i.e., equal status, common goals, intergroup cooperation, and support of authorities) into the intentional structuring of campus spaces for facilitating meaningful interracial interactions and their associated positive outcomes. In addition, in this concluding section, I offer a few more recommendations that can help institutions enhance their efforts to construct campuses in which meaningful and educationally beneficial interracial interactions can flourish.

Gauging Prior Interactions and Perspectives

First, the evidence above suggests that it is important for college educators to understand Asian American students' prior experiences and corresponding perspectives in efforts to understand how to construct diversity programs and practices that can more effectively facilitate positive interactions among these students and their peers. As mentioned, existing evidence indicates that Asian American students enter college with a wide range of interracial interaction experiences. Moreover, it is possible that Asian American students who have experienced primarily negative pre-college interracial interactions and have an aversion to such interactions identify with different types of interactions than their counterparts who already have a history of and value engaging in positive meaningful interracial dialogues.

Given the reality of differential pre-college interaction experiences, it might be valuable for postsecondary educators to consider engaging Asian American college students in ways that are tailored to their prior interactions and affinities for interracial contact. For example, educators could engage those who are less likely to seek out interracial interactions and have high levels of interaction anxiety in diversity programming by allowing them to take a more passive role in such programs and observing the potential benefits of positive and productive interracial coalitions or dialogues. In contrast, college educators might be freer to engage those with an affinity for interracial interactions in other meaningful ways, such as in the co-construction of diversity programming opportunities with and for their racially diverse peers.

Combating Racial Stereotypes

As discussed above, a wide range of pervasive and problematic racial stereotypes define Asian American college student experiences. The stereotypes that help define Asian American experiences depict Asian American men and women in a deceivingly positive light on the surface, while perpetuating gross misconceptions that can have salient negative consequences for Asian American students in higher education. These stereotypes contribute to the racialization of Asian American men as socially inferior and undesirable, while they contribute to the construction of Asian American women as exoticized sexual objects. For Asian American students in higher education, who are exposed to these stereotypes in the media and in daily interactions repeatedly, these stereotypes can have a profound conscious or subconscious impact on their thoughts, perceptions, and behaviors. One potential ramification of these behaviors is that they can induce Asian American college students' disengagement from interracial interactions or high levels of interaction anxiety within those interactions.

Given the salience of stereotypes and their potential impact on interracial interactions, it is important for college educators to consider the importance of excavating and fostering awareness of Asian American stereotypes to increase the likelihood that their Asian American students will engage in and benefit from meaningful interracial interactions. This is a particularly important point because Asian Americans are often excluded from racial discourse in American society or constructed as impervious to racial oppression and realities, which could lead to many Asian American students and the peers with whom they interact being deprived of previous opportunities to think critically about and gain a consciousness of stereotypes of Asian Americans in society and their harmful consequences. Providing space for Asian American students and their peers to discuss, examine, and understand the nature of Asian American stereotypes can help foster a heightened awareness of these overgeneralizations and their consequences could ensure that they do not enter the interracial interactions in harmful ways and contribute to negative interracial dialogue experience for Asian Americans.

Constructing Common Ground

The research that is synthesized in this chapter underscores the value of educators identifying, understanding, and utilizing common ground among people from different racial groups to maximize the quality of their interracial interactions. Excavating common ground among students from different racial communities can create bonds that permit them to empathize across racial lines and have open and honest discussions about important political and social issues. Therefore, college educators should intentionally identify and emphasize common ground to maximize the likelihood that they are constructing spaces and activities that are conducive to productive interracial contact in postsecondary education.

There are many ways that postsecondary educators can excavate and foster common ground among Asian American college students and their peers. One way in which postsecondary educators can highlight common ground between Asian American and other students is by engaging them in dialogue about common experiences of racial oppression among Asian Americans and other communities of color. Another way in which educators can excavate common ground among Asian American students and their different-race peers in college is by focusing on other social identities and associated struggles that these students share as a result of those identities. For example, educators can identify and shed light on the socioeconomic challenges faced by Southeast Asian Americans and their Black, Latino, Native American, and Pacific Islander counterparts to highlight the reality and salience of social oppression. And, this recognition of such common struggles can lead to higher levels of empathy among students for their other-race peers and provide a foundation for deeper discussions about other forms of social oppression.

Facilitating Inter-Ethnic Interactions

While Asian American college students can benefit from interacting across racial lines, they can also derive significant benefits from interacting with their Asian American peers from different ethnic backgrounds (Robinson, 2012). As I discuss in previous chapters, different Asian American ethnic groups have distinct histories, cultures, languages, and communities. Asian American students also come from a wide range of generational statuses. Consequently, students from various Asian American ethnic populations also have diverse worldviews and experiences.

College educators can acknowledge the aforementioned diversity within the Asian American population and capitalize on it by constructing spaces and opportunities that facilitate educationally purposeful inter-ethnic dialogues among Asian American students. For example, engaging Asian American students from different ethnic groups in inter-ethnic dialogues can help maximize common ground and foster empathy among them to create conditions conducive to positive and meaningful inter-ethnic interactions and dialogue.

Given the importance of intentionally structuring diverse learning environments and interracial interactions in ways that minimize negative outcomes and produce positive ones, it is critical for educators to utilize existing theory and research to create optimal conditions on their campuses. In fact, such purposeful design of diverse learning environments and interactions is essential to reduce racial prejudice and foster positive developmental outcomes.

Chapter 6

Asian American Success in College

In 1966, the New York Times *published an article, titled "Success Story, Japanese American Style." The article solidified societal perceptions of Asian Americans as a model minority and evidence of a well-functioning meritocracy and widespread access to the American Dream.*

In 1987, the cover of Time Magazine *featured six Asian American youth and the phrase "Asian American Whiz Kids." The article constituted one of many articles that were released by popular magazines to underscore the academic superiority of Asian American students in the 1980s.* Fortune, Newsweek, Time, *and* U.S. News *and* World Report, *to name a few, also published articles reinforcing the racial imagery of Asian Americans as a super minority.*

Over two decades later, the racialization of Asian American students as model minorities led, in part, to the racial construction of Asian American fathers and mothers as superior parents in public discourse. In 2011, Time Magazine *was one of several popular media outlets that published pieces aimed at facilitating dialogue about whether tough parenting and excessive academic expectations was the mechanism by which Asian American parents have been so successful at fostering academically successful children.*

In 2012, the Wall Street Journal *published an article that was titled "Rise of the Tiger Nation" and framed Asian Americans as "the country's best-educated, highest-earning and fastest-growing racial group" with "the distinction and occasional burden of immigrant success." The article was congruent with previously published articles in the* Wall Street Journal *and other popular media outlets, which frame the entire Asian American race as relatively free of problems and superior in work ethic and intellect.*

110

As I discuss in preceding chapters, stereotypes of Asian Americans as model minorities emerged in the 1960s and have persisted for decades. The persistence of these stereotypes is indicative of the reality that they are deeply embedded in the minds of people throughout the United States. In addition, media outlets, national policy reports, and other public discourse periodically reinforce and reify the place of these stereotypes in society. These racialized generalizations are problematic for several reasons. One significant way in which these racial stereotypes are harmful is that they hinder the development of a complex understanding of Asian American experiences and outcomes in education.

The absence of complex understandings of Asian American student success in higher education is particularly problematic given the current national emphasis on increasing college completion rates. Both the federal government and major national policy organizations have highlighted the importance of increasing college student success rates to ensure that the United States is a world leader in educational attainment. The College Board (2012), for example, has outlined a College Completion Agenda to ensure that a minimum of 55 percent of the nation's 25 to 34-year-olds hold at least an associate's degree by 2025. Although Asian Americans are often not the focus of college completion discourse, they can and should play a critical role in it.

It is important for leaders in the federal government and national policy organizations, as well as educators within institutions of higher education, to recognize that a failure to understand the ways in which various influences facilitate or hinder the success of Asian American students in higher education precludes the development of a comprehensive understanding of how to maximize success among all students and progress toward the nation's college completion agenda. Comparatively, a more informed and intricate grasp of the factors that positively and negatively affect Asian American college students' outcomes can productively inform larger discourse on how to maximize success in postsecondary education (Museus & Chang, 2009).

In contrast to simplistic racial stereotypes of Asian Americans as overachieving model minorities, the current chapter is aimed at synthesizing existing research to construct a more complex and realistic picture of Asian American college student success than what already exists. First, I provide an overview of two traditional perspectives of student success, and discuss their limitations. Second, I discuss several concepts that help clarify the role of community and campus cultures in shaping the success of Asian American students and other students of color in college. Third, I outline a couple useful perspectives that were derived from the voices and experiences of Asian American students and other students of color in higher education and can constitute useful conceptual tools for understanding the ways in which postsecondary institutions can and do facilitate success among Asian American students in higher education.

111

Before proceeding, it is important to note a couple important caveats. First, both theoretical perspectives and empirical research that focus specifically on Asian American college student persistence and completion are difficult to find. Therefore, in the following discussion, I draw heavily from theory and research on students of color in general. Second, the current discussion is based on the assumption that the greatest forthcoming advances in theory and research on Asian American student success will not be based on empirical testing of traditional theories, but rather will be a result of the development and testing of new theoretical frameworks that take into account the authentic voices and experiences of these populations. Consequently, in the current synthesis, I place primary emphasis on theories and research that are largely based on the voices of Asian American students and their peers of color.

TRADITIONAL FRAMEWORKS OF SUCCESS IN COLLEGE

There are two traditional frameworks that have emerged and dominated discourse on college student success: Tinto's (1975, 1987, 1993) student integration theory and Astin's (1984, 1999) student involvement theory. I provide an overview of these theoretical frameworks and their contributions briefly herein. I also discuss their limitations in advancing discourse around an understanding of Asian American college student success.

The most widely cited and studied theory of college success is Tinto's (1975, 1987, 1993) integration theory. Tinto's theory suggests that students enter postsecondary education with initial levels of commitment to their goals and their institutions. These commitments determine the degrees to which students become integrated into the academic and social subsystems of their campuses. These levels of integration, in turn, shape students' subsequent commitments to their goals and their institutions. Finally, these subsequent commitments determine their likelihood of succeeding in higher education. While most research testing Tinto's integration theory analyzes whether academic and social integration predict persistence and degree completion in college (see Braxton, 2000; Braxton, Sullivan, & Johnson, 1997), the theory is based on cultural foundations which have origins in the field of anthropology.

Tinto's (1987, 1993) integration theory is partly based on Van Gennep's (1960) stages of cultural transition. Van Gennep's work suggests that people transition through three stages to move from one status to another within a particular culture. First, individuals go through a stage of *separation*, or detachment from their former status. Second, they go through a stage of *liminality*, which refers to the transition period from the original to the second status. Finally, individuals go through a stage of *incorporation*, which refers to their adoption of the values and norms of the new status. Building on these stages, Tinto (1993) argued that students must "physically as well as socially dissociate from the communities of the past" to fully become incorporated into academic life and succeed in college (p. 96). Thus, the underlying foundations of Tinto's theory are based on an assumption that students who fail to separate from their precollege cultures and communities and assimilate into the cultures of their campuses are less likely to persist (Hurtado & Carter, 1997; Kuh & Love, 2000; Tierney, 1999).

Another theory that has garnered attention in the college student success literature is Astin's (1984, 1999) theory of student involvement, which hypothesizes that college students' involvement is associated with greater levels of satisfaction and increased likelihood of persistence to graduation in higher education. Astin asserts that the concept of student involvement refers to the amount of physical and psychological energy that students invest in various college activities and opportunities. Moreover, Astin's involvement theory argues that both the quality and quantity of energy that students invest in college activities and opportunities determine the likelihood that they will achieve greater learning outcomes and succeed. Astin suggests that, when college educators facilitate student involvement in particular activities and opportunities, such as interaction with faculty members and membership in student groups, they can facilitate positive learning and persistence outcomes. Noteworthy is the fact that Astin's involvement theory (1984, 1999) can be viewed as acultural in that it does not explicitly discuss the role of culture in the experiences and outcomes of college students.

These theories offer important concepts that have helped us better understand success among Asian American students. These theories also have limitations in explaining Asian American college student success, three of which I discuss herein. First, it could be argued that both of these theories are inherently culturally biased and disadvantage Asian Americans and other students of color (Rendón, Jalomo, & Nora, 2000; Tierney, 1992, 1999). Given that Asian American students and other students of color in college are more likely to come from cultures that are markedly different from the ones that they encounter at their PWIs, Tinto's (1975, 1987, 1993) expectation that students bear the burden of detaching from their pre-college communities and assimilate into the predominantly White cultures of their campuses disproportionately disadvantages these populations of color by expecting them to sever important ties to their traditional cultural heritages (Attinasi, 1989; Rendón et al., 2000; Tierney, 1992, 1999). In addition, while Astin's (1984, 1999) theory of student involvement is culturally neutral on the surface, it could be argued that its neutrality is inherently culturally biased because of the reality that the cultures of PWIs are likely to disproportionately limit the involvement opportunities to which Asian Americans and other students of color have access.

Second, scholars have noted that both of these theoretical frameworks are self-deterministic (e.g., Bensimon, 2007; Rendón et al., 2000). More specifically, the

113

frameworks disproportionately focus on student behaviors, but do not adequately emphasize the responsibility of postsecondary institutions to create environments that foster success among their students. This is a critical limitation, given that the ways in which institutions structure their campus environments and college educators' behaviors do influence the success of their students (Jayakumar & Museus, 2012). Again, given that most colleges and universities in the United States are predominantly White, and Asian Americans and other students of color are more likely to encounter cultural challenges adjusting to and navigating these institutions, the lack of focus on institutional responsibilities to create conditions that welcome, engage, and validate students is especially problematic for and disadvantages these populations.

A third limitation of these traditional theories is that they place disproportionate emphasis on student behavior and give insufficient attention to the psychological aspects of the college student experience. Indeed, much of the research that examines Tinto's (1975, 1987, 1993) theory measures academic and social behaviors, as indicators of integration into the respective social systems of campus, but does not specifically focus on the psychological dimensions of students' experiences (Hurtado & Carter, 1997). Although Astin (1984, 1999) explicitly underscored the psychological component of involvement, his definition of quality focused on the quality of activities in which students participate (e.g., participation in honors program and faculty–student interaction). Knowledge of the types of activities in which students participate is important, but it is not sufficient for understanding college experiences and success because it does not take into account the reality that White students and students of color can experience the same high-quality activity in drastically different ways. Moreover, Asian American college students and other students of color can experience even the high-quality activities at PWIs in negative ways, if these experiences are characterized by significant cultural dissonance, prejudice, or discrimination. It is important to note that this discussion is not intended to be an exhaustive list of limitations and they are not mutually exclusive.

IMPACT OF COMMUNITY AND CAMPUS CULTURAL CONTEXTS ON ASIAN AMERICAN SUCCESS IN COLLEGE

Multiple perspectives have emerged that illuminate the role that community and campus cultures play in the experiences and outcomes of Asian American and other students in college. In this section, I discuss two perspectives that can be used to understand the ways in which communities and families influence Asian American student success: the cultural mechanisms and community cultural wealth frameworks. Then, I discuss several concepts that higher education scholars have offered to explain the ways in which campus cultures impact Asian American and other college students' success: the Intercultural Perspective of Minority Student Persistence and the Culturally Engaging Campus Environments (CECE) Model.

Cultural Mechanisms

The cultural mechanisms perspective of Asian American success has primarily been discussed in K-12 education contexts and focuses on how community, family, and parental cultural values can affect Asian American students' success (Min, 2003; Zhou & Kim, 2006). For example, researchers have discussed how, in some communities, residential segregation and poverty contribute to the development of cultures that promote self-defeating behaviors among students (e.g., welfare dependency, drug addiction, and school failure) (Wilson, 1996). They argue that those who are raised in these self-defeating cultures can develop an opposition to dominant society's norms and values, and such resistance to the dominant culture can hinder their education (Fordham, 1996; Kohl, 1994). In contrast, the cultural mechanisms perspective indicates that cultural values that stress the value of education and making sacrifices for family explain the superior academic achievement that some ethnic groups exhibit (Min, 2003; Ngo & Lee, 2007).

The application of this cultural mechanisms perspective to the understanding of Asian American student success in college should be done with caution for at least a few reasons. First, this perspective can attribute some Asian American ethnic groups' relatively high levels of success to their cultural values, while blaming the cultures of other Asian American ethnic groups or other groups of color for their relatively low levels of educational success (Zhou & Kim, 2006). Second, the notion that cultural values are deterministic in the context of understanding college success can reinforce stereotypes of Asian American students as model minorities. Third, an overemphasis on community and family values in explanations of Asian American student success, like the traditional frameworks discussed above, fails to emphasize the role and responsibility of postsecondary institutions in determining success outcomes.

It is also important to avoid simplistic notions of cultural mechanisms and acknowledge that they interact with structural factors that also influence success. Zhou and Kim (2006), for example, underscore the interaction of cultural and structural influences by analyzing Chinese and Korean immigrant communities that originated from countries in which education is the principal means of social mobility, competition for access to high-quality education is normal, and families invest in the education of their children. Zhou and Kim demonstrated that the majority of members within these Asian American communities were socialized in cultures that emphasized values of education and competition, so they utilized these cultural values and material resources to develop complex supplementary

115

education structures to facilitate student success within their communities. In contrast, Asian American communities whose members come from primarily agrarian cultures without competitive education systems and abundant material resources, such as some Southeast Asian refugees from rural areas, might face barriers in constructing such community structures (Museus, in press-b).

The cultural mechanisms perspective has not been applied to the examination of Asian American students in higher education. The small body of research that does exist in this area clearly suggests that community and family influences do play a role in shaping Asian American students' educational trajectories (Kiang, 2002, 2009; Museus, in press-b; Museus, Maramba, Palmer, Reyes, & Bresonis, 2013). Indeed, evidence indicates that parental expectations of academic success, parental valuing of education, and parental sacrifice and students' feelings of responsibility to repay their parents for these sacrifices are all associated with motivation and success among these students. It is important to note that excessive pressure from parents, combined with pressures to confirm to model minority stereotypes, can create situations in which Asian American students feel like they can never do well enough or fulfill others' expectations of them (Museus, in press-b; Museus & Park, 2012), although there is no evidence that such experienced excessive pressure is a frequent occurrence in the lives of Asian American college students.

Community Cultural Wealth

While the cultural mechanisms perspective focuses on the ways in which communities and families motivate and pressure Asian American students to succeed, the concept of community cultural wealth offers a broader perspective regarding the ways in which the cultures in Asian American and other communities of color can equip students with the tools to succeed (Yosso, 2005). Specifically, Yosso highlighted the notion that deficit perspectives often frame students of color as lacking the capital, but argued that these students acquire valuable knowledge and skills in their cultural communities that constitute forms of capital that students possess and can help them succeed in the education system and society.

There are six forms of community cultural wealth. First, *aspirational capital* has to do with the ability of Asian American and other communities of color to maintain hopes and dreams for the future, despite perceived or real barriers, which enables children of color to dream of potential opportunities and achievements beyond their present circumstances (Gándara, 1982, 1995). Second, *linguistic capital* includes the intellectual and social capacities that Asian American students and their peers of color acquire in multiple languages or styles (Faulstich Orellana, 2003). Third, *familial capital* refers to the cultural knowledge in the form of Asian American and other racial minority communities' cultural history, memory, and intuition (see Delgado Bernal, 1998, 2002). Fourth, *social capital* refers to the social networks, and their corresponding resources, to which Asian American students and other students of color in postsecondary education have access, which can aid them in navigating society's institutions (Stanton-Salazar, 2001). Fifth, *navigational capital* refers to the skills that Asian American college students and their peers of color develop to maneuver through social institutions that are not created by or for people of color. Finally, *resistant capital* is grounded in the legacy of social oppression and has to do with the knowledge and skills that Asian American students and other student of color in college develop through oppositional behavior that resists social subordination (Freire, 1970a, 1973; Solórzano & Delgado Bernal, 2001).

The community cultural wealth framework is particularly useful for those who are interested in understanding the strengths that Asian American students can bring with them to college. The community cultural wealth framework also challenges dominant deficit perspectives and deviant minority stereotypes of Southeast Asian Americans; it complicates the picture regarding the many different community contextual factors that can hinder or promote success among Asian Americans and other communities of color in general. There is a need, however, for theory and research that examines how these forms of capital manifest in Asian American students' experiences and to develop a better understanding regarding how college educators can incorporate these forms of cultural wealth into policies, programs, and practices to engage and validate Asian American students and other students of color in college.

Cultural Integrity

In addition to the aforementioned cultural perspectives, which underscore the role of communities and families in the experiences and success of Asian American students and other students of color, higher education scholars have generated several concepts that advance current understandings of the ways in which campus cultures can and should influence the success of Asian Americans and students of color in college. For example, Tierney (1992, 1999) underscored the need to move beyond Tinto's (1975, 1987, 1993) assumptions about the necessity of cultural separation and assimilation to facilitate success, a process that he referred to as *cultural suicide*. Building on the work of Deyhle (1995), Tierney emphasized the notion of *cultural integrity*, or affirming students' cultural backgrounds and identities through programs and practices that engage students' cultural backgrounds in positive ways to provide more relevant education and promote success among students of color in college. The concept of cultural integrity sparked a new body of literature that examines the ways in which institutions of higher education can and should construct environments that engage and respond to the cultural backgrounds of Asian American students and their peers of color.

117

Cultural Validation

Similar to cultural integrity is the concept of cultural validation. Rendón (1994) first highlighted the importance of the concept of cultural validation. She asserted that postsecondary institutions that construct campus environments that function to validate the cultural backgrounds of students of color make it easier for those undergraduates to engage in the academic and social life of their respective institutions. Scholars have begun to analyze this concept of validation (Museus & Quaye, 2009; Nora, Urick, & Cerecer, 2011; Rendón & Muñoz, 2011), and, in doing so, they have underscored the importance of institutions constructing spaces, curricula, programs, and practices that are aimed at serving students of color in higher education.

Cultural Belonging

Hurtado and Carter (1997) also acknowledged the importance of moving beyond the Tinto (1975, 1987, 1993) integration model and developing alternative perspectives of success among students of color. Noting the limitations of focusing on student behaviors and the need to acknowledge the psychological component of students' experiences in college, the authors argued for a focus on students' subjective sense of belonging or fitting into the cultures of their college and university campuses. They applied Bollen and Hoyle's (1990) concept of *sense of belonging* to the college context and illuminated the value of focusing on racial and ethnic minority students' overall perception of social cohesion within their respective campus cultures. The concept of sense of belonging has offered higher education researchers a psychological alternative method of measuring students' connections to the cultures of their campuses, and emerging evidence suggests that it is a valuable framework through which to view students' sense of connection to their institutions (Locks et al., 2008; Museus & Maramba, 2011).

Bicultural Socialization

Building on the work of de Anda (1984) and Valentine (1971), Rendón et al. (2000) offered the concept of *bicultural socialization* to underscore how college students of color can develop the skills to navigate multiple cultures (e.g., the cultures of their communities and campuses) simultaneously and effectively. The notion of bicultural socialization suggests that students who originate from cultures that are incongruent with the dominant cultures of their respective campuses can effectively navigate both cultures without severing ties to either one (de Anda, 1984; Rendón et al., 2000; Valentine, 1971). An individual's ability to develop bicultural socialization skills is, in part, a function of the amount of overlap between the two cultures, their access to cultural agents who can facilitate

118

socialization within the two cultures, their access to feedback, their approach to problem-solving, and their degree of bilingualism, to name a few. This concept of *bicultural socialization* highlights the fact that postsecondary institutions and the cultural agents within them can and sometimes do facilitate the ability of individuals to successfully navigate the cultures of their communities and their institutions simultaneously.

Cultural Integration

To move beyond discussions of academic and social integration, Museus (2011b) sought to reclaim the term *integration* and redefine it as a more culturally responsive process for which institutions and college educators could take responsibility. Recognizing the limitations of the common fragmentation of the academic, social, and cultural aspects of students' lives, Museus offered the concept of *cultural integration* to underscore how institutions can begin thinking about integrating three components of students' lives—academic, social, and cultural—into specific academic programs, courses, projects, spaces, and activities (Figure 6.1). Specifically, postsecondary institutions can and should purposefully incorporate academically engaging activity, the nurturing of meaningful social connections, and the engagement of cultural knowledge and validation into programs, courses, projects, spaces, and activities (Museus, 2011b; Museus, Lam, et al., 2012). Purposefully utilizing such integration can create conditions in which Asian American college students and other college students of color are able to strengthen their connections to the academic sphere of the institutions, the social subsystem of their campuses, and their own cultural heritages simultaneously.

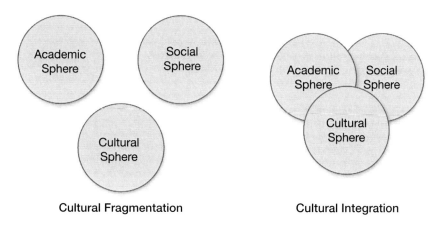

Cultural Fragmentation　　　　　**Cultural Integration**

Figure 6.1　Cultural Fragmentation and Cultural Integration.

Source: Museus (2011c).

119

These cultural concepts have made substantial contributions to current levels of understanding of the experiences and outcomes of college students of color, but they do not offer holistic models that explain the processes by which institutions impact students' experiences and outcomes. At least two frameworks for understanding college student persistence and completion have been created using the voices of Asian American students and their peers of color: the Intercultural Perspective of Minority Student Persistence and the Culturally Engaging Campus Environments (CECE) Model. I discuss these frameworks in the following sections.

AN INTERCULTURAL PERSPECTIVE OF PERSISTENCE AMONG STUDENTS OF COLOR IN COLLEGE

A few researchers have attempted to generate new holistic frameworks of minority student success that are independent of Tinto's theory, generated from the voices of students of color, and attempt to explain college student persistence and degree completion processes (e.g., Kuh & Love, 2000; Museus, in press-b; Museus & Quaye, 2009). Kuh and Love (2000), for example, proposed a cultural perspective of student departure consisting of eight culturally based propositions that help explain minority student persistence. The cultural perspective posited that the level of incongruence between students' precollege cultures and dominant campus cultures is negatively related to persistence, and students who experience a high level of distance between those two cultures must either acclimate to the dominant culture of their campus or become immersed in one or more subcultures to successfully find membership in and persist through college. They also posited that, when those subcultures value academic achievement, they are more conducive to the success of their members.

Museus and Quaye (2009) subsequently simultaneously analyzed Kuh and Love's cultural perspective, existing literature, and the voices of 30 Asian Americans and other students of color to generate a new *intercultural perspective* that confirmed, revised, and built upon various elements of the aforementioned cultural perspective. For example, Museus and Quaye's intercultural perspective suggests that it is extreme *cultural dissonance*, tension resulting from incongruence between students' cultural knowledge and the new cultural information that they encounter, that is inversely related to success. They also noted that, while Kuh and Love focused on the importance of connecting with subcultures that value achievement, connections to both collective and individual agents that value achievement and validate students' cultural backgrounds can facilitate students' success. Their propositions include the following:

1. Minority students' college experiences are shaped by their cultural meaning-making systems.

120

2. Minority students' cultures of origin moderate the meanings that they attach to college attendance, engagement, and completion.

3. Knowledge of minority students' cultures of origin and immersion are required to understand those students' abilities to negotiate their respective campus cultural milieus.

4. Cultural dissonance is inversely related to minority students' persistence.

5. Minority students who experience a substantial amount of cultural dissonance must acclimate to the dominant campus culture or establish sufficient connections with cultural agents at their institution to persist.

6. The degree to which campus cultural agents validate minority students' cultures of origin is positively associated with reduced cultural dissonance and greater likelihood of persistence.

7. The quality and quantity of minority students' connections with various cultural agents on their respective campuses is positively associated with their likelihood of persistence.

8. Minority students are more likely to persist if the cultural agents to whom they are connected emphasize educational achievement, value educational attainment, and validate their traditional cultural heritages.

Although Museus and Quaye's (2009) intercultural perspective provides a useful framework for understanding success among Asian American students and other students of color, it does not offer a holistic model of minority student success that lends itself to being easily quantified, statistically tested, and (in)validated. In light of the important role of quantitative research in the testing and (in)validation of theoretical frameworks, such perspectives might be valuable but have limited impact unless they can be translated into quantitatively testable models. The Culturally Engaging Campus Environments (CECE) Model offers such a theoretical perspective, and it is to this model that I now turn.

THE CULTURALLY ENGAGING CAMPUS ENVIRONMENTS MODEL OF SUCCESS AMONG RACIALLY DIVERSE STUDENT POPULATIONS IN COLLEGE

In this section, I provide an overview of the CECE Model of success among diverse populations (Museus, in press-a). This theoretical framework, which is displayed in Figure 6.2, constitutes an explanatory model for understanding Asian American and other students' success in college. Moreover, the model was primarily constructed from the concepts and perspectives delineated above and research on Asian American undergraduates and other students of color in college.

The CECE Model posits that a variety of *external influences* (i.e., finances, employment, family influences) shape *individual influences* (i.e., sense of belonging,

121

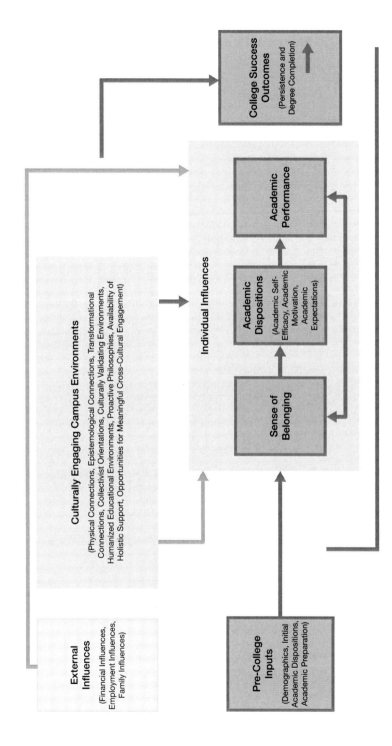

Figure 6.2 The Culturally Engaging Campus Environments (CECE) Model of College Success.

Source: Museus (in press-a).

academic dispositions, and academic performance) and *success* among racially diverse college student populations. The model also suggests that college students enter higher education with *pre-college inputs* (i.e., demographic characteristics, initial academic dispositions, academic preparation) that influence individual influences and success. The focal point of the model underscores the *environmental* (i.e. culturally engaging campus environments) and individual influences on college success. Specifically, the focal area of the model suggests that the degree to which culturally engaging campus environments exist at a particular post-secondary institution is positively associated with more positive individual factors and ultimately greater college student success. Finally, the model posits that the aforementioned individual influences are positively associated with greater likelihood of college persistence and degree attainment.

In the following subsections, I focus on providing an overview of the focal point of the model, which includes environmental and individual influences. The key environmental influences on success among racially diverse college student populations refer to the culturally engaging campus environments constructs. The individual influences include racially diverse students' sense of belonging, academic dispositions (academic self-efficacy, academic motivation, and academic expectations), and academic performance.

Culturally Engaging Campus Environments

The CECE Model posits that students who encounter more culturally engaging campus environments (i.e., environments that reflect the cultures and respond to the needs of the communities from which students come) are more likely to (1) have a greater sense of belonging, more positive academic dispositions, and better academic performance and (2) ultimately be more likely to persist and graduate. The model suggests that there are nine elements of culturally engaging campus environments that can and do function to engage students' racially diverse cultural identities and reflect their diverse needs as they navigate higher education.

Physical Cultural Connections. First, the CECE Model postulates that the extent to which undergraduates are able to connect with faculty, staff, and peers with whom they share common backgrounds is positively related to their success in college. This proposition is consistent with existing scholarship suggesting that Asian American and other students who are able to connect with institutional agents who have similar backgrounds as them or have experiences in common with them are more likely to succeed in higher education (Burrell, 1980; Guiffrida, 2003, 2005; Harper & Quaye, 2007; Museus, 2008b, 2010, 2011c; Museus & Neville, 2012; Museus & Quaye, 2009; Museus & Ravello, 2010; Sedlacek, 1987).

Epistemological Cultural Connections. Second, the CECE Model suggests that campuses that provide opportunities for students to develop, maintain, and strengthen *epistemological cultural connections* to their home communities can positively influence their experiences and success. Specifically, opportunities for the creation and maintenance of epistemological connections refer to the ways in which campuses provide space for students to acquire and share knowledge about their home communities. The inclusion of this construct is congruent with existing research that indicates that Asian American and other students' abilities to acquire and share knowledge about the needs of their communities of origin are associated with developing greater connections with their institutions, having higher levels of motivation, and being more likely to succeed (e.g., Guiffrida, 2003, 2005; Harper & Quaye, 2007; Kiang, 2002, 2009; Museus, 2008b, 2011c; Museus, Lam, et al., 2012).

Transformational Cultural Connections. Third, the proposed model posits that *transformational cultural connections* can positively influence the experiences and outcomes of racially diverse populations. Transformational connections occur when institutions provide students with opportunities to give back to and positively transform their communities of origin through various means, such as activities designed to spread awareness about issues in their community, engage in community activism, participate in service-learning opportunities, or be involved in problem-based research opportunities that help address challenges in their communities of origin. Consistent with the inclusion of transformational connections in the CECE Model, existing research indicates that activities allowing Asian American and other students in college to positively impact their communities are positively associated with stronger connections to their institutions, and such connections are associated with success in higher education (Astin & Sax, 1998; Eyler & Giles, 1999; Guiffrida, 2003; Harper & Quaye, 2007; Museus, 2008b, 2011c; Museus, Lam, et al., 2012; Museus & Quaye, 2009).

Collectivist Cultural Orientations. Fourth, the CECE Model suggests that environments with more *collective cultural orientations*, in contrast to more individualistic ones, are more conducive to positive college experiences and success among racially diverse students. Indeed, evidence indicates that Asian Americans and their peers of color who originate from more collectivist cultural orientations might face unique challenges navigating postsecondary educational institutions with individualistic cultural orientations (Dennis, Phinney, & Chuateco, 2005; Thompson & Fretz, 1991). Moreover, existing evidence supports the potential impact of collective approaches to facilitate success among Asian American students and other students of color (Fullilove & Treisman, 1990; Guiffrida, 2006).

Culturally Validating Environments. Fifth, the CECE Model posits that *culturally validating environments* are positively associated with success. In other words, when college educators validate the cultural backgrounds and identities of diverse students, they are more likely to have positive experiences in college and succeed (Barnett, 2011a, 2011b; Museus & Quaye, 2009; Nora et al., 2011; Rendón & Muñoz, 2011; Rendón, 1994). Cultural validation refers to the extent to which postsecondary institutions value the cultural backgrounds and identities of their students. This cultural validation construct is congruent with extant empirical research that indicates that such validation can positively shape the adjustment, sense of belonging, academic dispositions, and success of Asian American and other students in college (Barnett, 2011a; Gloria, Castellanos, Lopez, & Rosales, 2005; Museus & Quaye, 2009; Rendón, 1994; Rendón et al., 2000; Tierney, 1992, 1999).

Humanized Educational Environments. Sixth, the proposed model posits that the extent to which students encounter *humanized educational environments* is positively related to college experiences and success. Humanized educational environments refer to college environments that are characterized by caring, commitment, and meaningful relationships. And, consistent with the CECE Model, research indicates that such humanization contributes to the success of Asian American and other college student populations (Guiffrida, 2003; Rendón & Muñoz, 2011; Museus, 2011a; Museus & Ravello, 2010; Nora, 2001; Nora & Crisp, 2009).

Proactive Philosophies. Seventh, the CECE Model suggests that the extent to which *proactive philosophies* exist on college campuses can partially determine the likelihood of success among racially diverse student populations on those campuses. That is, the model indicates that, when faculty and staff go beyond making information and support available to making extra efforts to bring that information and support to students and maximize their likelihood of success, they can increase the rates of persistence and attainment among the racially diverse college student populations they serve. This construct is congruent with existing evidence that highlights the positive influences of such proactive philosophies and practices on Asian American and other college students' success (Guiffrida, 2005; Jenkins, 2006; Museus & Neville, 2012; Museus & Ravello, 2010; Rendón, 1994; Rendón & Muñoz, 2011).

Availability of Holistic Support. The eighth aspect of the culturally engaging campus environments construct in the CECE Model is the *availability of holistic support*. The availability of holistic support refers to the extent to which students have access to a faculty or staff member who they are confident will provide the information they need, offer the help that they seek, or connect them with the information or support that they require. While empirical research examining the impact of holistic support is limited, the small body of literature that does exist indicates that such holistic approaches facilitate success among Asian American students and other students of color (e.g., Guiffrida, 2005; Jenkins, 2006; Museus & Ravello, 2010). Specifically, when racially diverse

125

students do not have to seek out and track down necessary information and support across their institutions on their own, but instead can access one or more institutional agents that serve as conduits to the broader social and support networks on their respective campuses, they are more likely to succeed (Museus & Neville, 2012).

Opportunities for Meaningful Cross-Cultural Engagement. Finally, the CECE Model suggests that *opportunities for meaningful cross-cultural engagement* positively influence success among racially diverse college student populations. Specifically, the model indicates that opportunities to engage in positive purposeful interactions with peers of different cultural backgrounds can positively influence college experiences and success. While the relationship between such cross-cultural engagement and college persistence and degree completion has not been extensively empirically analyzed, higher education researchers have documented that climates that promote meaningful cross-cultural engagement are associated with many positive outcomes that are associated with success among Asian American and other college students (e.g., antonio, 2004; antonio et al., 2004; Astin, 1993; Chang, 2001; Chang et al., 2004; Gruenfeld, Thomas-Hunt, & Kim, 1998; Gurin et al. 2003; Hurtado, 2005; Jayakumar, 2008; Locks et al., 2008; Milem et al., 2005; Nelson-Laird, Engberg, & Hurtado, 2005; Pettigrew & Tropp, 2006; Sáenz et al., 2007; Zuniga, Williams & Berger, 2005).

Individual Influences

The final construct that constitutes a predictor of success outcomes in the proposed CECE Model consists of *individual influences*. Specifically, the proposed model posits that students' sense of belonging, academic dispositions, and academic performance exhibit significant influences on their college persistence and degree completion.

Sense of Belonging. First, the CECE Model posits that *sense of belonging* is a critical predictor of success among racially diverse college student populations. Researchers have offered and utilized the sense of belonging construct as an alternative to Tinto's academic and social integration variables (Hurtado & Carter, 1997). Consistent with the inclusion of sense of belonging in the proposed model is the fact that, although research on the linkages between sense of belonging and persistence and completion is sparse, a small but growing body of literature suggests that sense of belonging is a valid construct among students of color and a potentially powerful predictor of success (Hausmann, Schofield, & Woods, 2007; Hoffman, Richmond, Morrow, & Salomone, 2002; Lee & Davis, 2000; Locks et al., 2008; Museus & Maramba, 2011). For example, controlling for a variety of background, integration, commitment, and support variables, Hausmann et al. examined a single-institution sample of 365 Black and White undergraduates using growth modeling techniques and found that sense of belonging was a positive predictor of intent to persist in college.

Academic Dispositions. The second individual factor in the proposed model is *academic dispositions.* A significant body of literature indicates that academic dispositions influence success among racially diverse college student populations. For example, existing evidence indicates that *academic self-confidence* (i.e., confidence in one's own intellectual abilities to succeed) is a significant predictor of college success. Indeed, prior research demonstrates that higher levels of academic self-confidence or self-efficacy are positively associated with both college grades and persistence (Bong, 2001; Brown, Lent, & Larkin, 1989; Gloria & Kurpius, 1996; Hackett, Betz, Casas, & Rocha-Singh, 1992; Lent, Brown, & Larkin, 1984, 1986, 1987; Multon, Brown, & Lent, 1991; Robbins, Lauver, Le, Davis, & Langley, 2004). Robbins et al. (2004), for example, conducted a meta-analysis of 109 empirical studies and concluded that undergraduates' confidence in their own academic abilities is a significant predictor of persistence and degree completion outcomes in college.

Another important academic disposition that scholars have highlighted as an important factor in predicting college outcomes is *academic motivation* (Guiffrida, 2006). While sparse, existing studies do show a positive correlation between academic motivation and both grade-point average (GPA) and persistence among students of color (Allen, 1999; Côté & Levine, 1997; Dennis et al., 2005; Vallerand & Bissonnette, 1992). Allen (1999), for example, analyzed a sample of 1,000 first-year students to examine the relationships among student background, motivation, performance, and persistence, and concluded that motivation was a strong predictor of persistence among students of color. Thus, while more research on the topic is warranted, the small body of research that examines the relationship between motivation and academic outcomes in college suggest that it is a valid predictor of undergraduate success.

A third and final academic disposition highlighted herein is *academic expectations*. The inclusion of intent to persist in the proposed CECE Model is consistent with existing empirical evidence, which indicates that expectations to earn a bachelor's degree are an important predictor of college student persistence and degree completion (Bean & Metzner, 1985; Cabrera, Nora, & Castañeda, 1993; Cabrera, Castañeda, Nora, & Hengstler, 1992).

Academic Performance. The final individual influence in the proposed model is *academic performance.* Consistent with this model, existing evidence suggests that academic performance exhibits one of the strongest influences on persistence and degree completion (e.g., Byun, Meece, & Irvin, 2012; Museus, 2010; Museus, Nichols, & Lambert, 2008; Nora & Cabrera, 1996). For instance, Byun et al. (2012) conducted a logistic regression analysis of a nationally representative sample of 6,000 four-year college attendees from urban, rural, and suburban background and concluded that college GPA was one of the most

127

powerful predictors of bachelor's degree completion for all three groups. In sum, a substantial body of existing research indicates that culturally engaging campus environments and the aforementioned individual influences are important predictors of college student persistence and degree completion.

IMPLICATIONS FOR INSTITUTIONAL POLICY AND PRACTICE

The preceding discussion has several implications for institutional policy and practice in higher education and I offer a few of these recommendations in this section. They include adopting a cultural assets perspective of Asian American students, constructing culturally engaging campus environments, fostering cultural integration, and conducting campus climate assessments to ensure that policy and practice is based on sound empirical data. However, given the paucity of theory and research that focuses on Asian American college student success, it is important to emphasize that readers should consume these implications with caution until higher education scholars generate a solid knowledgebase from which more definitive conclusions about the factors that influence success among these students can be drawn.

Adopting a Cultural Assets Perspective

In constructing programs and practices to foster success among Asian American college students, institutions of higher education should adopt an assets perspective of these undergraduates. Assuming an assets perspective might mean learning about the community cultural wealth that Asian American students bring to college, and then intentionally constructing programs and curriculum that engage these forms of cultural wealth. For example, college educators could learn about the social capital that Asian American college students bring with them to higher education and leverage these community networks in ways that enhance the curriculum through collaborations, service learning activities, and other methods. Educators could also identify which Asian American students have developed navigational and resistant capital and collaborate with them in the development of activities that engage them as mentors who can help their peers cultivate these forms of capital. College educators could engage Asian American college students' linguistic capital, which could be especially valuable in research and service projects that are executed within Asian American communities as well. Engaging these forms of community cultural wealth can help educators empower and validate Asian American college students, while enriching the learning environment for all students on campus.

Constructing Culturally Engaging Campus Environments

The preceding discussion underscores the value of cultural perspectives in understanding Asian American college students' success, especially the importance of fostering these students' development of connections to the cultures of both their communities and campuses. Indeed, college educators should make meaningful efforts to ensure that they are constructing and perpetuating culturally engaging campus environments in order to strengthen these connections. For example, constructing programs, classrooms, and practices that foster physical connections, cultivate epistemological connections, encourage transformational connections, value collectivist orientations, and validate students' cultural backgrounds can minimize the incongruence between the cultures of students' respective Asian American communities and campuses and enhance the likelihood of their persistence and completion. Similarly, constructing humanized educational environments, programs and practices that are based on proactive philosophies, and mechanisms for providing holistic support can strengthen Asian American college students' connections to their campuses and increase their likelihood of success.

Focusing on Cultural Integration

In order to begin creating culturally engaging campus environments, college educators can focus their time and energy on utilizing cultural integration in the construction of institutional policies and programs that are aimed at serving Asian American college students. College classrooms and programmatic offices are just two important spaces in which educators can intentionally embed academic learning, connection, and trust building to strengthen social bonds, and cultural elements that engage and validate the cultural backgrounds and identities of their Asian American students. Indeed, both classroom curricula and co-curricular programming should be constructed with the value of cultural integration in mind so that the strength of the connections that students feel with those environments is maximized.

Conducting Campus Environmental Assessments

It is critical for institutions of higher education to invest time and energy in assessing the nature of their campus environments to enhance their abilities to maximize success among Asian American college students. Today, it is common for colleges and universities to assess the levels of involvement and engagement on their campuses. While such assessments can be and are often useful, as the discussion above demonstrates, measuring the behaviors of students is not sufficient, in and of itself, for informing the purposeful construction of campus spaces, programs, curricula, and practices to effectively serve Asian American students. Rather, evaluating whether and to what extent Asian American and other college students encounter environments that evidence indicates are conducive to positive educational experiences and outcomes is also important in institutions' ability to inform the construction of campus spaces, programs, curricula, and practices that can help maximize optimal outcomes among these students.

There is still much to be learned about Asian American student success in higher education. The current discussion, however, is intended to initiate an important discussion about theory and research that illuminates the ways in which college and university campuses can and do construct environments that facilitate success among these undergraduates. College educators should utilize this knowledge to construct environments on their campuses that are conducive to success among Asian American students in postsecondary education.

Chapter 7

Future Directions for Research on Asian American Students in College

In the preceding chapters of this volume, I utilize theory and research from several disciplines and invoke scholarship on both students of color in general and Asian American college students in particular to present a relatively comprehensive picture of the lives of Asian American college students. Nevertheless, scholarly research on Asian American students' experiences and outcomes in higher education remain sparse. Consequently, one major conclusion regarding the state of research on Asian American students in higher education that can be drawn from the current synthesis is that there is an urgent need for more theory and research on Asian American college students to both inform the development of policies and programs that can effectively serve this population, as well as inform larger discourse about diversity and equity in postsecondary education research and discourse.

Analyzing Critical Asian American Populations

In 2012, my colleagues and I analyzed and synthesized more than 300 pieces of literature on Asian Americans and Pacific Islanders (AAPIs) in both K-12 and higher education and outlined a national agenda for future research on AAPIs in education (Museus, antonio, & Kiang, 2012). Our agenda included a recommendation that future scholarship on AAPIs be focused on generating knowledge of several critical populations within the AAPI umbrella category. We used the term "critical populations" to refer to AAPI groups that have a substantial presence in society and higher education, and for which little knowledge exists. Although I focus on the Asian American population in the current discussion, rather than the AAPI community, I borrow from our earlier recommendations to advance knowledge on these populations and reiterate the importance of generating a knowledgebase on these groups.

- **Southeast Asian Americans** suffer from significant disparities in educational attainment. While they are often invoked in discussions about inequalities within the Asian American population in higher education, they are seldom the focus of theory and research in higher education. Although some scholars are beginning to generate knowledge of Southeast Asian American students' experiences in higher education (e.g., Chhuon & Hudley, 2008; Kiang, 2002, 2009; Lin et al., 2009; Museus, in press-b; Museus, Lam, et al., 2012; Vue, 2013), more research that illuminates the challenges and success of these populations is warranted.

- **South Asian Americans** exhibit high rates of educational attainment compared with other racial and ethnic groups. Nevertheless, with few exceptions (e.g., Abbas, 2002; Cole & Ahmadi, 2010), this population is virtually invisible in higher education research and discourse. In light of the post-9/11 increase in xenophobia aimed at those of South Asian descent, scholarship that examines and excavates their unique experiences, challenges, and successes is warranted.

- **Multiracial Asian Americans** is another population that is virtually invisible in higher education research and discourse. The vast majority of literature that does exist on mixed-race Asian Americans explores identity formation in college (Renn, 2000, 2003, 2004, 2008). In addition, a few studies have begun to analyze these students' experiences with prejudice and discrimination in higher education (Museus, Lambe, & Kawamata-Ryan, 2012; Museus, Lambe, Robinson, Knepler, & Yee, 2009; Talbot, 2008). Nevertheless, empirical examinations of mixed-race Asian Americans in college remain sparse and, given the significant presence of multiracial Asian Americans in society, more scholarship on this population is critical (Museus et al., 2009; Museus, Lambe, & Kawamata-Ryan, 2012).

- **Transracial Asian American Adoptees** are another virtually invisible and misunderstood Asian American population in postsecondary education research and discourse. Literature on this population does exist outside of the field of education (e.g., Galvin, 2003; Johnston, Swim, Saltsman, Deater-Deckard, & Petrill, 2007), but research that examines the identities, challenges, and experiences encountered by Asian American adoptees as they navigate postsecondary education is virtually non-existent. Thus, it is imperative that higher education scholars begin expanding knowledge of this group.

- **Low Socioeconomic Asian Americans** is used to refer to Asian Americans who are from low-income backgrounds or the first in their families to attend college. Although these Asian American populations face significant inequalities and many salient challenges (e.g., Museus,

2011b; Museus & Vue, in press; Teranishi, Ceja, antonio, Allen, & McDonough, 2004), there is little scholarship to illuminate the experiences of this Asian American subgroup. Postsecondary education policymakers and educators would benefit from a better understanding of the struggles and successes of this population.

- **Lesbian, Gay, Bisexual, Transgender, Queer, and Asexual Asian Americans** are another virtually invisible population in higher education. With few exceptions (Pepin & Talbot, 2013), postsecondary education scholars have not examined the identities and experiences of lesbian, gay, bisexual, transgender, queer, and asexual Asian Americans in-depth. Given that these students are double minorities who might experience social oppression as a result of both their race and sexual orientation, it is important for higher education scholars to expand current levels of understanding about these individuals.

- **Undocumented Asian Americans** have garnered limited attention in research and discourse in postsecondary education. Nevertheless, only a few higher education scholars have engaged in research to increase current levels of understanding of this segment of the Asian American population (Buenavista & Chen, 2013; Buenavista & Tran, 2010; Buenavista et al., 2009). This portion of the Asian American population is particularly vulnerable given the relentless attacks on undocumented immigrants. Thus, scholarship that examines this population can not only contribute to larger debates about immigration and immigrant education, but can also help postsecondary education policymakers and educators help better understand how they can most effectively meet the needs of this group within the larger Asian American category.

- **Asian American Military Recruits and Veterans** are increasingly present on college and university campuses, and their experiences are not well understood. Research that unpacks the experiences of these Asian Americans can shed light on issues related to the impact of militarization on education. Few studies have been conducted on military veterans in postsecondary education (Kiang, 1991), and this is another population that warrants attention from higher education scholars.

- **Asian Americans in Community Colleges** include a substantial proportion of the Asian American college student population and a significant segment of two-year college students (Kiang, 1992; Lew, Chang, & Wang, 2005). Nevertheless, empirical inquiries that analyze the experiences and outcomes of Asian Americans at two-year colleges are sparse (Yang, Rendón, & Shearon, 1994). Given that many Asian Americans at two-year colleges are likely to come from more modest

133

backgrounds and face significant challenges, scholars should make efforts to better understand the experiences of this population to produce more authentic understandings of Asian Americans in postsecondary education.

This list of critical populations is certainly not intended to be exhaustive, but is aimed at underscoring some of the Asian American subgroups that could most use urgent attention from higher education scholars. Indeed, the empirical examination of these various Asian American subgroups is essential to developing a rich knowledgebase to inform policy and practice that can best serve the diverse groups that comprise the larger Asian American community.

Critique of Social Systems of Oppression

In the field of postsecondary education, analyses that focus on critiquing social systems of oppression and how they impact the lives of Asian Americans are difficult to find. However, such analyses could contribute to significant advances in understandings of the Asian American experience. Specifically, higher education scholars can and should engage in critical analyses of how racism intersects with other systems of oppression to shape the experiences of Asian Americans in the United States.

The intersections among racism, classism, and sexism are particularly important in understanding how intersectionality shapes the experiences of Asian Americans in higher education. Indeed, more examinations of how racism intersects with socioeconomic oppression to deny low socioeconomic Asian American populations educational opportunities are warranted. Similarly, the ways in which racism and sexism intersect to mutually impact the environmental contexts, experiences with discrimination, and behaviors of Asian American men and women in higher education could make a substantial contribution to the knowledgebase.

Unpacking the Influence of Critical Contexts

I reiterate earlier calls that education scholars can and should focus attention and energies on unpacking the complex influences that transnational, national, community contexts on the lives of Asian American students (e.g., Museus, antonio, & Kiang, 2012). Indeed, a significant body of literature has now illuminated the various ways that campus contexts impact the experiences of Asian American students (see Chapters 5 and 6). More research, however, is needed on how pre-migration cultures of origin, transnational migrations, national policies, and community structures hinder or promote the development and success of Asian American students in college.

134

Although some studies have been conducted on the ways in which these international, national, and community contexts influence Asian American students' experiences (e.g., Buenavista et al., 2009; Buenavista & Chen, 2013; Kiang, 2002, 2009; Lin et al., 2009; Zhou & Kim, 2006), such analyses are few and far between. Moving forward, higher education scholars should conduct more research that examines how transnational contexts contribute to the economic, social, and political conditions of Asian American students and their communities. They should make efforts to analyze how national policies, such as legislation related to undocumented immigrants and the increasing emphasis on loans in financial aid packages, influence Asian American students' experiences. Finally, scholars should build upon existing research on how connections to cultural communities and families influence Asian American experiences in college (e.g., Chhuon & Hudley, 2008; Kiang, 2002, 2009; Museus, in press-b; Museus, antonio, & Kiang, 2012; Museus, Lam, et al., 2012; Museus & Quaye, 2009) to examine the ways in which community organizations can detract from or contribute to Asian American students' higher education experience, development and learning outcomes, and success.

Conducting Historical Analysis and Narrative Construction

In this volume, I underscore the importance of conducing analyses of Asian American history and constructing an Asian American historical narrative in society and in postsecondary education. The pursuit of the development of such historical analyses and subsequent Asian American presence in the history of American society in general and higher education in particular yields many significant implications. As mentioned, for example, such an historical narrative can solidify a history or shared struggles and successes, which can provide the foundation for the further development of Asian American identity and consciousness.

Scholars interested in conducting historical analyses of Asian Americans in higher education could contribute to the knowledgebase in several ways. One way to contribute to an historical Asian American narrative is to analyze critical events in Asian American higher education history. Another method of contributing to an historical narrative for Asian Americans in postsecondary education is by engaging in critical analyses of the ways in which Asian Americans have been racialized in higher education throughout various phases in history. Similarly, scholars could examine how researchers have analyzed and depicted Asian American populations in postsecondary education over time. This (re)constructive history is necessary for Asian Americans to understand their contributions and place in American higher education.

New Theory Development and Testing

As I mention earlier in this volume, it could be argued that the most significant future advances in our understandings of Asian American college student success will not be those that utilize traditional theories that were created for majority populations to analyze the experiences of Asian American students in higher education. Rather, in the future, scholars who generate new theoretical perspectives and conceptual models that are grounded in the voices of Asian American students and invest energy in testing these frameworks will contribute to substantial advances in knowledge about Asian Americans in postsecondary education.

Although multiple useful theoretical frameworks have now been generated to understand Asian American identity, it is difficult to find empirical inquiries that have applied these frameworks to analyze Asian American experiences, evaluated the explanatory power of these models, or utilized the voice of Asian American students in higher education to revise and refine these identity models. Such investigations would not only function to generate an understanding of the utility of the various identity models, but they could also help advance the development of Asian American identity theories and build a knowledge base that could provide a more thorough understanding of Asian American identity processes.

Regarding Asian American college student success theory and research, the aforementioned CECE Model offers one example of a conceptual framework that is grounded in the voices of Asian American students and their diverse peers, and has the potential to generate more complex and accurate understandings of the ways in which campus environments influence the experiences and outcomes of Asian Americans in postsecondary education. Thus, future research can advance current levels of understanding regarding the validity of the CECE Model for Asian Americans, as well as the different subpopulations within this racial group.

Conducting Disaggregated Data Analysis

Several scholars have called on researchers, policymakers, and educators to disaggregate data and conduct more complex analyses of Asian American college students to generate more intricate understandings of this population (Hune, 2002; Kiang, 2002, 2009; Museus, 2009a, 2011b, 2013; Museus & Truong, 2009; Ngo & Lee, 2007)). Many examples of both disaggregated qualitative and quantitative analyses now exist, and reinforce that disaggregated analyses are essential to illuminate the complexities of Asian American communities, identities, and experiences (Chapter 3; CARE, 2008, 2010, 2011; Hune, 2002; Kiang, 2002, 2009; Museus, 2009a, 2011b, 2013; Museus & Truong, 2009; Ngo & Lee, 2007). For example, disaggregated analyses of statistical data have repeatedly revealed drastic ethnic, socioeconomic, and educational inequalities within the larger Asian American population.

Less common than the aforementioned disaggregated quantitative analyses are examinations or disaggregated qualitative data. Such analyses are critical in generating in-depth understandings of the unique experiences of subgroups within the Asian American population and a comprehension of how various demographic characteristics and identities intersect to influence the experiences of Asian American students in college (Museus & Truong, 2009). And, these analyses can be especially useful for producing a knowledgebase about Asian American subgroups for which such a foundation of knowledge does not currently exist, such as in the case of the critical populations delineated above. Therefore, it is prudent for postsecondary education scholars to invest time and energy in conducting disaggregated qualitative analyses of critical Asian American student subpopulations in higher education.

Conducting More Complex Data Analyses

Researchers who are interested in studying Asian American students in postsecondary education should also consider the importance of advancing existing understandings of this population by analyzing how various racial and cultural processes are associated with important outcomes in college. Indeed, there is a tendency for researchers who study racial and cultural influences on the experiences of people of color to illuminate the ways in which these individuals experience particular racial realities of cultural challenges. However, future scholarship can move beyond these descriptive analyses and advance understandings of Asian American students' racial realities by conducting more in-depth examinations that unpack how various racial realities impact these undergraduates' behaviors, relationships, thought processes, self-perceptions, and decisions in postsecondary education.

Indeed, a substantial body of literature clarifies the reality that stereotypes of Asian Americans permeate society and that they influence the experiences of Asian American students in college (e.g., Chou & Feagin, 2008; Lewis et al., 2000; Museus, 2008a; Museus & Park, 2012; Museus & Kiang, 2009; Museus & Truong, in press; Suzuki, 2002; Tran & Chang, 2013; Wu, 1995). Yet, understandings regarding *how* these stereotypes influence Asian American students' behaviors (e.g., overcompensation via hypermasculinity), perceptions of themselves if they are unable to live up to the unrealistic expectations of the model minority stereotype, and important decisions (e.g., major choices) in higher education have only begun to emerge. Researchers should make efforts to develop a deeper understanding of how this stereotype and other racial constructions of Asian Americans operate and influence their lives on a daily basis.

137

Examination of Diverse Outcomes

Higher education discourse is often dominated by discussions of academic performance, college persistence, and degree completion. Yet, some Asian Americans have reported that they define success using a variety of indicators in addition to persistence and degree completion, such as happiness, occupational attainment, and having a positive impact on society (Museus et al., 2013). Including such outcomes in the examination of Asian American students' experiences could be an effective means to illuminating some of the challenges that these students face. For example, examining Asian American students' happiness or satisfaction in college can reveal that, while succeeding at relatively high rates in the aggregate, they are one of the least satisfied racial groups in higher education (Kuh, 2005), suggesting that they do face salient challenges during the college years. In addition, empirical analyses of occupational mobility after college reveal the existence of a "glass ceiling" that prevents Asian Americans from reaching levels of occupational attainment equal to their peers with similar levels of education (Lee, 2002; Yan & Museus, 2013). If postsecondary scholars expand their foci to examine these outcomes and center them in discourse on college students, they might be able to broaden that discourse to consider and encompass more holistic understandings of Asian American students' experiences, challenges, and outcomes in higher education.

CONCLUSION

In contrast to the oversimplified racial stereotypes of Asian Americans that permeate society, the current volume illuminates the complexities that characterize the lives of Asian American college students. Multiple interconnected layers of environmental context, evolving political and social processes, and intersecting identities all interact in intricate ways to determine these students' experiences and outcomes in higher education. Moreover, the juxtaposition of these complexities with the limited literature on Asian American students in college underscores the need for the development of a more robust knowledgebase that can inform postsecondary education policy and practice aimed at serving this population in meaningful ways. This volume constitutes one minor step in the construction of more holistic understandings of this rapidly growing and diverse community.

References

Abbas, T. (2002). The home and the school in the educational achievements of South Asians. *Race, Ethnicity and Education*, *5*(3), 291–316.

Aberson, C. L., & Haag, S. C. (2007). Contact, perspective taking, and anxiety as predictors of stereotype endorsement, explicit attitudes, and implicit attitudes, *Group Processes & Intergroup Relations*, *10*(2), 179–201.

Abueg, F. R., & Chun, K. M. (1996). Traumatization stress among Asian and Asian Americans.

In A. J. Marsella, M. J. Friedman, E. T. Gerrity, & R. M. Scurfield (Eds.), *Ethnocultural aspects of posttraumatic stress disorder: Issues, research, and clinical applications* (pp. 285–299). Washington, DC: American Psychological Association.

Accapadi, M. M. (2012). Asian American identity consciousness: A polycultural model. In D. Ching & A. Agbayani (Eds.), *Asian Americans and Pacific Islanders in higher education: Research and perspectives on identity, leadership, and success* (pp. 57–94). Washington, DC: NASPA Foundation.

Allen, D. (1999). Desire to finish college: An empirical link between motivation and persistence. *Research in Higher Education*, *40*(4), 461–485.

Allport, G. W. (1954). *The nature of prejudice.* Reading, MA: Addison-Wesley Publishing Company.

Amato, S. (2009). Community honors memory of hate crime victim a decade later. *Indiana Daily Student.* Retrieved from http://www.idsnews.com/news/story.aspx?id=68871.

Ancis, J. R., Sedlacek, W. E., & Mohr, J. (2000). Student perceptions of campus cultural climate by race. *Journal of Counseling and Development*, *78*(2), 180–185.

antonio, a. l. (2001a). Diversity and the influence of friendship groups in college. *The Review of Higher Education*, *25*(1), 63–89.

antonio, a. l. (2001b). The role of inter-racial interaction in the development of leadership skills and cultural knowledge and understanding. *Research in Higher Education*, *42*(5), 593–617.

antonio, a. l. (2004). Diversity and the influence of friendship groups in college. *The Review of Higher Education, 25*(1), 63–89.

antonio, a. l., Chang, M. J., Hakuta, K., Kenny, D. A., Levin, S., & Milem, J. F. (2004). Effects of racial diversity on complex thinking in college students. *Psychological Science, 15*(8), 507–510.

Astin, A. W. (1984). Student involvement: A developmental theory for higher education. *Journal of College Student Personnel, 25*, 297–308.

Astin, A. W. (1993). *What matters in college? Four critical years revisited.* San Francisco, CA: Jossey-Bass.

Astin, A. W. (1999). Student involvement: A developmental theory for higher education. *Journal of College Student Development, 40*(5), 518–529.

Astin, A. W., & Sax, L. J. (1998). How undergraduates are affected by service participation. *Journal of College Student Development, 39*(3), 251–263.

Attinasi, L. C. Jr. (1989) Getting in: Mexican Americans' perceptions of university attendance and the implications for freshman year persistence. *The Journal of Higher Education, 60*(3), 247–77.

Austin, A. W. (2004). *From concentration camp to campus.* Chicago, IL: University of Illinois Press.

Barnett, E. A. (2011a). Faculty validation and persistence among nontraditional community college students. *Enrollment Management Journal: Student Access, Finance, and Success in Higher Education, 5*(2), 97–119.

Barnett, E. A. (2011b). Validation experiences and persistence among community college students. *The Review of Higher Education, 34*(2), 193–230.

Bean, J. P., & Metzner, B. S. (1985). A conceptual model of nontraditional student attrition. *Review of Educational Research, 55*, 485–540.

Bell, D. A. (1980). Jr. Brown v. Board of Education and the interest convergence dilemma. *Harvard Law Review, 93*(3), 518–534.

Bell, D. (1987). *And we will not be saved: The elusive quest for racial justice.* New York: Basic Books.

Bell, D. (1992). *Faces at the bottom of the well: The permanence of racism.* New York: Basic Books.

Bell, L. A. (1997). Theoretical foundations for social justice education. In M. Adams, L. A. Bell, & P. Griffin (Eds.), *Teaching for diversity and social justice: A sourcebook* (pp. 3–15). New York: Routledge.

Bensimon, E. (2007). The underestimated significance of practitioner knowledge in the scholarship on student success. *Review of Higher Education, 30* (4), 441–469.

Better, S. (2007). *Institutional racism: A primer on theory and strategies for social change* (2nd edition). Boulder, CO: Rowman & Littlefield Publishers.

Birman, D. (1994). Acculturation and human diversity in a multicultural society. In E. J. Trickett, R. J. Watts, & D. Birman (Eds.), *Human diversity: Perspectives on people in context* (pp. 261–284). San Francisco, CA: Jossey-Bass.

Boehnlein, J. K., & Kinzie, J. D. (1997). Cultural perspectives on posttraumatic stress disorder. In T. W. Miller (Ed.), *Clinical disorders and stressful life events. International Universities Press Stress and Health Series. Monograph* (vol. 7, pp. 19–43). Madison, CT: International Universities Press.

Bollen, K. A., & Hoyle, R. H. (1990). Perceived cohesion: A conceptual and empirical examination. *Social Forces, 69*(2), 479–504.

Bong, M. (2001). Role of self-efficacy and task-value in predicting college students' course performance and future enrollment intentions. *Contemporary Educational Psychology, 26*(4), 553–570.

Bonilla-Silva, E. (2006). *Racism without racists: Colorblind racism and the persistence of inequality in the United States.* Lanham, MD: Rowman & Littlefield.

Bowman, N. B., Brandenberger, J. W., Hill, P. L., & Lapsley, D. K. (2011). The long-term effects of college diversity experiences: Well-being and social concerns 13 years after graduation. *Journal of College Student Development, 52*(6), 729–739.

Bowman, N. A., & Griffin, T. M. (2012). Secondary transfer effects of interracial contact: The moderating role of social status. *Cultural Diversity & Ethnic Minority Psychology, 18*(1), 35–44.

Braxton, J. M. (2000). Introduction. In J. M. Braxton (Ed.), *Reworking the student departure puzzle* (pp. 1–8). Nashville, TN: Vanderbilt University Press.

Braxton, J. M., Sullivan, A. S., & Johnson, R. M. (1997). Appraising Tinto's theory. In J. C. Smart (Ed.), *Higher education: Handbook of theory and research* (vol. 12, pp. 71–96). San Francisco, CA: Jossey-Bass.

Brayboy, B. M. J. (2005). Toward a tribal critical race theory in education. *The Urban Review, 37*(5), 425–446.

Brown, S. D., Lent, R. D., & Larkin, K. C. (1989). Self-efficacy as a moderator of scholastic aptitude-academic performance relationships. *Journal of Vocational Behavior, 35*, 64–75.

Bryant-Davis, T. (2007). Healing requires recognition: The case for race-based traumatic stress. *The Counseling Psychologist, 35*(1), 135–143.

Bryant-Davis, T., & Ocampo, C. (2005). Racist incident-based trauma. *The Counseling Psychologist, 33*(4), 479–500.

Buenavista, T. L., & Chen, A. C. (2013). Intersections and crossroads: A counter-story of an undocumented Pinay college student. In S. D. Museus, D. Maramba, & R. Teranishi (Eds.), *The misrepresented minority: New insights on Asian Americans and Pacific Islanders, and the implications for higher education.* Sterling, VA: Stylus Publishing.

Buenavista, T. L., Jayakumar, U. M., & Misa-Escalante, K. (2009). Contextualizing Asian American education through critical race theory: An example of U.S. Pilipino college student experiences. In S. D. Museus (Ed.), *Conducting research on Asian Americans in higher education. New Directions for Institutional Research* (no. 142, pp. 69–81). San Francisco, CA: Jossey-Bass.

141

Buenavista, T. L., & Tran, T. (2010). Undocumented immigrant students. In E. Chen & G. Yoo (Eds.), *Encyclopedia of contemporary Asian American issues* (pp. 253–257). Westport, CT: Greenwood Press.

Bulhan, H. A. (1985). *Frantz Fanon and the psychology of oppression*. New York: Plenum Press.

Burck, J. (1999). Korean graduate student killed on his way to church Sunday. *The Herald Times*. Retrieved from www.heraldtimesonline.com/.../hate-hits-home-070599. PDF.

Burrell, L. F. (1980). Is there a future for Black students on predominantly White campuses? *Integrate Education*, *18*, 23–27.

Byun, S., Meece, J. L., & Irvin, M. J. (2012). Rural–nonrural disparities in postsecondary educational attainment revisited. *American Educational Research Journal*, *49*(3), 412–437.

Cabrera, A. F., Castañeda, M. B., Nora, A., & Hengstler, D. (1992). The convergence between two theories of college persistence. *The Journal of Higher Education*, *63*(2), 143–164.

Cabrera, A. F., Nora, A., & Castañeda, M. B. (1993). College persistence: Structural equation modeling test of an integrated model of student retention. *The Journal of Higher Education*, *64*(2), 123–139.

Calmore, J. (1992). Critical race theory, Archie Shepp, and fire music: Securing an authentic intellectual life in a multicultural world. *Southern California Law Review*, *65*, 2129–2231.

Carter, R. T. (2007). Racism and psychological and emotional injury: Recognizing and assessing race-based traumatic stress. *The Counseling Psychologist*, *35*(1), 13–105.

Carter, R. T., Forsyth, J. M., Mazzula, S. L., & Williams, B. (2005). Racial discrimination and race-based traumatic stress: An exploratory investigation. In R. T. Carter (Ed.), *Handbook of racial-cultural psychology and counseling: Training and practice* (vol. 2, pp. 447–476). Hoboken, NJ: John Wiley.

Carter, R. T., & Forsyth, J. M. (2009). A guide to the forensic assessment of race-based traumatic stress reactions. *The Journal of the American Academy of Psychiatry and the Law*, *37*, 28–40.

Chan, S. (1991). *Asian Americans: An interpretive history*. Boston, MA: Twayne.

Chang, M. J. (2001). Is it more than about getting along? The broader educational relevance of reducing students' racial biases. *Journal of College Student Development*, *42*(2), 93–105.

Chang, M. J. (2008). Asian evasion: A recipe for flawed resolutions. *Diverse Issues in Higher Education*, *25*(7), 26.

Chang, M. J., Astin, A. W., & Kim, D. (2004). Cross-racial interaction among undergraduates: Some consequences, causes and patterns, *45*(5), 529–552.

Chang, M. J., Chang, J. C., & Ledesma, M. C. (2005). Doing the real work of diversifying our institutions. *About Campus*, May/June, 9–16.

Chang, M. J., Park, J. J., Lin, M. H., Poon, O. A., & Nakanishi, D. T. (2007). *Beyond myths: The growth and diversity of Asian American college freshmen, 1971–2005*. Los Angeles, CA: Higher Education Research Institute.

Chang, R. S. (1993). Towards and Asian American legal scholarship: Critical Race Theory, post-structuralism, and narrative space. *California Law Review, 81*(5), 1243–1323.

Cheryan, S., & Bodenhausen, G. V. (2000). When positive stereotypes threaten intellectual performance: The psychological hazards of "model minority" status. *Psychological Science, 11*, 399–402.

Chew, P. K. (1994). Asian Americans: The "reticent" minority and their paradoxes. *William and Mary Law Review, 36*(1), 1–94.

Chhuon, V., & Hudley, C. (2008). Factors supporting Cambodian American students' successful adjustment into the university. *Journal of College Student Development, 49*(1), 15–30.

Chickering, A. W. (1969). *Education and identity.* San Francisco, CA: Jossey-Bass

Chien, J. W. (1990). Lobbying for justice: Lessons from a graduate student. *Amerasia Journal, 16*(1), 119–122.

Ching, D., & Agbayani, A. (2012). *Asian Americans and Pacific Islanders in higher education: Research and perspectives on identity, leadership, and success.* Washington, DC: NASPA Foundation.

Cho, S. K. (2003). Converging stereotypes in racialized sexual harassment: Where the model minority meets Suzie Wong. In A. K. Wing (Ed.), *Critical race feminism: A reader* (pp. 349–356). New York: New York University Press.

Chon, M. (1995). On the need for Asian American narratives in law: Ethnic specimens, native informants, storytelling and silences. *UCLA Asian Pacific American Law Journal, 3*, 4–32.

Chou, R., & Feagin, J. R. (2008). *The myth of the model minority: Asian Americans facing racism.* Boulder, CO: Paradigm.

Choy, S. (2000). *Low-income students: Who they are and how they pay for their education.* Washington, DC: U.S. Department of Education, Office of Educational Research and Improvement, National Center for Education Statistics.

Clark, R., Anderson, N. B., Clark, V. A., & Williams, D. R. (1999, October). Racism as a stressor for African Americans. *American Psychologist, 54*(1), 805–816.

Cole, D., & Ahmadi, S. (2010). Reconsidering campus diversity: An examination of Muslim students' experiences. *The Journal of Higher Education, 81*(2), 121–139.

Cole, P. (1999). *Honoring the life of Won-Joon Yoon and condemning racist hatred in Bloomington.* Bloomington, IN: City of Bloomington.

College Board (2012). *The college completion agenda 2012 progress report.* New York: Author.

Coloma, R. S. (2006). Disorienting race and education: Changing paradigms on the schooling of Asian Americans and Pacific Islanders. *Race, Ethnicity and Education, 9*(1), 1–15.

Constantine, M. G., & Sue, D. W. (2007). Perceptions of racial microaggressions among Black supervisees in cross-racial dyads. *Journal of Counseling Psychology, 54*(2), 142–153.

143

Côté, J. E., & Levine, C. (1997). Student motivation, learning environments, and human capital acquisition: Toward an integrated paradigm of student development. *Journal of College Student Development*, *38*(3), 229–243.

Crenshaw, K. (1989). Demarginalizing the intersection of race and sex: A Black feminist critique of antidiscrimination doctrine, feminist theory and antiracist politics. *University of Chicago Legal Forum 1989*, 139–167.

Crenshaw, K. (1993). Mapping the margins: Intersectionality, identity politics, and the violence against women of color. *Stanford Law Review*, *43*, 1241–1299.

Crenshaw, K., Gotanda, N., Peller, G., & Thomas, K. (Eds.). (1996). *Critical race theory: The key writings that formed the movement.* New York: New Press.

Cress, C. M., & Ikeda, E. K. (2003). Distress under duress: The relationship between campus climate and depression in Asian American college students. *NASPA Journal*, *40*(2), 74–97.

Crisp, R. J., & Turner, R. N. (2011). Cognitive adaptation to the experiences of social and cultural diversity. *Psychological Bulletin*, *137*(2), 242–266.

de Anda, D. (1984). Bicultural socialization: Factors affecting the minority experience. *Social Work*, *29*(2), 101–107.

Delgado, R. (1984). The imperial scholar: Reflections on a review of civil rights literature. *University of Pennsylvania Law Review*, *132*, 561–578.

Delgado, R. (1989). Storytelling for oppositionists and others: A plea for narrative. *Michigan Law Review*, *87*(8), 2411–2441.

Delgado, R. (1992). The imperial scholar revisited: How to marginalize outsider writing, ten years later. *University of Pennsylvania Law Review*, *140*, 1349–1372.

Delgado, R., & Stefancic, J. (2001). *Critical race theory: An introduction.* New York: New York University Press.

Delgado Bernal, D. (1998). Using a Chicana feminist epistemology in educational research. *Harvard Educational Review*, *68*(4), 555–582.

Delgado Bernal, D. (2002). Critical race theory, Latino critical theory, and critical raced-gendered epistemologies: Recognizing students of color as holders and creators of knowledge. *Qualitative Inquiry*, *8*, 105–126.

Dennis, J. M., Phinney, J. S., & Chuateco, L. I. (2005). The role of motivation, parental support, and peer support in the academic success of ethnic minority first-generation college students. *Journal of College Student Development*, *46*(3), 223–236.

Denson, N. (2009). Do curricular and cocurricular diversity activities influence racial bias? A meta-analysis. *Review of Educational Research*, *79*(2), 805–838.

Denson, N., & Chang, M. J. (2009). Racial diversity matters: The impact of diversity-related student engagement and institutional context. *American Educational Research Journal*, *46*(2), 322–353.

Denson, N., & Zhang, S. (2010). The impact of student experiences with diversity on developing graduate attributes. *Studies in Higher Education*, *35*(5), 529–543.

Deyhle, D. (1995). Navajo youth and Anglo racism: Cultural integrity and resistance. *Harvard Educational Review*, *65*(3), 403–444.

Dovidio, J. F., Gaertner, S. L., Kawakami, K., & Hodson, G. (2002). Why can't we just get along? Interpersonal biases and interracial distrust. *Cultural Diversity and Ethnic Minority Psychology*, *8*(2), 88–102.

Dumke, G. S. (1969). Controversy on campus: Need for peace and order. *Vital Speeches*, *35*(11), 332–335.

Duster, T. (1991). *The diversity project*. Berkeley, CA: Institute for the Study of Social Change.

Eng, D. L. (2001). *Racial castration: Managing masculinity in Asian America*. Durham, NC: Duke University Press.

Espinoza, L., & Harris, A. P. (1997). Embracing the Tar-Baby: LatCrit theory and the sticky mess of race. *California Law Review*, *85*(5), 1585–1645.

Espiritu, Y. L. (1993). *Asian American panethnicity: Bridging institutions and identities*. Philadelphia, PA: Temple University Press.

Espiritu, Y. L. (2008). *Asian American women and men: Labor, laws, and love* (2nd edition). Lanham, MD: Rowman & Littlefield Publishers.

Essed, P. (1991). *Understanding everyday racism: An interdisciplinary theory*. Newbury Park, CA: Sage Publications.

Evans, N. J., Forney, D. S., Guido, F. M., Patton, L. D., & Renn, K. A. (2009). *Student development in college: Theory, research, and practice*. San Francisco, CA: Jossey-Bass.

Eyler, J. S., & Giles, D. E., Jr. (1999). *Where's the learning in service-learning?* San Francisco, CA: Jossey-Bass.

Faulstich Orellana, M. (2003) *In other words: en otras palabras: learning from bilingual kids' translating/interpreting experiences*. Evanston, IL: School of Education and Social Policy, Northwestern University.

Feagin, J. R. (2006). *Systemic racism: A theory of oppression*. New York: Routledge.

Findlay, S., & Kohler, N. (2010). Too Asian? *Maclean's*. Retrieved from http://oncampus.macleans.ca/education/2010/11/10/too-asian/.

Fordham, S. (1996). *Blacked out: Dilemmas of race, identity, and success at Capital High*. Chicago, IL: University of Chicago Press.

Freire, P. (1970a). *Education for critical consciousness*. New York: Continuum Publishing Company.

Freire, P. (1970b). *Pedagogy of the oppressed*. New York: Herder and Herder.

Freire, P. (1973). *Pedagogy of the oppressed*. New York: The Seabury Press.

Fullilove, R. E., & Treisman, E. M. (1990). Mathematics achievement among African American undergraduates at the University of California, Berkeley: An evaluation of the Mathematics Workshop Program. *Journal of Negro Education*, *59*(3), 463–478.

Gaertner, S. L., & Dovidio, J. F. (1986). The aversive form of racism. In J. F. Dovidio & S. L. Gaertner (Eds.), *Prejudice, discrimination, and racism* (pp. 61–89). Orlando, FL: Academic Press.

Galvin, K. (2003). International and transracial adoption: Communication research agenda. *Journal of Family Communication, 3*(4), 237–253.

Gándara, P. (1982) Passing through the eye of the needle: high-achieving Chicanas. *Hispanic Journal of Behavioral Sciences, 4*, 167–179.

Gándara, P. (1995) *Over the ivy walls: the educational mobility of low-income Chicanos.* Albany, NY: State University of New York Press.

Garcia, R. (1995). Critical race theory and Proposition 187: The racial politics of immigration law. *Chicano-Latino Law Review, 17*, 118–148.

Gee, H. (1999). Beyond Black and White: Selected writings by Asian Americans within the Critical Race Theory Movement. *St. Mary's Law Journal, 30*(3), 759–799.

Gloria, A. M., Castellanos, J., Lopez, A., & Rosales, R. (2005). An examination of academic nonpersistence decisions of Latino undergraduates. *Hispanic Journal of Behavioral Sciences, 27*, 202–223.

Gloria, A. M., & Kurpius, S. E. R. (1996). The validation of the cultural congruity scale and the university environment scale with Chicano/a students. *Hispanic Journal of Behavioral Sciences, 18*(4), 533–549.

Gomez, A., Dovidio, J. F., Huici, S. L., Gaertner, S. L., & Cuadrado, I. (2008). The other side of we: When out-group members express common identity. *Personality and Social Psychology Bulletin, 34*(12), 1613–1626.

Government Accountability Office [GAO]. (2007). *Information sharing could help institutions identify and address challenges that some Asian American and Pacific Islanders face.* Washington, DC: United States Government Accountability Office.

Grillo, T. (1995). Anti-essentialism and intersectionality: Tools to dismantle the master's house. *Black Women's Law Journal, 10*, 16–30.

Gruenfeld, D. H., Thomas-Hunt, M. C., & Kim, P. H. (1998). Cognitive flexibility, communication strategy, and integrative complexity in groups: Public versus private reactions to majority and minority status. *Journal of Experimental Social Psychology, 34*(2), 202–226.

Guiffrida, D. A. (2003). African American student organizations as agents of social integration. *Journal of College Student Development, 44*(3), 304–319.

Guiffrida, D. (2005). Othermothering as a framework for understanding African American students' definitions of student-centered faculty. *The Journal of Higher Education, 76*(6), 701–723.

Guiffrida, D. A. (2006). Toward a cultural advancement of Tinto's theory. *The Review of Higher Education, 29*(4), 451–472.

Gurin, P. Y., Dey, E. L., Gurin, G., & Hurtado, S. (2003). How does racial/ethnic diversity promote education? *Western Journal of Black Studies, 27*(1), 20–29.

Gurin, P., Nagda, B. A., & Lopez, G. E. (2004). The benefits of diversity in education for democratic citizenship. *Journal of Social Sciences*, *60*(1), 17–34.

Hackett, G., Betz, N. E., Casas, J. M., & Rocha-Singh, I. A. (1992). Gender, ethnicity, and social cognitive factors predicting the academic achievement of students in engineering. *Journal of Counseling Psychology*, *39*(4), 527–538.

Hamamoto, D.Y. (1994). *Monitored peril: Asian Americans and the politics of TV representation*. Minneapolis, MN: University of Minnesota Press.

Hardiman, R., & Jackson, B.W. (1997). Conceptual foundation for social justice courses. In M. Adams, L. A. Bell, & P. Griffin (Eds.), *Teaching for diversity and social justice: A sourcebook* (pp. 16–29). New York: Routledge.

Harper, S. R., & Hurtado, S. (2007). Nine themes in campus racial climates and implications for institutional transformation. In S. R. Harper & L. D. Patton (Eds.), *Responding to the realities of race on campus. New Directions for Student Services* (no. 120, pp. 7–24). San Francisco, CA: Jossey-Bass.

Harper, S., Patton, L., & Wooden, O. (2009). Access and equity for African American students in higher education: A critical race historical analysis of policy efforts. *Journal of Higher Education*, *80*(4), 389–414.

Harper, S. R., & Quaye, S. J. (2007). Student organizations as venues for Black identity expression and development among African American male student leaders. *Journal of College Student Development*, *48*(2), 127–144.

Harrell, S. P. (2000). A multidimensional conceptualization of racism-related stress: Implications for the well-being of people of color. *American Journal of Orthopsychiatry*, *70*(1), 42–45

Harris, A. P. (2003). Race and essentialism in feminist legal theory. In A. K. Wing (Ed.), *Critical race feminism: A reader* (2nd edition, pp. 34–41). New York: New York University Press.

Hausmann, L. R. M., Schofield, J. W., & Woods, R. L. (2007). Sense of belonging as a predictor of intentions to persist among African American and White first-year college students. *Research in Higher Education*, *48*(7), 803–839.

Helms, J. E. (1994). The conceptualization of racial identity and other racial constructs. In E. J. Trickett, R. J. Watts, & D. Birman (Eds.), *Human diversity: Perspectives on people in context* (pp. 285–311). San Francisco, CA: Jossey-Bass.

Hoffman, M., Richmond, J., Morrow, J., & Salomone, K. (2002). Investigating "sense of belonging" in first-year college students. *Journal of College Student Retention*, *4*(3), 227–256.

Hune, S. (2002). Demographics and diversity of Asian American college students. In M. K. McEwen, C. M. Kodama, A. N. Alvarez, S. Lee, & C. T. H. Liang (Eds.), *Working with Asian American college students. New Directions for Student Services* (no. 97, pp. 11–20). San Francisco, CA: Jossey-Bass.

Hurtado, S. (2005). The next generation of diversity and intergroup relations. *Journal of Social Issues*, *61*(3), 595–610.

Hurtado, S., & Carter, D. (1997). Effects of college transition and perceptions of the campus racial climate on Latina/o college students' sense of belonging. *Sociology of Education, 70,* 324–345.

Hurtado, S., Milem, J. F., Clayton-Pedersen, A. R., & Allen, W. R. (1998). Enhancing campus climates for racial/ethnic diversity: educational policy and practice. *The Review of Higher Education, 21*(3), 279–302.

Ibrahim, F., Ohnishi, H., & Sandhu, D.S. (1997). Asian-American identity development: A culture specific model for South Asian-Americans. *Journal of Multicultural Counseling and Development, 25*(1), 34–50.

Indiana University Newsroom (2013). *IU selects recipients of scholarship honoring memory of Won-Joon Yoon.* Retrieved from http://homepages.indiana.edu/news/page/normal/1036.html.

Jayakumar, U. M. (2008). Can higher education meet the needs of an increasingly diverse and global society? Campus diversity and cross-cultural workforce competencies. *Harvard Educational Review, 78*(4), 615–651.

Jayakumar, U. M. (2012). The role of student agency, student empowerment, and social praxis in shaping supportive cultures at traditionally White institutions. In S. D. Museus & U. M. Jayakumar (Eds.), *Creating campus cultures: Fostering success among racially diverse student populations* (pp. 130–149). New York: Routledge.

Jayakumar, U. M., & Museus, S. D. (2012). Mapping the intersection of campus cultures and equitable outcomes among racially diverse student populations. In S. D. Museus & U. M. Jayakumar (Eds.), *Creating campus cultures: Fostering success among racially diverse student populations* (pp. 1–27). New York: Routledge.

Jenkins, D. (2006). *What community college policies and practices are effective in promoting student success? A study of high- and low-impact institutions.* New York: Community College Research Center.

Johnson, K. (1997). Racial hierarchy, Asian Americans and Latinos as "foreigners," and social change: Is law the way to go? *Oregon Law Review, 76,* 347–368.

Johnston, K. E., Swim, J. K., Saltsman, B. M., Deater-Deckard, K., & Petrill, S. A. (2007). Mothers' racial, ethnic, and cultural socialization of transracially adopted Asian children. *Family Relations, 56,* 390–402.

Jones, J. M. (1997). *Prejudice and Racism* (2nd edition). New York: McGraw-Hill.

Katayama, M. (1990). Doing the right thing: The critical role of students in the tenure campaign. *Amerasia Journal, 16*(1), 109–117.

Kiang, P. N. (1991). About face: Recognizing Asian & Pacific American Vietnam veterans in Asian American Studies. *Amerasia, 17*(3), 22–40.

Kiang, P. N. (1992). Issues of curriculum and community for first-generation Asian Americans in college. *New Directions for Community Colleges, 80,* 97–112.

Kiang, P. N. (2002). Stories and structures of persistence: Ethnographic learning through research and practice in Asian American Studies. In Y. Zou & H. T. Trueba (Eds.), *Advances in ethnographic research: from our theoretical and methodological roots to post-modern critical ethnography* (pp. 223–255). Lanham, MD: Rowman & Littlefield.

Kiang, P. N. (2004). Checking Southeast Asian American realities in Pan-Asian American agendas. *AAPI Nexus: Policy, Practice & Community*, *2*(1), 48–76.

Kiang, P. N. (2008). Crouching activists, hidden scholars: Reflections on research and development with students and communities in Asian American Studies. In C. R. Hale. (Ed.), *Engaging contradictions: Theory, politics, and methods of activist scholarship* (pp. 299–318). Berkeley: CA. University of California Press.

Kiang, P. N. (2009). A thematic analysis of persistence and long-term educational engagement with Southeast Asian American college students. In L. Zhan (Ed.), *Asian American voices: Engaging, empowering, enabling* (pp. 21–58). New York: NLN Press.

Kibria, N. (1998): The contested meanings of "Asian American": Racial dilemmas in the contemporary US. *Ethnic and Racial Studies*, *21*(5), 939–958.

Kim, B. S. K., Atkinson, D. R., & Yang, P. H. (1999). The Asian values scale: Development, factor analysis, validation and reliability. *Journal of Counseling Psychology*, *46*, 342–352.

Kim, C. J. (1999). The racial triangulation of Asian Americans. *Politics and Society*, *27*(1), 105–138.

Kim, J. (1981). *Processes of Asian American identity development: A study of Japanese American women's perceptions of their struggle to achieve positive identities as Americans of Asian ancestry*. Unpublished Dissertation. University of Massachusetts, MA.

Kim, Y. K., Chang, M. J., & Park, J. J. (2009). Engaging with faculty: Examining rates, predictors, and educational effects for Asian American undergraduates. *Journal of Diversity in Higher Education*, *2*(4), 206–218.

Kinzie, J. D. (1989). Therapeutic approaches to traumatized Cambodian refugees. *Journal of Traumatic Stress*, *2*, 75–91.

Kodama, C. M., McEwen, M., Liang, C. T. H., & Lee, S. (2002). An Asian American perspective on psychosocial student development theory. In M. K. McEwen, C. M. Kodama, A. N. Alvarez, S. Lee, & C. T. H. Liang (Eds.), *Working with Asian American college students. New Directions for Student Services* (no. 97, pp. 45–60). San Francisco, CA: Jossey-Bass.

Kohl, H. (1994). *"I won't learn from you" and other thoughts on creative maladjustment*. New York: New Press.

Korematsu v. United States, 323 US 214 (1944).

Kotori, C., & Malaney, G. D. (2003). Asian American students' perceptions of racism, reporting behaviors, and awareness of legal rights and procedures. *NASPA Journal*, *40*(3), 56–76.

Kuh, G. D. (2005). Getting off the dime. In *Exploring different dimensions of student engagement: 2005 annual report*. Bloomington, IN: Center for Postsecondary Research.

Kuh, G. D., & Love, P. G. (2000). A cultural perspective on student departure. In J. M. Braxton (Ed.), *Reworking the student departure puzzle* (pp. 196–212). Nashville, TN: Vanderbilt University Press.

149

Lee, R. M., & Davis, C. (2000). Cultural orientation, past multicultural experience, and a sense of belonging on campus for Asian American college students. *Journal of College Student Development*, *41*(1), 110–115.

Lee, S. J. (1994). Behind the model-minority stereotype: Voices of high- and low-achieving Asian American students. *Anthropology & Education Quarterly*, *25*(4), 413–429.

Lee, S. (2002). Do AAPI faculty face a glass ceiling in higher education? *American Educational Research Journal*, *39*(3), 695–724.

Lee, S. J., & Kumashiro, K. K. (2005). *A report on the status of Asian Americans and Pacific Islanders in education: Beyond the "model minority" stereotype.* Washington, DC: National Education Association.

Lent, R. W., Brown, S. D., & Larkin, K. C. (1984). Relation of self-efficacy expectations to academic achievement and persistence. *Journal of Counseling Psychology*, *31*(3), 356–362.

Lent, R. W., Brown, S. D., & Larkin, K. C. (1986). Self-efficacy in the prediction of academic performance and perceived career options. *Journal of Counseling Psychology*, *33*(3), 265–269.

Lent, R. W., Brown, S. D., & Larkin, K. C. (1987). Comparison of three theoretically derived variables in predicting career and academic behavior: Self-efficacy, interest congruence, and consequence thinking. *Journal of Counseling Psychology*, *34*(3), 293–298.

Lew, J., Chang, J. C., & Wang, W. W. (2005). The overlooked minority: Asian Pacific American students at community colleges. *Community College Review*, *33*(2), 64–84.

Lewis, A. E., Chesler, M., & Forman, T. A. (2000). The impact of "colorblind" ideologies on students of color: Intergroup relations at a predominantly White university. *The Journal of Negro Education*, *69*(1/2), 74–91.

Li, G., & Wang, L. (2008). *Model minority myth revisited.* Charlotte, NY: Information Age Publishing.

Lin, N. J., Suyemoto, K. L., & Kiang, P. N. (2009). Education as catalyst for inter-generational refugee family communication about war and trauma. *Communication Disorders Quarterly*, *30*, 195–207.

Littleford, L. N., O'Dougherty Wright, M., & Sayoc-Parial, M. (2005). White students' intergroup anxiety during same-race and interracial interactions: A multimethod approach. *Basic and Applied Social Psychology*, *27*(1), 85–94.

Liu, A. (2009). Critical Race Theory, Asian Americans, and higher education: A review of research. *InterActions: UCLA Journal of Education and Information Studies*, *6*.

Liu, W. M. (2002). Exploring the lives of Asian American men: Racial identity, male role norms, gender role conflict, and prejudicial attitudes. *Psychology of Men and Masculinity*, *3*(2), 107–118.

Locks, A. M., Hurtado, S., Bowman, N. A., & Oseguera, L. (2008). Extending notions of campus climate and diversity to students' transition to college. *The Review of Higher Education*, *31*(3), 257–285.

Loes, C., Pascarella, E., & Umbach, P. (2012). Effects of diversity experiences on critical thinking skills: Who benefits? *Journal of Higher Education, 83*(1), 1–25.

Loo, C. (1993). An integrative-sequential treatment model for posttraumatic stress disorder: A case study of the Japanese American internment and redress. *Clinical Psychology Review, 13,* 89–117.

Lowe, L. (1996). *Immigrant acts: On Asian American cultural politics.* Durham, NC: Duke University Press.

Matsuda, G. (1990). "Only the beginning": Continuing the fight for empowerment. *Amerasia Journal, 16*(1), 159–169.

Matsuda, M. J. (1991). Voices of America: Accent, antidiscrimination law, and jurisprudence for the last reconstruction. *Yale Law Journal, 100,* 1329–1407.

Matsuda, M. J. (1996). *Where is your body? And other essays on race, gender, and the law.* Boston, MA: Beacon Press.

Matz, M. (1999). Bloomington mourns death of Korean student. *United Methodist News Feature.* Retrieved from http://archives.umc.org/umns/news_archive1999.asp?p tid=&story={5C9A2FCD-10C4-4A07-A081-9C6B61A3D855}&mid=3368.

McEwen, M. K., Kodama, C. M., Alvarez, A. N., Lee, S., & Liang, C. T. H. (2002). *Working with Asian American college students. New Directions for Student Services* (no. 97). San Francisco, CA: Jossey-Bass.

McEwen, M. K., Roper, L. D., Bryant, D. R., & Langa, M. J. (1990). Incorporating the development of African American students into psychosocial theories of student development. *Journal of College Student Development, 31*(5), 429–436.

Milem, J. F., Chang, M. J., & antonio, a. l. (2005). *Making diversity work on campus: A research-based perspective.* Washington, DC: Association of American Colleges and Universities.

Min, P. G. (2003). Social science research on Asian Americans. In J. A. Banks & C. M. Banks (Eds.), *Handbook of research on multicultural education* (pp. 332–348). New York: Macmillan.

Minami, D. (1990). Guerilla war at UCLA: Political and legal dimensions of the tenure battle. *Amerasia Journal, 16*(1), 81–107.

Multon, K. D., Brown, S. D., & Lent, R. W. (1991). Relation of self-efficacy beliefs to academic outcomes: A meta-analytic investigation. *Journal of Counseling Psychology, 38*(1), 30–38.

Museus, S. D. (2007). Using qualitative methods to assess diverse institutional cultures. In S. R. Harper & S. D. Museus (Eds.), *Using qualitative methods in institutional assessment. New Directions for Institutional Research* (no. 136, pp. 29–40). San Francisco, CA: Jossey-Bass.

Museus, S. D. (2008a). The model minority and the inferior minority myths: Understanding stereotypes and their implications for student involvement. *About Campus, 13*(3), 2–8.

151

Museus, S. D. (2008b). The role of ethnic student organizations in fostering African American and Asian American students' cultural adjustment and membership at predominantly White institutions. *Journal of College Student Development*, *49*(6), 568–586.

Museus, S. D. (2009a). A critical analysis of the invisibility of Southeast Asian American students in higher education research and discourse. In L. Zhan (Ed.), *Asian voices: Engaging, empowering, and enabling* (pp. 59–76). New York: NLN Press.

Museus, S. D. (Ed.) (2009b). *Conducting research on Asian Americans in higher education. New Directions for Institutional Research* (no. 142). San Francisco, CA: Jossey-Bass.

Museus, S. D. (2009c). Editor's notes. In S. D. Museus (Ed.), *Conducting research on Asian Americans in higher education. New Directions for Institutional Research* (no. 142, pp. 1–5). San Francisco, CA: Jossey-Bass.

Museus, S. D. (2010). Understanding racial/ethnic differences in the direct and indirect effects of loans on degree completion. *Journal of College Student Retention: Theory, Research, and Practice*, *11*(4), 499–527.

Museus, S. D. (2011a). Generating Ethnic Minority Success (GEMS): A collective-cross case analysis of high-performing colleges. *Journal of Diversity in Higher Education*, *4*(3), 147–162.

Museus, S. D. (2011b). Mixing quantitative national survey data and qualitative interview data to understand college access and equity: An examination of first-generation Asian Americans and Pacific Islanders. In K. A. Griffin & S. D. Museus (Eds.), *Using mixed-methods approaches to study intersectionality in higher education. New Directions for Institutional Research* (no. 151, pp. 63–75). San Francisco, CA: Jossey-Bass

Museus, S. D. (2011c). Using cultural perspectives to understand the role of ethnic student organizations in Black students' progress to the end of the pipeline. In D. H. Evensen & C. D. Pratt (Eds.), *The end of the pipeline: A journey of recognition for African Americans entering the legal profession*. Durham, NC: Carolina Academic Press.

Museus, S. D. (2013). Asian Americans and Pacific Islanders: A national portrait of growth, diversity, and inequality. In S. D. Museus, D. C. Maramba, & R. T. Teranishi (Eds.), *The misrepresented minority: New insights on Asian Americans and Pacific Islanders, and the implications for higher education*. Sterling, VA: Stylus.

Museus, S. D. (in press-a). The Culturally Engaging Campus Environments (CECE) Model: A new theory of college success among racially diverse student populations. In *Higher Education: Handbook of Theory and Research*. New York: Springer.

Museus, S. D. (in press-b). Unpacking the complex and multifaceted nature of parental influences on Southeast Asian American college students' educational trajectories. Manuscript accepted for publication in the *Journal of Higher Education*.

Museus, S. D., antonio, a. l., & Kiang, P. N. (2012). *The state of scholarship on Asian Americans and Pacific Islanders in education: Anti-essentialism, inequality, context, and relevance.* Honolulu, HI: Asian American and Pacific Islander Research Coalition.

Museus, S. D., & Chang, M. J. (2009). Rising to the challenge of conducting research on Asian Americans in higher education. In S. D. Museus (Ed.), *Conducting research on*

Asian Americans in higher education. New Directions for Institutional Research (no. 142, pp. 95–105). San Francisco, CA: Jossey-Bass.

Museus, S. D., & Griffin, K. A. (2011). Mapping the margins in higher education: On the promise of intersectionality frameworks in research and discourse. In K. A. Griffin & S. D. Museus (Eds.), *Using mixed-methods approaches to study inter-sectionality in higher education. New Directions for Institutional Research* (no. 151, pp. 15–26). San Francisco, CA: Jossey-Bass.

Museus, S. D., & Iftikar, J. (2013). *AsianCrit: Toward an Asian Critical Theory in education.* Paper presented at the 2013 Annual Meeting of the American Educational Research Association, San Francisco, CA.

Museus, S. D., & Iftikar, J. (in press). *Asian Critical Theory (AsianCrit).* In M. Y. Danico & J. G. Golson (Eds.), *Asian American society.* Thousand Oaks, CA: Sage Publications and Association for Asian American Studies.

Museus, S. D., & Kawamata-Ryan, T. (2012). *Mixed-race college students' strategies for coping with multiracial microaggressions in college: A qualitative inquiry.* Paper presented at the 2012 Annual Meeting of the Association for the study of Higher Education, Las Vegas, NV.

Museus, S. D., & Kiang, P. N. (2009). The model minority myth and how it contributes to the invisible minority reality in higher education research. In S. D. Museus (Ed.), *Conducting research on Asian Americans in higher education. New Directions for Institutional Research* (no. 142, pp. 5–15). San Francisco, CA: Jossey-Bass.

Museus, S. D., Lam, S., Huang, C., Kem, P., & Tan, K. (2012). Cultural integration in campus subcultures: Where the cultural, academic, and social spheres of college life collide. In S. D. Museus & U. M. Jayakumar (Eds.). *Creating campus cultures: Fostering success among racially diverse student populations* (pp. 106–129). New York: Routledge.

Museus, S. D., Lambe, S. A., & Kawamata-Ryan, T. (2012). *Mixed-Race college students' strategies for coping with multiracial microaggressions in college: A qualitative inquiry.* Paper presented at the 2012 Annual Meeting of the Association for the study of Higher Education, Las Vegas, NV.

Museus, S. D., Lambe, S. A., Robinson, T., Knepler, E., & Yee, A. (2009). *Multiracial microaggressions: Uncovering subtle forms of racial prejudice and discrimination in the experiences of people of mixed-race heritage.* Paper presented at the 2009 Annual Meeting of the Association for the Study of Higher Education, Vancouver, BC.

Museus, S. D., & Maramba, D. C. (2011). The impact of culture on Filipino American students' sense of belonging. *Review of Higher Education, 34*(2), 231–258.

Museus, S. D., Maramba, D. C., Palmer, R. T., Reyes, A., & Bresonis, K. (2013). An explanatory model of Southeast Asian American college student success: A grounded theory analysis. In R. Endo & Xue Lan Rong (Eds.), *Asian American educational achievement, schooling, and identities.* Charlotte, NC: Information Age Publishers.

Museus, S. D., Maramba, D. C., & Teranishi, R. T. (2013). *The misrepresented minority: New insights on Asian Americans and Pacific Islanders, and the implications for higher education.* Sterling, VA: Stylus Publishing.

153

Museus, S. D., & Neville, K. (2012). Delineating the ways that key institutional agents provide racial minority students with access to social capital in college. *Journal of College Student Development*, *53*(3), 436–452.

Museus, S. D., Nichols, A. H., & Lambert, A. (2008). Racial differences in the effects of campus racial climate on degree completion: A structural model. *The Review of Higher Education*, *32*(1), 107–134.

Museus, S. D., & Park, J. J. (2012). *The significance of race and racism in the lives of Asian American college students*. Paper to be presented at the 2012 Annual Meeting of the Association for the study of Higher Education, Las Vegas, NV.

Museus, S. D., & Quaye, S. J. (2009). Toward an intercultural perspective of racial and ethnic minority college student persistence. *The Review of Higher Education*, *33*(1), 67–94.

Museus, S. D., & Ravello, J. N. (2010). Characteristics of academic advising that contribute to racial and ethnic minority student success at predominantly White institutions. *NACADA Journal*, *30*(1), 47–58.

Museus, S. D., Ravello, J. N., & Vega, B. E. (2012). The campus racial culture: A critical race counterstory. In S. D. Museus & U. M. Jayakumar (Eds.), *Creating campus cultures: Fostering success among racially diverse student populations* (pp. 28–45). New York: Routledge.

Museus, S. D., & Truong, K. A. (2009). Disaggregating qualitative data on Asian Americans in campus climate research and assessment. In S. D. Museus (Ed.), *Conducting research on Asian Americans in higher education. New Directions for Institutional Research* (no. 142, pp. 17–26). San Francisco, CA: Jossey-Bass.

Museus, S. D., & Truong, K. A. (in press). *Racism and sexism in cyberspace: Engaging stereotypes of Asian American women and men to facilitate student learning*. Manuscript accepted for publication in *About Campus*.

Museus, S. D., & Vue, R. (in press). A structural equation modeling analysis of the role of socioeconomic status in Asian American and Pacific Islander students' transition to college. Manuscript accepted for publication in *The Review of Higher Education*.

Museus, S. D., Vue, R., Nguyen, T. K., & Yeung, F. (2013). A model of Southeast Asian American identity model: Merging theoretical perspectives and considering intersecting identities. In S. D. Museus, D. C. Maramba, & R. T. Teranishi (Eds.), *The misrepresented minority: New insights on Asian Americans and Pacific Islanders, and the implications for higher education*. Sterling, VA: Stylus Publishing.

Nadal, K. I. (2004). Pilipino American identity development model. *Multicultural Counseling and Development*, *32*(January), 45–62.

Nagata, D. K., & Cheng, W. J. Y. (2003). Intergenerational communication of race-related trauma by Japanese American former internees. *American Journal of Orthopsychiatry*, *73*(3), 266–278.

Nakanishi, D. T. (1990). Why I fought. *Amerasia Journal*, *16*(1), 139–158.

Nakanishi, D. T. (1995). Linkages and boundaries: Twenty-five years of Asian American Studies. *Amerasia Journal*, *21*(3), xvii–xxv.

Narui, M. (2011). Understanding Asian/American gay, lesbian, and bisexual experiences from a poststructural perspective. *Journal of Homosexuality*, *58*, 1211–1234.

National Commission on Asian American and Pacific Islander Research in Education [CARE]. (2008). *Facts, not fiction: Setting the record straight*. New York: Author.

National Commission on Asian American and Pacific Islander Research in Education [CARE]. (2010). *Federal higher education policy priorities and the Asian American and Pacific Islander community*. New York: Author.

National Commission on Asian American and Pacific Islander Research in Education [CARE]. (2011). *The relevance of Asian Americans and Pacific Islanders in the college completion agenda*. New York: Author.

Nelson-Laird, T. F., Engberg, M. E., & Hurtado, S. (2005). Modeling accentuation effects: Enrolling in a diversity course and the importance of social engagement. *Journal of Higher Education*, *76*(4), 448–476.

Ngo, B., & Lee, S. (2007). Complicating the image of model minority success: A review of Southeast Asian American education. *Review of Educational Research*, *77*(4), 415–453.

Nora, A. (2001). The depiction of significant others in Tinto's "rites of passages": A reconceptualization of the influence of family and community in the persistence process. *Journal of College Student Retention*, *3*(1), 41–56.

Nora, A., & Cabrera, A. F. (1996). The role of perceptions of prejudice and discrimination on the adjustment of minority students to college. *Journal of Higher Education*, *67*(2), 119–148.

Nora, A., & Crisp, G. (2009). Hispanics and higher education: An overview of research, theory, and practice. In J. C. Smart (Ed.), *Higher education: Handbook of theory and research* (vol. XXIV, pp. 317–353). New York, NY: Springer.

Nora, A., Urick, A., & Cerecer, P. D. (2011). Validating students: A conceptualization and overview of its impact on student experiences and outcomes. *Enrollment Management Journal: Student Access, Finance, and Success in Higher Education*, *5*(2), 97–119

Ogbar, J. O. G. (2001). Yellow power: The formation of Asian-American nationalism in the age of Black power. *Souls: A Critical Journal of Black Politics, Culture and Society*, *3*(3), 29–38.

Okihiro, G. Y. (1995). *Privileging positions: The sites of Asian American Studies*. Pullman, WA: Washington State University Press.

Omi, M., & Winant, H. (1994). *Racial formation in the United States: From the 1960s to the 1990s*. New York: Routledge.

Omi, M., & Winant, H. (1996). Contesting the meaning of race in the post-civil rights movement era. In S. Pedraza & R. Rumbaut (Eds.), *Origins and destinies: Immigration, race, and ethnicity in America* (pp. 470–478). Belmont, CA: Wadsworth.

Omi, M., & Winant, H. (2002). Racial formations. In T. E. Ore (Ed.), *Social construction of difference and inequality: Race, class, gender, and sexuality* (pp. 13–22). Columbus, OH: McGraw-Hill.

Osajima, K. H. (1995). Racial politics and the invisibility of Asian Americans in higher education. *Educational Foundations*, *9*(1), 35–53.

Park, I. J. K., Sulaiman, C., Schwartz, S. J., Kim, S. Y., Ham, L. S., & Zamboanga, B. L. (2011). Self-construals and social anxiety among Asian American college students: Testing emotion suppression as a mediator. *Asian American Journal of Psychology*, *2*(1), 39–50.

Park, J. J. (2008). Race and the Greek system in the 21st century: Centering the voices of Asian American women. *The NASPA Journal*, *45*(1), 103–132.

Park, J. J. (2009a). Are we satisfied? A look at student satisfaction with the diversity at traditionally White institutions. *The Review of Higher Education*, *32*(3), 291–320.

Park, J. J. (2009b). Taking race into account: Charting student attitudes towards affirmative action. *Research in Higher Education*, *50*(7), 670–690.

Park, J. J. (2009c). *When race and religion hit campus: An ethnographic examination of a campus religious organization*. Doctoral dissertation, University of California, Los Angeles, CA.

Park, J. J. (2012a). *Asian Americans and the benefits of campus diversity: What the research says*. New York: CARE.

Park, J. J. (2012b). When race and religion collide: The effect of religion on interracial friendship during college. *Journal of Diversity in Higher Education*, *5*(1), 8–21.

Park, J. J., Lew, J. W., & Chiang, W. (2013). Hybrid faith, hybrid identities: Asian American evangelical Christian students on campus. In S. D. Museus, D. C. Maramba, & R. T. Teranishi (Eds.), *The misrepresented minority: New insights on Asian Americans and Pacific Islanders, and the implications for higher education* (pp. 192–213). Sterling, VA: Stylus Publishing.

Pepin, S., & Talbot, D. (2013). *Negotiating the complexities of being Asian American and lesbian, gay, or bisexual.* In S. D. Museus, D. C. Maramba, & R. T. Teranishi (Eds.), *The misrepresented minority: New insights on Asian Americans and Pacific Islanders, and the implications for higher education* (pp. 272–293). Sterling, VA: Stylus Publishing.

Perry, B. (2008). *Silent victims: Hate crimes against Native Americans.* Tuscon, AZ: The University of Arizona Press.

Perry, B., & Robyn, L. (2005). Putting anti-Indian violence in context: The case of the Great Lakes Chippewas of Wisconsin. *American Indian Quarterly*, *29*(3/4), 590–625.

Peterson, M., & Spencer M. G. (1990). Understanding academic culture and climate. In W. G. Tierney (Ed.), *Assessing academic climates and cultures* (pp. 3–18). San Francisco, CA: Jossey-Bass.

Pettersen, W. (1966, January 9). Success story, Japanese American style. *Washington Post*, p. 20.

Pettigrew, T. F., & Tropp, L. R. (2006). A meta-analytic test of Intergroup Contact Theory. *Journal of Personality and Social Psychology*, *90*(5), 751–783.

Pettigrew, T. F., & Tropp, L. R. (2008). How does intergroup contact reduce prejudice? Meta-analytic tests of three mediators. *European Journal of Social Psychology*, *38*(6), 922–934.

Pew Research Center. (2012, July 12). *The rise of Asian Americans* (pp. 1–36). http://www.pewsocialtrends.org/files/2012/06/SDT-The-Rise-of-Asian-Americans-Full-Report.pdf.

Pierce, C. (1995). Stress analogs of racism and sexism: Terrorism, torture, and disaster. In C. Willie, P. Rieker, B. Kramer, & B. Brown (Eds.), *Mental health, racism, and sexism* (pp. 277–293). Pittsburgh, PA: University of Pittsburgh Press.

Poon, O. (2012). *Do Asian Americans benefit from race-blind college admissions policies?* New York: CARE.

Poon, O. (2013). "Think about it as decolonizing our minds": Spaces for critical race pedagogy and transformative leadership development. In S. D. Museus, D. C. Maramba, & R. T. Teranishi (Eds.), *The misrepresented minority: New insights on Asian Americans and Pacific Islanders, and the implications for higher education* (pp. 355–375). Sterling, VA: Stylus Publishing.

Portes, A., & Rumbaut, R. G. (1996). *Immigrant America: A portrait* (2nd edition). Berkeley, CA: University of California Press.

Poston, W. S. C. (1990). The biracial identity development model: A needed addition. *Journal of Counseling and Development, 69,* 152–155.

Prasso, S. (2005). *The Asian mystique.* New York: PublicAffairs.

Rendón, L. I. (1994). Validating culturally diverse students: Toward a new model of learning and student development. *Innovative Higher Education, 19*(1), 33–51.

Rendón, L. I., & Muñoz, S. M. (2011). Revisiting validation theory: Theoretical foundations, applications, and extensions. *Enrollment Management Journal: Student Access, Finance, and Success in Higher Education, 5*(2), 12–33.

Rendón, L. I., Jalomo, R. E., & Nora, A. (2000). Theoretical considerations in the study of minority student retention in higher education. In J. Braxton (Ed.), *Reworking the student departure puzzle* (pp. 127–156). Nashville, TN: Vanderbilt University Press.

Renn, K. A. (2000). Patterns of situational identity among biracial and multiracial college students. *Review of Higher Education, 23,* 399–420.

Renn, K. A. (2003). Understanding the identities of mixed-race college students through a developmental ecology lens. *Journal of College Student Development, 44,* 383–403.

Renn, K. A. (2004). *Mixed race students in college: The ecology of race, identity, and community.* Albany, NY: SUNY Press.

Renn, K. A. (2008). Research on biracial and multiracial identity development: Overview and synthesis. In K. A. Renn & P. Shang (Eds.), *Biracial and multiracial students. New Direction for Student Services* (no. 123, pp. 13–21). San Francisco, CA: Jossey-Bass.

Rhoads, R. A., Lee, J. J., & Yamada, M. (2002). Panethnicity and collective action among Asian American college students. *Journal of College Student Development, 43*(6), 876–891.

Ridley, C. R. (2005). *Overcoming unintentional racism in counseling and therapy: A practitioner's guide to intentional intervention* (2nd edition). Thousand Oaks, CA: Sage Publications.

157

Rios-Aguilar, C., & Kiyama, J. M. (2012). Funds of knowledge: A proposed approach to study Latina/o students' transition to college. *Journal of Latinos and Education, 11*(1), 2–16.

Robbins, S. R., Lauver, K., Le, H., Davis, D., & Langley, R. (2004). Do psychosocial and study skill factors predict college outcomes? A meta-analysis. *Psychological Bulletin, 130*(2), 261–288.

Robinson, T. E. (2012). *Exploring how White and Asian American students experience cross-racial interactions: A phenomenological study.* Boston, MA: University of Massachusetts, Boston.

Root, M. P. P. (1990). Resolving 'Other' status: Identity development of biracial individuals. *Women and Therapy, 9*, 185–205.

Root, M. P. P. (1998). Multiracial Americans: Changing the face of Asian America. In L. C. Lee & N. W. S. Zane (Eds.), *Handbook of Asian American psychology* (pp. 261–287). Thousand Oaks, CA: Sage Publications, Inc.

Rothenberg, P. S. (Ed.). (2007). *Race, class, and gender in the United States: An integrated study.* New York, NY: Worth Publishers.

Russell, M. (1992). Entering great America: Reflections on race and the convergence of progressive legal theory and practice. *Hastings Law Journal, 43*, 749–767.

Ryoo, J. J., & Ho, R. (2013). The perspectives and experiences of Asian American student activists. In S. D. Museus, D. C. Maramba, & R. T. Teranishi (Eds.), *The misrepresented minority: New insights on Asian Americans and Pacific Islanders, and the implications for higher education* (pp. 254–271). Sterling, VA: Stylus Publishing.

Sáenz, V. B., Ngai, H. N., & Hurtado, S. (2007). Factors influencing positive interactions across race for African American, Asian American, Latino and White college students. *Research in Higher Education, 48*(1), 1–38.

Saito, N. T. (1997a). Model minority, yellow peril: Functions of "foreignness" in the construction of Asian American legal identity. *Asian Law Journal, 4*, 71–95.

Saito, N. T. (1997b). Alien and non-alien alike: Citizenship, "foreignness," and racial hierarchy in American law. *Oregon Law Review, 76*, 261–345.

Sears, D. O. (1988). Symbolic racism. In P. A. Katz & D. A. Taylor (Eds.), *Eliminating racism: Profiles in controversy* (pp. 53–84). New York: Plenum Press.

Sedlacek, W. E. (1987). Black students on White campuses: 20 years of research. *Journal of College Student Personnel, 28*(6), 484–495.

Shek, Y. L. (2006). Asian American masculinity: A review of literature. *The Journal of Men's Studies, 14*(3), 379–391.

Shilpa, D., Pawan, D., Sunaina, M., & Partha, M. (2000). De-privileging positions: Indian Americans, South Asian Americans and politics of Asian American studies. *Journal of Asian American Studies, 3*(1), 67–100.

Smith, W. A., Allen, W. R., & Danley, L. L. (2007). Assume the position . . . You fit the description: Psychosocial experiences and racial battle fatigue among African American male college students. *American Behavioral Scientist, 51*, 551–578.

Solórzano, D. G. (1998). Critical race theory, race and gender microaggressions, and the experience of Chicana and Chicano scholars. *International Journal of Qualitative Studies in Education*, *11*(1), 121–136.

Solórzano, D., Ceja, M., & Yosso, T. (2000). Critical Race Theory, microagressions, and campus racial climate: The experiences of African American college students. *Journal of Negro Education*, *69*(1/2), 60–73.

Solórzano, D. G., & Delgado Bernal, D. (2001). Examining transformational resistance through a critical race and LatCrit theory framework. *Urban Education*, *36*(3), 308–342.

Solórzano, D., Villalpando, O., & Oseguera, L. (2005). Educational inequities and Latina/o undergraduate students in the United States: A Critical Race Analysis of their educational progress. *Journal of Hispanic Education*, *4*(3), 272–294.

Solórzano, D. G., & Yosso, T. J. (2001). From racial stereotyping and deficit discourse toward a Critical Race Theory in teacher education. *Multicultural Education*, *9*(1), 2–8.

Solórzano, D. G., & Yosso, T. J. (2002). A critical race counterstory of race, racism, and affirmative action. *Equity & Excellence in Education*, *35*, 155–168.

Son, D., & Shelton, J. N. (2011). Stigma consciousness among Asian Americans: Impact of positive stereotypes in interracial roommate relationships. *Asian American Journal of Psychology*, *2*(1), 51–60.

Spivak, G. (1987). *In other worlds*. London: Routledge.

Stanton-Salazar, R. D. (2001). *Manufacturing hope and despair: the school and kin support networks of US–Mexican youth.* New York: Teachers College Press.

Sue, D. W. (2003). Cultural competence in the treatment of ethnic minority populations. In D. W. Sue (Ed.), *Psychological treatment of ethnic minority populations.* Washington DC: APA Press.

Sue, D. W., Bucceri, J., Lin, A. I., Nadal, K. L., & Torino, G. C. (2007). Racial microaggressions and the Asian American experience. *Cultural Diversity and Ethnic Minority Psychology*, *13*(1), 72–81.

Sue, D. W., Capodilupo, C. M., & Holder, A. M. B. (2008). Racial microaggressions in the life experience of Black Americans. *Professional Psychology: Research and Practice*, *39*(3), 329–336.

Sue, D. W., Capodilupo, C. M., Torino, G. C., Bucceri, J. M., Holder, A. M. B., Nadal, K. L., & Esquilin, M. (2007). Racial microaggressions in everyday life: Implications for clinical practice. *American Psychologist*, *62*(4), 271–286.

Suinn, R., Ahuna, C., & Khoo, G. (1992). The Suinn-Lew Asian self-identity acculturation scale: Concurrent and factorial validation. *Educational and Psychological Measurement*, *52*(4), 1041–1046.

Suzuki, B. II. (1977). Education and the socialization of Asian Americans: A revisionist analysis of the "model minority" thesis. *Amerasia Journal*, *4*(2), 23–51.

Suzuki, B. H. (2002). Revisiting the model minority stereotype: Implications for student affairs practice and higher education. *Working with Asian American College Students: New Directions for Student Services* (no. 97, pp. 21–32). San Francisco, CA: Jossey-Bass.

Takaki, R. (1998). *Strangers from a different shore: A history of Asian Americans* (rev. edition). Boston, MA: Little, Brown & Company.

Talbot, D. M. (2008). Exploring the experiences and self-labeling of mixed-race individuals with two minority parents. In K. A. Renn & P. Shang (Eds.), *Biracial and multiracial students. New Direction for Student Services* (no. 123, pp. 23–31). San Francisco, CA: Jossey-Bass.

Tamura, E. (1993). The English-only effort, the anti-Japanese campaign, and language acquisition in the education of Japanese Americans in Hawaii, 1915–40. *History of Education Quarterly, 3*(1), 37–58.

Tamura, E. H. (2001a). Asian Americans in the history of education: An historiographical essay. *History of Education Quarterly, 41*(1), 58–71.

Tamura, E. H., (2001b). Introduction: Asian Americans and educational history. *History of Education Quarterly, 43*(1), 1–9.

Teranishi, R. T. (2007). Race, ethnicity, and higher education policy: The use of critical quantitative research. In F. K. Stage (Ed.), *Using quantitative data to answer critical questions. New Directions for Institutional Research.* (no. 133, pp. 37–49). San Francisco, CA: Jossey-Bass.

Teranishi, R. T., Ceja, M., antonio, a. l., Allen, W. R., & McDonough, P. M. (2004). The college-choice process for Asian Pacific Americans: Ethnicity and socioeconomic class in context. *The Review of Higher Education, 27*(4), 527–551.

The Brady Center to Prevent Gun Violence (2009). *Guns and hate: A lethal combination.* Washington DC: Author.

Thompson, C. E., & Fretz, B. R. (1991). Predicting the adjustment of Black students at predominantly White institutions. *Journal of Higher Education, 62*(4), 437–450.

Tierney, W. G. (1992). An anthropological analysis of student participation in college. *Journal of Higher Education, 63*(6), 603–618.

Tierney, W. G. (1999). Models of minority college-going and retention: Cultural integrity versus cultural suicide. *The Journal of Negro Education, 68*(1), 80–91.

Tinto, V. (1975). Dropout from higher education: A theoretical synthesis of recent research. *Review of Educational Research, 45*(1), 89–125.

Tinto, V. (1987). *Leaving college: Rethinking the causes and cures of student attrition.* Chicago, IL: University of Chicago Press.

Tinto, V. (1993). *Leaving college: Rethinking the causes and cures of student attrition* (2nd edition). Chicago, IL: University of Chicago Press.

Torres, V., Howard-Hamilton, M. F., & Cooper, D. L. (2003). *Identity development of diverse populations: Implications for teaching and administration in higher education.* San Francisco, CA: Jossey-Bass.

Tran, M., & Chang, M. J. (2013). To be mice of men: Gender identity and development of masculinity through participation in Asian American interest fraternities. In S. D. Museus, D. C. Maramba, & R. T. Teranishi (Eds.), *The misrepresented minority: New insights on Asian Americans and Pacific Islanders, and the implications for higher education* (pp. 68–92). Sterling, VA: Stylus Publishing.

Truong, K. A., McGuire, K. M., & Museus, S. D. (2011) *Caught in a catch-33: The experiences of doctoral students of color with secondhand racism.* Paper presented at the 2011 Meeting of the American Anthropological Association, Montreal, QC.

Truong, K. A., & Museus, S. D. (2012). Responding to racism and racial trauma in doctoral study: An inventory for coping and mediating relationships. *Harvard Educational Review, 82*(2), 226–254.

Uba, L. (1994). *Asian Americans: Personality patterns, identity, and mental health.* New York: The Guilford Press.

Umemoto, K. (1989). "On strike!" San Francisco State College strike, 1968–69: The role of Asian American students. *Amerasia Journal, 15*(1), 3–41.

U.S. Census Bureau (2011). *Overview of race and Hispanic origin: 2010.* Washington, DC: Author.

U.S. General Accounting Office (2007). *Asian Americans and Pacific Islanders' educational attainment. A report to congressional requesters.* Washington, DC: General Accounting Office.

Uyematsu, A. (1971). The emergence of yellow power in America. In A. Tachiki et al. (Eds.), *Roots: An Asian American reader* (pp. 9–13). Los Angeles, CA: University of California Press.

Valdez, F. (2000–2001). Race, ethnicity, and Hispanismo in a triangular perspective: The "essential Latina/o" and LatCrit Theory. *UCLA Law Review, 48*, 305–352.

Valdez, F. (2013) *LatCrit overview.* Retrieved from http://latcrit.org/content/about/conceptual-overview/.

Valentine, C. A. (1971). Deficit, difference, and bicultural models of Afro-American behavior. *Harvard Educational Review, 41*(2), 137–157.

Vallerand, R. J., & Bissonnette, R. (1992). Intrinsic, extrinsic, and amotivational styles as predictors of behavior: A prospective study. *Journal of Personality, 60*(3), 599–620.

Van Gennep, A. (1960). *The rites of passage.* Translated by M. B. Vizedom & G. I. Chaffee. Chicago, IL: University of Chicago Press.

Villalpando, O. (2004). Practical considerations of critical race theory and Latino critical theory for Latino college students. In A. M. Ortiz (Ed.), *Addressing the unique needs of Latino American students. New Directions for Student Services* (no. 105, pp. 41–50). San Francisco, CA: Jossey-Bass.

Volpp, L. (2001). "Obnoxious to their very nature": Asian Americans and constitutional citizenship. *Asian Law Journal, 8*, 71–85.

Vue, R. (2013). Searching for self, discovering community: An examination of the experiences of Hmong American college students. In S. D. Museus, D. C. Maramba, & R. T. Teranishi (Eds.), *The misrepresented minority: New insights on Asian Americans and Pacific Islanders, and the implications for higher education* (pp. 214–234). Sterling, VA: Stylus Publishing.

Wei, W. (1993). *The Asian American movement*. Philadelphia, PA: Temple University Press

Wei, W. (2004). A commentary on young Asian American activists from the 1960s to the present. In J. Lee & M. Zhou (Eds.), *Asian American youth: Culture, identity, and ethnicity* (pp. 299–312). New York: Routledge.

West, T. V., Pearson, A. R., Dovidio, J. F., Shelton, J. N., & Trail. T. E. (2009). Superordinate identity and intergroup roommate friendship development. *Journal of Experimental Social Psychology*, *45*, 1266–1272.

Wijeyesinghe, C. L. (2001). Racial identity in multiracial people: An alternative paradigm. In C. L. Wijeyesinghe & B. W. Jackson III (Eds.), *New perspectives on racial identity development: A theoretical and practical anthology*. New York: New York University Press.

Wijeyesinghe, C. L., Griffin, P., & Love, B. (1997). Racism curriculum design. In M. Adams, L. A. Bell, & P. Griffin (Eds.), *Teaching for diversity and social justice* (pp. 82–110). New York: Routledge.

Williams, D. R., & Williams-Morris, R. (2000). Racism and mental health: The African American experience. *Ethnicity & Health*, *5*(3/4), 243–268.

Wilson, W. J. (1996). *When work disappears: The world of the new urban poor*. New York: Vintage Books.

Wong, A. (2013). Racial identity construction among Chinese American and Filipino American undergraduates. In S. D. Museus, D. C. Maramba, & R. T. Teranishi (Eds.), *The misrepresented minority: New insights on Asian Americans and Pacific Islanders, and the implications for higher education* (pp. 93–118). Sterling, VA: Stylus Publishing.

Wright, E. K., & Balutski, B. J. N. (2013). The role of context, critical theory, and counternarratives in understanding Indigenous Pacific Islander identities and experiences. In S. D. Museus, D. C. Maramba, & R. T. Teranishi (Eds.), *The misrepresented minority: New insights on Asian Americans and Pacific Islanders, and the implications for higher education* (pp. 163–184). Sterling, VA: Stylus Publishing.

Wu, F. H. (1995). Neither black nor white: Asian Americans and affirmative action. *Boston College Third World Law Journal*, *15*, 225.

Yamamoto, E. K. (1997). Critical race praxis: Race theory and political lawyering practice in post-civil rights America. *Michigan Law Review*, *95*(4), 821–900.

Yan, W., & Museus, S. D. (2013). Asian American and Pacific Islander faculty and the glass ceiling in higher education. In S. D. Museus, D. C. Maramba, & R. T. Teranishi (Eds.), *The misrepresented minority: New insights on Asian Americans and Pacific Islanders, and the implications for higher education* (pp. 249–280). Sterling, VA: Stylus.

Yang, X., Rendón, L. I., & Shearon, R. W. (1994). A profile of Asian students in North Carolina community colleges. *Community College Review*, *22*(1), 19–32.

Yinger, J. M. (1994). *Ethnicity: Source of strength? Source of conflict?* New York: State University of New York Press.

Yosso, T. J. (2005). Whose culture has capital? A critical race theory discussion of community cultural wealth. *Race, Ethnicity and Education*, *8*(1), 69–91.

Yosso, T., Smith, W., Ceja, M., & Solórzano, D. (2009). Critical race theory, racial microaggressions, and campus racial climate For Latina/o undergraduates." *Harvard Educational Review*, *79*, 659–690.

Yu, T. (2006). Challenging the politics of the "model minority" stereotype: A case for educational equity. *Equity & Excellence in Education*, *39*, 325–333.

Zhou, M., & Kim, S. (2006). Community forces, social capital, and educational achievement: The case of supplementary education in the Chinese and Korean immigrant communities. *Harvard Educational Review*, *76*(1), 1–29.

Zuniga, X., Williams, E. A., & Berger, J. B. (2005). Action-oriented democratic outcomes: The impact of student involvement with campus diversity. *The Journal of College Student Development*, *46*(6), 660–678.

Index

Note: 'F' after a page number indicates a figure.